COMPOSE YOURSELF!

COMPOSE YOURSELF!

SONGWRITING AND CREATIVE MUSICIANSHIP

IN FOUR EASY LESSONS

DAVID ALZOFON

Klaf Rackner Mediaworks

Klaf Rackner Mediaworks

Printed in the United States of America

ISBN: 1453724958

for Susan

Table of Contents

Preface

The book you are holding is the one I wish I'd had when I embarked on the musician's path in the 1960s: a practical introduction to music that values theory, but values musical creativity even more.

When I picked up the guitar at age thirteen, The Beatles were all the rage. So were The Rolling Stones, Bob Dylan, Jimi Hendrix, Cream, Creedence Clearwater, The Doors, Carlos Santana, The Beach Boys, The Mamas and the Papas, Donovan, The Grateful Dead, and countless other gods and goddesses of rock 'n' roll, folk, rock, folk/rock, acid rock, surf rock, swamp rock, Southern rock, and Motown.

The harmonies were hot, the rhythms were cool, melody mattered—it was easy to fall in love with music back then. But it wasn't an easy time to be a beginner. If you wanted to learn guitar, you copied licks from records, which was frustrating and tedious. Teachers tended to guard their secrets instead of sharing them on YouTube—hardly a surprise, since YouTube didn't even exist. Neither did laptops, CDs, DVDs, or magazines such as *Guitar Player* or *Guitar Techniques*. Books on theory and technique were, on the whole, poorly written and confusing. Note-for-note transcriptions? You've got to be kidding. You were lucky if you knew anyone who could explain how to tune a guitar, let alone why.

So there you were, on your own, thrashing about in the dark. Now it's a brave new world out there. We have instructional videos by the thousands online, and armies of skillful teachers who've graduated from vocational programs in pop and rock in British trade schools, or similar schools in the States, such as Musicians Institute, L.A., Berklee College of Music, Boston, or Roberts Music Institute, Seattle. Books, software, and other tools of education have also gotten better and better with every passing year. Students who want to can learn as much in their first year now as students learned in five years or more back in the '60s.

Which raises a question: With all of the great educational opportunities available today, what could possibly justify yet another book on music theory and composition?

Plenty! If you've ever taken a course in poetry, creative writing, painting, drawing, or sculpture, you know that you begin writing, painting, drawing, or sculpting on the first day of class. But music is different. It takes a year, maybe two, maybe even four, to get past the fundamentals and begin composing, and by then you may have had the creativity wrung right out of you. What is needed now, just as much as it was way back then, is a course that cultivates creativity right away, before students drown under a mass of rules.

The importance of theory is undeniable, but the long delay in creative work in music is a clue that something is missing. More than that, it undermines a student's natural gifts and desire for self-expression. It hasn't always been like this. In the Renaissance and Baroque, instrumentalists were expected to be co-creators of the music they performed. A lutenist, for example, was expected to improvise ornaments and divisions on repeated verses. Then came the printing press, and by the end of the eighteenth century, composers and audiences had begun to expect exact renditions of printed scores. In the nineteenth century, "composer" and "performer" split into separate career paths, and the artificial division became ingrained in school curricula.

In popular music, however, creativity has always been a part of the job description. The accent is not so much on talent as it is on craftsmanship. When I was in school, the results were easy to see. While I struggled with four-part harmony, counterpoint, and analysis, my friends in rock, blues, and jazz made rapid progress in writing songs and improvising solos. Something was out of whack. I wasn't sure what, but I trusted in the system. While there was no deliberate harm being done, I realize now that my intuitions were correct. There really is a better way.

Compose Yourself was conceived as a cure for the common music education. It invites everyone, not just the "talented," to enjoy the creative side of music, and right away, not later. Decades of meditation, research, and experimentation have led to a unique teaching program that blends the best of academic wisdom and pop music instruction, plus language instruction, and even a smattering of computer science. But ultimately the course owes its existence to the influence of two gifted teachers, Jef Raskin (1943 – 2005, creator of the Macintosh computer), and Howard Roberts (1929 – 2002, jazz guitarist, music educator, and founder of Musicians Institute, L.A.).

In order to convey the impact these teachers had on me, it will be necessary to rev up the time machine and roll the clock back to the summer of 1963, my thirteenth year. This was when I first picked up the guitar, and when I first failed at musical creativity. Surfing was my obsession at the time, and I often went to the beach with a friend named Mike who had a reputation as a pianist. I had no idea how good he was until one day when he launched into a rhapsody by Liszt on the old upright piano at his parents' house. When he noticed my jaw dragging on the floor, he instantly began banging out something that sounded like Jerry Lee Lewis.

"Wow! What's that?" I asked, as he finished off with a *Great Balls of Fire* flourish.

"Oh, that? That's just something I made up. You wouldn't believe how easy it is to make up that stuff you hear on the radio."

Easy to make up that stuff I heard on the radio? When I wasn't surfing, I *lived* for pop music. The idea that an ordinary mortal such as Mike, let alone *me*, could compose a song such as the ones I loved set my brain on fire. "So, can you show me?" I asked, trying not to sound overeager.

"I thought we were going surfin'," he said, begging off politely. And so we went. Mike never did get around to showing me how to compose, but I could not forget what he said. A few months later, I sat down beside a swimming pool with a battered old hand-me-down guitar and a dozen chords, determined not to get up until I'd written a song, preferably a hit song. The July sun melted the glue under the bridge of my guitar and the soundboard cracked and caved in, but the songs never came. Not even close.

Thus began a quest that led to four years of music in college, many additional years of private lessons in theory and performance, a book (*Mastering Guitar*, Fireside Books, 1981), and a position as an Assistant Editor at *Guitar Player Magazine*, where my primary responsibilities were editing instruction columns and reviewing new books, most of them instruction books.

By the mid-1980s, I had done all my homework, everything I should have done, everything prescribed by my teachers, not once but many times over. And yet, perhaps like you, I still didn't feel that I "got it." I could compose—I had composed over a hundred exercises and pieces for the book—but Mike had said it was "easy," and I knew that I was still struggling. I also knew that most music students shared my sense of frustration, and that none of my professors had a magic potion for musical enlightenment. *Something was missing.* Back on that fateful day in 1963 when I had tried and failed to write a song, I had asked a friend whose abilities with guitar I respected what had gone wrong. "Composers are born, not made," he said, with a streetwise air of authority. "Either you got it or you don't." At the time, I refused to believe him. But now I was beginning to think that maybe he'd been right.

In 1985, I gave up on music, sold all my guitars, and changed careers, moving over to Silicon Valley to write software documentation. By a strange coincidence, *Guitar Player* had rented Apple their first building on Bandley Drive in Cupertino, so the move was a short one. Unfortunately, my dreams of stock option riches never materialized. But in a supreme twist of fate, this is where I finally found the solution to the musical riddles that bedeviled me. They came from Jef Raskin, my boss at a little start-up company called Information Appliance.

"Genius" is a much overused term these days, but it certainly applied to Jef.[1] He had written the original 400-plus-page spec for the Macintosh while he'd been at Apple, named the new computer after his favorite apple, and hired and led the development team for a couple of years before Steve Jobs took over. It also happened that he was a great keyboard artist and recorder player who had been a music professor at UC San Diego before coming to Silicon Valley. When Jef hired me, he imposed one condition: I had to get a new guitar and play it once in awhile at work. I thought he was joking, but the only time he threatened to fire me was when I lagged on that commitment. Jef revived my interest in music, and later gave me lessons in composition, the only lessons on that subject that ever worked. His unique teaching method was a major source of inspiration for *Compose Yourself.*

---

1 In the interests of economy and symmetry, Jef spelled his name with one "f."

The second major influence was Howard Roberts, jazz guitarist and founder of G.I.T. (Guitar Institute of Technology), which evolved into Musicians Institute, Los Angeles. As a freelance writer and editor, I worked with Howard ("HR") on his popular *Guitar Player Magazine* column from the early 1970s to the early 1980s, helped him with a book on his Sonic Shapes concept, and attended several Howard Roberts Guitar Seminars, which ultimately led to the launch of G.I.T. It is impossible to overstate HR's influence on several generations of musicians, and I am grateful to have been one of them.

Nowadays it's unusual for a music teacher to ask a student how an interval, a melody, or a chord progression affects them emotionally, which is just one of many signs that music has drifted in the direction of science. Over the long haul, this subtle bias can lead students toward a habitual dissociation from their emotions, which is unfortunate, because music has more in common with poetry than chemistry.

Jef and Howard were both particularly adept at expressing emotion through music, and this is what made lessons with them so powerful, leading to moments when knowledge seemed to pass like a live spark, directly and wordlessly, with Zen-like immediacy. At the same time, Jef and Howard were both as brilliant with the English language as they were with the musical language. Because of this, they were able to articulate theoretical ideas in simple terms without sacrificing depth. A well-chosen metaphor, a casual joke, and a good laugh made for an atmosphere in which catching that live spark was more likely. Both Howard and Jef loved to laugh. Both of them were leaders in fields where cutthroat competition was the norm, and yet I never heard either of them utter an unkind word about anyone.

It is my hope that *Compose Yourself* will convey some of their inspirational spirit while generating a few of those all-important musical sparks.

Prelude

People spend thousands of dollars on stereos. Sometimes tens of thousands. There is a specialist industry right here in the States which builds stereo gear to a standard you wouldn't believe. Tubed amplifiers which cost more than a house. Speakers taller than me. Cables thicker than a garden hose. Some army guys had that stuff. I'd heard it on bases around the world. Wonderful. But they were wasting their money. Because the best stereo in the world is free. Inside your head. It sounds as good as you want it to. As loud as you want it to be.

– Jack Reacher, in Killing Floor, *a novel by Lee Child[1]*

Intro

Listening to music is great. Performing it is greater. But making your own music? That has to be the greatest thrill of all. Some people are lucky—they have the knack. But most of us who venture into composition and improvisation for the first time quickly discover just how difficult it is to put two notes together. Perhaps we stumble across a lick or two, or maybe the beginnings of a song, but that's where it ends. We know the music is there inside of us, but it remains tantalizingly out of reach.

What causes this invisible barrier? Talent plays a role, but it's not decisive. Most of us are well-equipped to craft a good piece of music. More often than not, the stumbling block lies in the way we're taught. As the most technical of all the arts, music invites a technical approach to creativity: theory, drills, exercises, memorization, analysis. But in the wee hours of the morning when we call upon the muse for inspiration and she's not picking up the phone, it doesn't necessarily mean that she doesn't care. It may simply be a sign that the line isn't connected, because the learning that was supposed to help us has hindered us instead. What we really need is a new path to creative musicianship, a path that anyone—not just the talented—can follow.

---

1 Quoted with the author's permission. *Killing Floor* is also the title of a blues song by Howlin' Wolf.

What's It All About?

An awakening. *Compose Yourself* awakens and develops your *Musical I.Q.* What's that? Your *Musical Imagination Quotient*, the least understood, least appreciated, yet most powerful, most valuable musical asset you have.

As an illustration, consider a recent product release from Fender, a replica of Eddie Van Halen's famous "Frankenstrat" guitar, the one he rode to fortune and fame in the '80s. In case you haven't heard the story, Eddie put the Frankenstrat together from spare parts in an effort to blend the best traits of Fender and Gibson rock guitars. The price of the original was in the neighborhood of $260. The price of the replica is—brace yourself—$25,000. The replica is as true to the original as humanly possible, so what accounts for the extra $24,740?

Eddie's virtuosity and star power, of course. But that's a superficial answer. Virtuosity and star power are *effects*, not causes. What's behind them is Eddie Van Halen's incredible musical imagination. Without the products of his imagination, which turned the world of rock on its head and continue to thrill and amaze us, the Fender replica would not be worth much more than $260 plus inflation. This is just a way of saying that you already own the most valuable musical instrument in the world: your musical imagination.

If a high Musical I.Q. is your most valuable musical asset, it is also the most underrated. Music instruction courses typically make no effort to develop it independently, as they routinely do with more tangible, measurable musical skills, such as sight-singing or scales. So let's take a moment to get acquainted. Just close your eyes, relax, and contemplate each of the following sounds: (1) The voice of a favorite singer. (2) A distant train whistle in the night. (3) The crack of thunder. (4) Crickets chirping outside your window. (5) The national anthem played by a brass band. (6) The same anthem played on accordion. (7) One of your favorite songs. (8) The same song as played on a violin, a piano, or a Frankenstrat.

Were you able to hear these sounds in the theatre of your mind? Maybe it took some effort. Maybe it was easy. It doesn't matter. If you heard anything at all, then you have a musical imagination. And if you have it, you can improve it. You don't need talent to succeed. Talent helps, but it's a gift. Imagination, on the other hand, is something we all have, and it responds to exercise.

Imagination also thrives in a playful environment, which makes it uncomfortable in the company of intellectual formality. Maybe that's why J.S. Bach didn't own a single theory book at the time of his death, or why some famous singers, songwriters, composers, and performers—George Gershwin, Frank Sinatra, Keith Richards, The Beatles, Jimi Hendrix, Lindsey Buckingham, Danny Elfman, and Eddie Van Halen, to name a few—never learned to read music. These brilliant musicians weren't necessarily contrary or eccentric. It could be that their prodigious talent was just trying to tell them something, such as "Musical imagination is inside of you, not on the page," or "Beware the left brain."

While some musicians have done splendidly without theory, a high Musical I.Q. still has something in common with a high mathematical I.Q. Consider the intricate architecture of a fugue by J.S. Bach, for example, or Mozart, who as a child covered the walls of his nursery with math problems. As an adult, he said that he could hear an entire symphony all at once, as if looking at an exploded parts diagram of a Viennese clock. He would tinker with the parts while holding a dinner conversation, then rush to his desk and write the whole thing down, page after page, without a single mistake. That's imagination on steroids.

From these examples and countless others, it's clear that Musical I.Q. has a dual nature: freewheeling on the one hand, mathematically precise on the other. Taking this into account, *Compose Yourself* tries to strike a balance between the intellectual side of music and the playful side, where creativity lies.

Genius is not a prerequisite for the course. There are many great poets other than Shakespeare, and many musicians have done extremely well on a fraction of Mozart's monumental talent. Bill Courtial, one of the most exceptional jazz guitarists I've ever known, once told me that when he was improvising, he never thought more than two measures ahead. In other words, you could build a brilliant career on just two measures' worth of musical imagination. And two measures' worth will be plenty to see you through the end of *Compose Yourself.*

What Will I Get Out of It?

Fluency in the musical language. Eventually you should be as able to compose songs, solos, or instrumental music as easily as you now compose sentences and paragraphs in English. Yes, this is a lifelong pursuit, but *Compose Yourself* will help you take that all important first step and ensure that you're headed in the right direction forever after.

How Does It Work?

We use drills borrowed from language courses to allow you to become creative immediately. In French classes, for example, you begin speaking and improvising simple sentences right away, with just a handful of words. Your vocabulary and grammar continue to expand, and one day you find yourself fluent in French. Similarly, we use games of imitation and variation on simple musical ideas to achieve musical fluency, meaning the ability to spontaneously compose or improvise whole musical sentences that have rhyme and reason.

Compose Yourself is not a substitute for higher level theory and performance courses. It simply ensures that your creativity doesn't get left at the curb when you undertake a disciplined study of music. It trains you to think flexibly and inventively, rather than in the by-the-numbers, right-or-wrong mode encouraged by theory.

The four easy lessons of *Compose Yourself* can also be compared to four lessons in juggling. You will learn how to juggle three musical elements: rhythm, harmony, and melody. The fourth lesson puts them all together and shows you how to write a song.

These four lessons are not the whole story—far from it—but they're enough to awaken and tune up your Musical I.Q., which is all you need to open the door to musical creativity.

What Style of Music Is Taught?

Fluency in a new language is the goal; the dialect you "speak" is up to you, so the course adapts to any style. We focus on songwriting because popular music is what we grow up with. It is the music we play in our heads, the soundtrack to our lives. Everyone knows Elvis, and everyone knows The Beatles, but the method will work no matter what you are interested in, whether it's Mozart or metal, Rachmaninoff or Radiohead.

What Are the Prerequisites?

Compose Yourself is not for beginners, but it's not for experts, either. It's for intermediate instrumentalists and songwriters who have a burning desire to create their own music. The course could have been written for any level, from beginner to pro, but moderately experienced players with a passion for music have the most to gain from it in the shortest time, so they are the intended audience.

The course was conceived with guitar in mind, but it will work for other instruments, too. Guitarists must know the so-called "garden-variety" or "cowboy" chords and how to change between them fairly quickly while strumming. Pianists need similar skills. If you like to read magazines such as *Guitar Player*, *Guitarist*, or *Guitar Techniques*, or if you browse the music scores and "how to write a song" books at the local bookstore, then you're an ideal candidate for the course.

Knowledge of music fundamentals, especially how to read music, is also required. You should at least know a few major scales and be able to sight-read simple melodies in the "easy" keys. Yes, a few rare and exceptional artists have achieved fortune and fame without knowing how to read a single note. But a book is a book. It depends on words and symbols to communicate, which limits our choices.

If you don't read music, you shouldn't hesitate to learn. Knowing how to read notes can no more cripple your musical creativity than knowing how to read words can cripple your ability to write a poem. Resistance to musical literacy isn't necessarily a sign of being gifted; only creative output can determine that. Musicians who resist sight-reading are probably resisting the way it is taught, rather than some inherent evil in music notation itself.

The course was designed for use in groups of at least two players, but if you're going solo, a cheap handheld recorder can take the place of a playing partner. A recorder is also useful for capturing your musical ideas, which will become important in *Lesson 4 – Secrets of Songwriting*. High-end digital equipment is all right, but there's nothing wrong with economy class. The focus should be on ideas and imagination, not hardware.

On Your Marks, Get Set, Compose!

So if you're ready, grab your instrument, tune up, and turn the page. And if you need inspiration now or any time in the future, just watch the Disney film Ratatouille, and every time Chef Gusteau says "cook," think "compose."

Lesson 1 – Juggling Rhythm

Rhythm is the least musical event that is still musical.

– Jef Raskin, creator of the Macintosh[1]

Intro

From here to the end of the course, your mission is simple: *Learn how to juggle*. Juggle what? Three musical elements:

- **Rhythm**: Patterns of time woven in long or short, accented or unaccented pulses and notes

- **Harmony**: *Chords*, which are groups of three or more notes that sound well together, and *chord progressions*, which are a parade of chords.

- **Melody**: A single line of notes that elicits a mood or tells a story. Melody is a form of poetry, and a good melody moves us like a good poem—more so, perhaps, because it appeals directly to the emotions.

It may not be easy to become an accomplished juggler, but it's far from impossible. All you have to do is take it one ball at a time. We'll start with rhythm because it's the only musical element that is musical all by itself. A chord progression or a melody is lifeless without the organizing force of rhythm, but a drum solo—pure, unadulterated rhythm—can be musical without any help from harmony or melody.

---

1 See the *Preface.*

Rhythm means patterns of time, from the regular, clockwork pulse of the beat to the coy maneuverings of melody. From these rhythmic building blocks, composers construct the larger forms of time that make up songs, dances, and symphonies.

Putting it another way, time is the composer's canvas, and chords and melody are like brushstrokes that fill it with tonal color. But there's a crucial difference: a painter's canvas is on the outside, where all can see. A composer's canvas is on the inside, made from the cloth of imagination. This means that as a composer, you have to create the frame, as well as the painting. But if you etch the rhythmic forms of time into your consciousness, it will free your imagination to paint in tonal colors across measures, sections, phrases, and periods, the most common structural units of musical composition.

A keen sense of rhythm and time structure is one of the chief traits that distinguish professional musicians from amateurs. It is also one of the least acknowledged. Yet there is no doubt that rhythmic consciousness is every bit as essential as a sense of pitch. Where do the pros get this magical awareness of time? Talent and years of experience certainly help. While it may not be possible to duplicate such experience in one easy lesson, you can greatly accelerate your progress and make the most of your talent by isolating rhythm and the forms of time and drilling them over and over until they become part of your thinking.

And it can be fun, too, if you make a game out of it. This lesson will introduce three games that will recur in every lesson. Together they make up the inner game of music.

Rhythmic I.Q.

We have all tapped a foot to the beat. But this is a passive response to an outside stimulus. In contrast, *creative* rhythm requires a high Rhythmic I.Q. (Imagination Quotient). This means an ability to shape time in your mind, like a sculptor shaping marble or clay. With the help of a high Rhythmic I.Q., you can let your imagination race ahead of the music you're playing, sketching what is yet to come. This may be a new idea to you, but it's not terribly exotic. You already do something similar when you mentally compose a sentence before you speak or write.

As musicians, we have a tendency to overrate our Rhythmic I.Q. After all, we've spent a lifetime tapping our foot to the beat, reading rhythmic notation, and performing scales and pieces. If you've performed a solo instrumental, then you know how difficult it is to conjure up a rhythm out of thin air, especially onstage. Experiences such as these make us feel like experts, but in reality most of our rhythmic experience has been *passive*, not creative. We reproduce rhythms created by others, and if we improvise, we mix and mingle rhythm with everything else we're doing. None of this encourages our Rhythmic I.Q. to develop as fully as it might were we to give it our undivided attention.

Having a high Rhythmic I.Q. means having a three-dimensional awareness of rhythm: past, present, and future. *Lesson 1* will elevate your Rhythmic I.Q. through improvised "dialog drills" between you and a playing partner. A recording device is an acceptable substitute for a live partner. These easy-to-perform drills introduce the four most common rhythmic units in music:

- **Motive**: One measure[2]
- **Section**: Two measures
- **Phrase**: Four measures
- **Period**: Eight measures

What Is a "Motive"?

Strictly speaking, a *motive* (also called a *motif*) is a brief, distinctive fragment of rhythm and melody, such as the "Dit-dit-dit-dah" theme in Beethoven's *Fifth Symphony*.

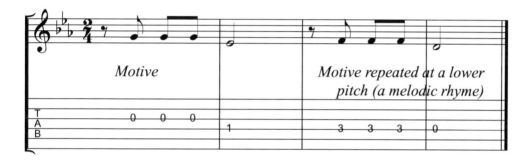

1-1. "Thus fate knocks at the door," Beethoven said of his "fate motif," the four most famous notes in the history of music. The repetition of the motif at a different pitch level, such as Beethoven does in measures 3-4, creates a "melodic rhyme." A melodic rhyme exists between any similar sounding group of notes. Just as with poetic rhyme, melodic rhyme adds layers of meaning to melody. Melodic rhyme is one of the "motifs" of Lesson 3.

Another well-known example of a motif is the menacing shark theme from *Jaws*. Because this lesson concerns rhythm only, the term *motive* will be used in a limited sense to mean any one-measure rhythmic pattern.

Game 1: Parroting

The Parrot Game is a rhythmic dialog reminiscent of the listen-and-repeat drills you've done in language classes. The object of the game is to perfectly parrot a rhythmic motive, in other words, to repeat it exactly. Two players are required. If you don't have a partner, you can record the examples and imitate them as you play them back. It is important to have a metronome

---

2 Rhythm exists on several levels: The *pulse* is the steady beat that gets your foot tapping. The *meter* is a uniform grouping of beats created by a recurring accent on the first beat of every group—the first of every four beats, for example. Each group of beats is called a *measure*. Every measure contains the same number of beats. The most common meters are two, three, or four beats per measure. The most popular meter is 4/4 (also called common meter). A measure of 4/4 time contains four quarter notes and is counted "ONE, two, three, four."

ticking in the background, or to tap your foot to establish a steady beat at a moderate tempo. *Tempo* means the pace of beats, or more literally, the beats per minute (*bpm*).

One person will be the "Player," the other will be the "Parrot." The Player plays a rhythmic motive and the Parrot imitates it. In effect, the Player says: "Polly want a cracker?" And the Parrot says it back exactly the same way: "Polly want a cracker?"

The setup is simple: Player and Parrot begin by tapping feet in unison. This establishes the tempo and a connection between the two musicians. The Player then plays a one-measure rhythmic motive that ends on the downbeat[3] of the next measure. The count continues in silence, which gives the Parrot time to think, and then the Parrot repeats the motive, ending on the downbeat of the fourth measure.

The Player then goes on to a new motive unless the Parrot has made a mistake, in which case the Player repeats the motive until the Parrot gets it right:

Both tap and count   "Player" beats out a rhythm   "Parrot" imitates rhythm (cont.)

1-2. Both players tap together. The Player plays the motive, and the Parrot imitates it, either immediately or after taking a measure or two to think before performing. Quarter-note rests have been used to emphasize the "ONE-two-three-four" count in each measure.

How do you play the motives? Any way you want. You can sing, clap, thump the guitar or pound the piano—it doesn't matter, as long as the Parrot echoes the rhythm perfectly. Twenty motives will be found below (*Ex. 1-3*). Players should switch roles every ten motives:

- Player 1 plays motives 1 through 10, while Player 2 parrots each one
- Player 2 plays motives 11 through 20, and Player 1 parrots each one
- Player 2 plays motives 1 through 10, and Player 1 parrots each one
- Player 1 plays motives 11 through 20, and Player 2 parrots each one

If you record the examples yourself, you will have to play the Parrot in all twenty examples. Performance tip: Exaggerate the accent on the count of "ONE," rather than leave listeners in doubt. It will help you feel the whole measure as a unit of time, which is vital to thinking like a composer or improviser.

---

3 The *downbeat* is the "ONE!" count, the accented beat at the beginning of each measure, so called because the conductor swings the baton downward on the "ONE" count.

1-3. Twenty One-Measure Rhythmic Motives for the Parrot Game

1-3. Quarter note rests appear in the score in order to stress the importance of counting the beats out loud: "ONE, two, three, four." Experiment with meters other than 4/4, if you wish.

Game 2: Q&A

The Q&A ("Question and Answer") Game is an improvised musical dialog. It is like the Parrot Game, but the response is *similar* to the motive, not the *same as* the motive. The "Questioner" plays the motive as before, and the "Answerer" improvises a response. Here are a couple of sample rounds:

1-4. The Q&A Game is like a dialog. One player plays a rhythmic motive, the other player improvises a variation on the motive.

In the Q&A Game, the Questioner repeats each motive four times, and the Answerer improvises four different responses. The order of play is the same as in the Parrot Game. Simply recycle the twenty motives used in the Parrot Game (*Ex. 1-3*). You can also compose new motives in 3/4 (*waltz time*), or 2/2 (*cut time*), or with a pickup beat.[4]

---

4 A *pickup beat* is an unaccented beat that leads into the accented first beat of the next measure. The shifted accent continues throughout the phrase. For example, 3/4 time is normally counted "ONE, two, three; ONE, two, three," like "MEX-i-co, MEX-i-co." With a pickup beat, 3/4 would be counted "three, ONE, two; three, ONE, two," like saying "Ba-NA-na, Ba-NA-na."

Sections – A Popular Rhythmic Unit

A two-measure rhythmic idea is called a *section*. Sections are not just a classical concept; they are common in all musical styles, from classical to pop:[5]

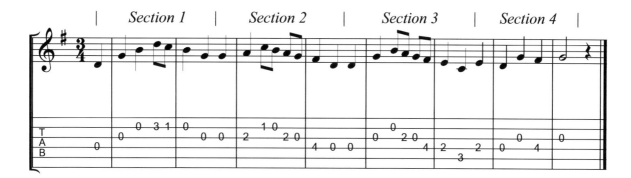

1-5. The Ash Grove, a traditional Welsh folk song, is made up of four two-measure sections. A stronger division occurs at the fourth measure, creating two four-measure phrases (more or less complete musical thoughts, like phrases in a sentence). Each section in The Ash Grove begins with a pickup beat (see footnote 4), but like all sections, each encompasses two downbeats.

1-6. Musette, by J.S. Bach (1685 – 1750). This piece is also made up of four two-measure sections. Like The Ash Grove, the sections pair up to create two four-measure phrases. The second phrase begins in measure 5, as signaled by the repetition of melody from measure 1.

---

5 Copyright restrictions rule out quotations from popular music, but if you look at the scores of a few songs, you will find sections everywhere.

| Section 1 | Section 2 | Section 3 | Section 4 |

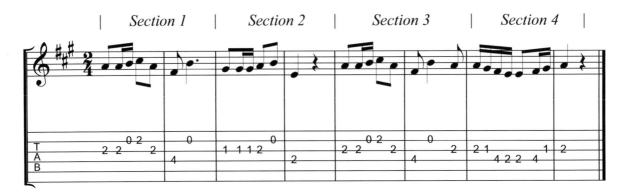

1-7. Là ci darem la mano, Wolfgang Amadeus Mozart (1756 – 1791). This famous aria from Don Giovanni combines four two-measure sections into two four-measure phrases. The end of the first phrase is signaled by the question tone "E" and the quarter-note rest in measure 4. The second phrase begins with the repetition of melodic material in measure 5, but the ending is different, an extremely valuable compositional device (repeat the phrase, vary the ending).

Sections are like musical bon-bons—short and sweet—which is one reason for their popularity as a compositional unit. The two downbeats of a section give it stability and make it easy for audiences to track the composer's ideas. The two downbeats are like the twin towers of a suspension bridge holding up the stream of notes flowing between them. The traffic is sometimes heavy or sometimes light, but the towers are firm—a useful reference when improvising.

Sections and the Parrot Game

The Player plays the example section, ending on the downbeat of measure 3. Both players keep the beat through measures 3 and 4. This gives the Parrot enough time to organize his thoughts. The Parrot imitates the example section in measures 5 and 6 and ends on the downbeat of measure 7. Both players keep the beat in measure 8. Then the Player begins a new example for the Parrot to imitate:

Player plays the rhythm   Parrot's think-time   Parrot repeats the rhythm (cont.)

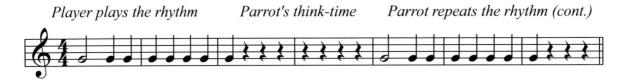

1-8. The Player and Parrot trade roles every ten sections, as described above.

1-9. Twenty Sections for Parroting

The Q&A Game – Improvising Sections

Use the twenty sections in *Ex. 1-9*, but improvise variations on them. The Questioner and the Answerer should trade roles every few sections, as shown below:

Questioner plays section　　　　*Think time*　　　*Answerer replies*　　　*Think time*

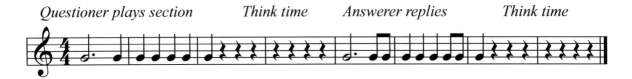

1-10. The answering variation may have fewer notes than the Question. (Quarter note rests emphasize the importance of counting every beat out loud, or at least mentally.)

Improvising Phrases and Periods

A complete definition of the term *phrase* would include rhythm, harmony, and melody, so for now we'll define a phrase simply as a four-measure rhythmic idea. Phrases don't always contain four measures, but this definition will do for now. Like a phrase in English, a musical phrase expresses a single idea, but it isn't weighty enough to stand on its own. It requires at least one other balancing phrase to round off the idea. Here, for example, is the first phrase of a Renaissance melody.

1-11. First phrase from Almain, *by Francis Cutting (1550 – 1595)*

This phrase asks a question, leaving us in suspense, awaiting an answer. The answer comes in the form of a balancing phrase of equal length that ends on a final-sounding note (see next page):

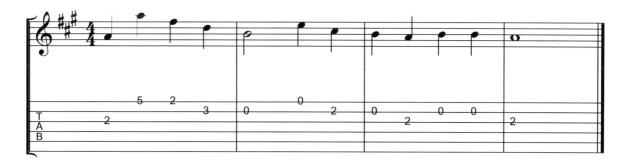

1-12. Second phrase from Cutting's Almain

Now the thought is complete. Two phrases in the form of question and answer, such as Cutting's *Almain*, make up a musical form called a *period*. *The Ash Grove* (*Ex. 1-5*), *Musette* (*Ex. 1-6*), and *Là ci darem la mano* (*Ex. 1-7*) are also examples of period form. A period is comparable to an English sentence. It has a subject (the first phrase) and a predicate (the second phrase). Sometimes the two phrases are called the *antecedent* and *consequent*. The antecedent starts something and the consequent finishes it. They are related, like cause and effect, yin and yang, breathe in and breathe out, night and day, wax on, wax off.

Ten Phrases for the Parrot Game

As with motives and sections, the Player plays, and the Parrot imitates (an exact repetition). The phrase ends in measure 4, but the Parrot may have up to two measures to think (both players maintain the beat). Then the Parrot begins the imitation, as shown below:

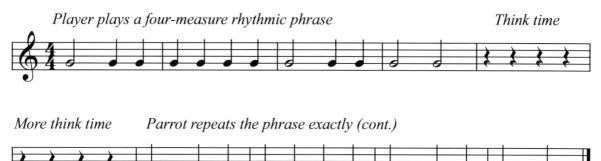

1-13. It takes a sharp parrot to "listen and repeat" a four-measure phrase.

Parroting a four-measure phrase is more difficult than parroting a two-measure section, so the Player may have to repeat the example a few times before the Parrot gets it. If the Parrot fails after four tries, go on to the next example. Play the game again the following day, and the Parrot should improve. You're learning a new language, and everyone learns at a different rate. Almost anyone can develop a strong Rhythmic I.Q. All that's required is perseverance.

Ten phrases for playing the Parrot Game are provided below, in *Ex. 1-14*. Phrases are longer and more demanding, so you may want to trade roles after each phrase. Be sure that you eventually play both roles with all ten examples.

1-14. Ten Four-Measure Phrases for the Parrot Game

[9]

[10]

Period Form and the Q&A Game

Playing the Q&A Game with four-measure phrases results in a four-measure Question followed by a four-measure Answer. This is the rhythmic blueprint for an eight-measure period, a complete musical thought. Periods have been fundamental structural units in countless songs and instrumental pieces throughout the history of music, including the present day.

Play the Q&A Game with the ten phrases given in *Ex. 1-14*. Be flexible about the think-time you allow each other between Question and Answer. If you need an adrenalin rush, begin the Answer phrase on the next beat after the Question phrase. Otherwise take your time, and begin the Answer after you've worked it out mentally. But *always* maintain the beat. Repeat each example four times to allow the Answerer a chance to improvise four different responses. Trade roles after each example, as shown below.

The Questioner plays a four-measure phrase...

The Answerer improvises a four-measure answer, and voila! Period form!

1-15. Period form—a complete musical thought with similarities to a sentence—is a matter of joining Question and Answer phrases. When playing the Q&A game with phrase-length rhythms, you are practicing the improvisation of complete musical thoughts in period form. Needless to say, this will significantly enhance your musical fluency.

Game 3: "As If"

Music is the language of emotion. To add an emotional element to your rhythmic improvisation, you might think about an emotional moment in your life, and then improvise a two-period, sixteen-measure rhythm, *as if* you were telling someone how you felt. The As If Game acquires greater depth when we add harmony and melody to the mix. With greater mastery of technique, it becomes the whole game of music.

Jamming

When both players begin playing at once, you have a jam. It can be a lot of fun and the dialog with your partner can be interesting. Just make sure that one player steps back a pace and plays the role of accompaniment, allowing the "soloist" leeway to take off and play in and around the beat. Trade roles often.

Rhythmic Improv Exercise for Guitar

The following exercise works best for guitar, though it could be adapted for keyboard. No special skill is needed. Eight-year-olds have been known to master it in five minutes. The exercise has several benefits:

- It will raise your Rhythmic I.Q.
- It's fun, like playing *Guitar Hero*, but with a real guitar.
- It builds the endurance you need to get through an entire song or piece.
- It builds a vocabulary of grooves for composition and improvisation.

Even experts have trouble defining "groove," a word that resembles "groovy," an antique term from the 1960s. *Groovy* may be gone, but groove lives on, especially among musicians. For our purposes, it is the lively, danceable, beat-driven rhythm at the heart of pop music of all kinds, from ska to metal. To paraphrase blogger-musician Steve Telehus, the groove is what makes you want to get up and dance, even if you don't know how.

When musicians talk about being "in the groove," they're describing the feeling of having a solid sense of metronomic time and knowing when to push or pull against it by coming in slightly before or after the beat. Audiences can feel it like a live current when musicians are in the groove.

The idea of the exercise is simple: Just tune in a music video on the Internet and play along. In this exercise, the guitar is a percussion instrument. You don't play chords except by muffling the strings or letting them ring out.

- Right hand: Begin by tapping your left foot to the beat. Match your right arm to the motion of your foot and strum on the downstrokes only. You now have the beat. Next, imitate the rhythm, using both upstrokes and downstrokes. Keep playing for the entire length of the song.

- Left hand: Use two "chords." For the first, just clasp the strings lightly, muffling them. All you want is a solid, percussive "chunk" when the pick (or hand) hits the strings. For the second chord, open your left hand and let the open strings ring out. Open your left hand whenever you feel like it. For some snappy percussive effects, slap the strings with the left-hand fingers or smack the strings against the fretboard with your right hand.

After the song is over, try to imitate the groove from memory. Then improvise new rhythms. The vocabulary of grooves you build will come in handy when you get to *Lesson 4 – Secrets of Songwriting*. You are also elevating your Rhythmic I.Q. by learning to track motives, sections, and phrases, a skill that will free you to be more ingenious with chords and melody in later lessons.

The exercise also has applications in various styles. See Texas-style blues-rock guitarist Anthony Stauffer's site, StevieSnacks.com, and check out the premium lessons on "the grip," "muting," and "raking" for insights into how the skills can be applied to real music. Also of interest are singer/songwriter Clare Dowling's reggae guitar lessons on YouTube, beginning with *How to Play Reggae Guitar Lesson Pt 1* and continuing through three other related lessons.

Focused Listening

"Focused listening" means paying strict attention to one feature of a musical composition. It resembles isolating and working one set of muscles in weightlifting. The mere act of sorting out what you are hearing sharpens your musical ear. It also improves your ability to use the feature you're focusing on in your own compositions and improvisations.

Rhythm is rich in possibilities for focused listening. Let's try just one: the downbeat, the first beat in each measure. Follow these steps:

- Listen to a piece of music and tap your foot to the beat.

- Find the count. Most rock and pop songs have four beats to the measure, so the count is likely to be "One, two, three, four; One, two, three, four," and so forth.

- Count "One!" loudly, while reducing all the other counts to a whisper: "One! two, three, four, One! two, three, four...." Don't hesitate to exaggerate the "One!"

This will make it conspicuous how the downbeat anchors the flow of melody and harmony in each measure. The organization of time between downbeats is flexible. Long notes, short notes, between-the-beat notes—all freely cavort around the master impulse of the downbeat.

Notice how counting downbeats allows you to sense the flow of thought in a phrase. Most phrases are four measures long and contain four downbeats.

Listen to the same piece several times, counting downbeats and sensing how the arc of each phrase tells a story, like the scenes in a drama. At this point you are beginning to hear the piece the way the composer heard it.

Repeat this exercise often. An awareness of the organizing power of the downbeat will improve your comprehension of musical grammar and your power to control the flow of musical thought in your own compositions and improvisations.

Outro

The first time I heard Jef Raskin[6] at the keyboard, I thought it was a recording of a majestic pipe organ booming out Baroque counterpoint. The elegant music was emanating from his office at Information Appliance in Palo Alto. As I stood in the hallway outside and listened, I couldn't place the composer. Was it Bach? Telemann? An unsung hero of the Baroque? When I turned the corner, there was Jef, sitting at his DX7 synthesizer, improvising a five-part fugue while reading the *Wall Street Journal* propped up on the music stand in front of him.

It took me about a nanosecond to ask him for composition lessons. Unfortunately, it took five more years and the demise of the company before he could afford the time. But it was worth the wait, if not the demise of our dream of challenging Microsoft and Apple. As a recognized authority in the field of human cognition and learning,[7] Jef had unique qualifications as a teacher. He was also a former music professor at UC San Diego who had joined Apple as employee number thirty-three, where he led the user documentation department before becoming Manager of Advanced Systems. The blend of all of these disciplines, as well as Jef's natural genius, led to his unique approach to teaching composition, the only method I've ever experienced that worked.

It was shortly after Information Appliance went out of business that I reminded Jef of his promise to give me a few lessons in composition when he got the time. He didn't answer. He just steepled his fingers together and went into a spell of deep thought. The first thing he said when he came out of it was that he wanted to treat *"this"* (teaching composition) like a programming problem.

Programming begins by dividing a complex task into simpler tasks and rebuilding from the simplest task of all. Jef observed that rhythm was "the least musical event that was still musical," so that's where we began. For more than a month, he gave me assignments in writing one- and two-part rhythmic compositions, which he would critique after we performed them on tambourine, conga drum, and clave sticks. Surprisingly, he had a lot of things to say, even about the least of them.

This was my introduction to a fundamental principle of Jef's teaching method: *Limited material, unlimited freedom.* A confession: At first, I *hated* working with nothing but half-note and quarter-note rhythms, but in contrast to the assignments I had received in college music classes, these were simple, manageable, and most important—*open-ended.* There were no right or wrong answers, which freed my creativity. Even the resentment I felt toward the limitations became a creative force.

---

6 See the *Preface.*
7 See *The Humane Interface*, by Jef Raskin, Addison-Wesley, 2000.

Jef would probably have said that his teaching method was based on computer programming and cognitive science, but I think that juggling may have had more to do with it. In addition to his other talents, Jef was an expert juggler, and he taught juggling the same way that he taught composition: one ball at a time.

Music, juggling, photography, archery, ping pong, radio-controlled glider design, advanced mathematics, computer science, race car driving, bicycling—Jef was not just a dilettante at all of these things. He was surprisingly *good* at all of them. For example, one day he showed me a surfcasting pole he had designed after watching fishermen on the beach near his home. They laughed when he brought it down to the water, because it looked like a homemade piece of junk. And it was: even the ferrules were plugged in backward. But they quit laughing when he slung his weighted line over the tops of the waves, well beyond the reach of the best surfcasting pole on the beach. He was showing me how he had modeled the physics of the pole on the Macintosh when I asked him how he'd managed to master so many skills. He replied without hesitation that he saw no difference between quantum physics and fishing—"all knowledge is digital," he said, with an impish gleam in his eye.

The truth is that I have an ulterior motive in telling these tales of Jef's genius. I'm hoping they will inspire you to stick with the exercises in *Lesson 1* for at least a few weeks. I'm all too aware that many readers will wonder if it's necessary. That's how I felt, even with a live teacher giving me feedback. But have faith that these exercises will open the door to a new kind of musical thinking for you, the precise sort of thinking that Mozart displayed when he composed symphonies while conversing at the dinner table.

Spend ten to twenty minutes a day on focused listening and rhythmic improvisation for the next week, and you will begin to hear music in a new way. You can even improvise rhythmic sections and phrases when you're taking a walk. Visualize the notes on the page. Eventually you will find yourself flying high above the landscape of time when you compose or improvise. That pleasurable feeling of standing outside the music while in the middle of it is a sign that your Musical I.Q. is rising. It is one of the secrets of learning how to think in whole musical thoughts, rather than note-to-note. It is also vital preparation for *Lesson 2 – The Harmonic Journey*, where you will learn how to juggle two musical elements at once.

Incidentally, in case you're curious, Jef never charged a dime for the composition lessons. *Limited material, unlimited freedom* was matched by *Zero cost, infinite value.*

Interlude – The Elements of Harmony

There is geometry in the humming of the strings. There is music in the spacings of the spheres.

– Pythagoras (c. 570 – c. 495 BC)

Intro

Presumably you're already familiar with intervals, chords, and the other elements of harmony, but it may have been awhile since you studied them, so this review has been provided to make sure that no student is left behind in *Lesson 2 – The Harmonic Journey*, which concerns improvising chord progressions. Even if what follows is new to you, it shouldn't be too difficult. And if you're already an expert, you may find answers to some intriguing questions, such as these:

- Why do scales have seven tones?
- Where do the scale tones come from?
- Where do triads come from?
- What makes a minor chord "sad"?
- What chord changed the history of music?
- What makes a chord progression feel like it's going somewhere?
- What does Renaissance music have in common with Renaissance painting, and why should a modern musician such as you care?

Historical Overview of Harmony

Harmony—the art of combining musical sounds in chords and arranging chords in meaningful chains called *chord progressions*—is the crowning achievement of Western music. In other cultures, melody and rhythm have great subtlety and complexity, but nowhere has harmony evolved as highly as it has in the West. A quick review of how this came about will enhance your understanding of the musical language and your ability to use it.

According to legend, ground zero for Western harmony was a blacksmith's shop on the island of Samos in the northern Aegean Sea, some twenty-five hundred years ago. The Greek philosopher-mathematician Pythagoras was walking by when he noticed the unusually harmonious ringing of the blacksmith's hammers. At the time, Pythagoras was locking horns with a rival school of philosophy that held that good taste and intuition were the ultimate guides to musical aesthetics. As the father of geometry, not to mention the leader of a mystical cult of mathematics, Pythagoras believed that music, like the whole universe, must be ruled by numbers. But *what* numbers?

The blacksmith explained that the hammers were weighted in simple ratios. With that in mind, Pythagoras conducted some experiments and found what he wanted: a musical system based on mathematical relationships. European musicians inherited Pythagorean wisdom in the form of the Greek modes (exotic scales) and a faith in mathematical analysis, but his original ideas had been lost or relegated to the category of esoteric mysticism by then, which is why he seldom receives more than a footnote in music theory books. Pythagoras's obscurity is not surprising, because he forbade his students from writing about his philosophy under pain of death, and most of what we know about him was written centuries after he died. Nevertheless, Pythagoras got the ball rolling, and his discoveries continue to resonate around the globe in just about every kind of instrument north of a didgeridoo.

The modern art of harmony arose during the late Middle Ages, when European composers began interweaving melodies in a style called *polyphony*, or counterpoint. As the voices of singers converged, they formed chords, and harmony began to emerge as an independent study. Through the Renaissance and later, polyphony evolved into *homophony* (one melody accompanied by chords) and tonality was born.

Tonality is a musical system in which a single tone—the *tonic* or *key tone*—is the center of all harmonic and melodic movement. The name of the tonic or the key tone is identical to the name of the scale that represents it. For example, in the key of D major, the tonic (or key tone) is the tone D, and the D major scale reinforces its central role (see *I-1* on the following page):

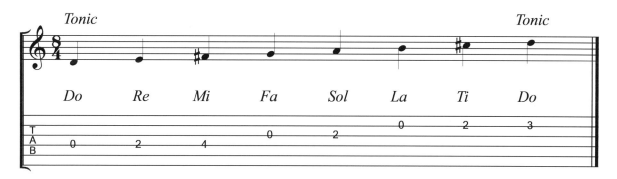

I-1. The D major scale establishes the supremacy of the tone D.

When we say "the key of D major," we're describing the *tonality* of a piece, not just the scale. *Key* is a broader, more inclusive term than *scale*. The D major scale is a *component* of the key of D major, but not the *whole* of it. As shown in the example above, a scale is a set of seven specific tones. A composition in the *key* of D major, however, may use tones and chords outside of the D major scale,[1] as long as they support the harmonic and melodic supremacy of the tonic D.

Tonality also offers a resource not found in the medieval modal system or in non-Western music: *modulation*, which means "changing key centers," whether temporarily or for extended periods. For example, when a composition in D major modulates to a nearby key, such as A major, the tone A becomes the new tonic, and the A major scale becomes the basis of melody and harmony. The key of D major may be gone, but it is not forgotten, because we feel as if we're coming home again when it returns.

Tonality and Perspective

Tonality has been around for centuries. Nowadays we take it for granted because we hear it everywhere, from rock to pop to advertising jingles, Broadway shows, symphonies, opera, and movie soundtracks.

But it wasn't always so.

Tonality arose during the Renaissance at the same time that perspective appeared in visual art. This was more than mere coincidence. Both art forms dramatized Renaissance ideals, especially the dawning consciousness of the worth of the individual, and an interest in everyday life and the details and details of human personality and psychology.

This change in consciousness was reflected in literature as early as 1400, in the poetry of Geoffrey Chaucer, who wrote about ordinary people who are as recognizable and real today as they were in the fourteenth century. Painters, too, began to show an interest in depicting people as they were, warts and all, rather than as emblems of religious doctrine or social status.

---

1 In Western music, the octave is divided into twelve equal half steps (the *chromatic scale*), leading to twenty-four potential key centers (twelve major and twelve minor). Any of the twelve tones of the chromatic scale may appear in a tonal composition, no matter what key it's in.

Objects no longer floated in space, as they had in medieval art, but obeyed the laws of optics. The more distant an object was, the smaller it became. The illusion of perspective was created by the *vanishing point*, a single point on the horizon where all light rays in the picture frame converged. Perspective had the effect of bringing the viewer into a realistic scene. It was a way of saying that the world was a rational place, governed by natural law, and you, the observer, could trust your perceptions of it, rather than what an authority figure, such as the pope or the king, might say.

Similarly, tonality established a vanishing point in music. Modal counterpoint, which preceded tonality, was the musical equivalent of medieval tapestry. In the music of composers such as Adam de la Halle (1237? – 1288), John Dunstable (1390 – 1453), and Guillaume Dufay (1397 – 1474), melodies floated and meandered without as firm a sense of an ultimate goal as we expect from music today. This is not to say that the music of these composers was inferior—medieval music is beautiful and remains popular even today—but with the rise of tonality, harmony and melody began to converge on a single tone, the tonic, like light rays converging on the horizon. It took several centuries to fully realize the implications of the change.

Tonality admitted harmonies that had been forbidden by the Church in the Middle Ages, such as sensual thirds and sixths, discordant sevenths and seconds, and even the dreaded tritone,[2] "the Devil in music." The approved intervals—"perfect" unisons, fourths, fifths, and octaves—submerged individual voices into one blended, concordant sound. The new, rebel intervals combined or clashed in ways that emphasized the individuality of the singing voices. These harmonies and discords, which we now take for granted, were, in their day, revolutionary, humanizing intervals.

Tonality has evolved continuously over the centuries. Equal-tempered tuning, which first appeared on the fretboards of lutes in the early sixteenth century, enabled composers to play in all twelve major and minor keys. More important, it gave them the ability to change key centers, or modulate, to any key. J.S. Bach (1685-1750) celebrated the new freedom with the *Well-Tempered Clavier*, a set of forty-eight preludes and fugues in all major and minor keys.

Polyphony reached its apex in Bach, partly because he was so superior that later composers didn't see any point in imitating him. Instead, in the mid-1700s, composers began to prize simplicity and elegance over the ornate complexity of Baroque counterpoint. Their inspiration came from the aesthetic ideals of the Golden Age of Greece, which were undergoing a revival because the constant siege of Greece by the Ottoman Empire (Turkish Moslems) had driven scholars into Italy, where they began to lecture to artisans, professors, and courtiers.

The new wave of Renaissance thinking ultimately led to the Classical period and the symphonies of Haydn, Mozart, and Beethoven. In their hands, modulation, which Bach had used for brief excursions into alternate tonal centers, was used to expand the formal architecture of music.

---

2 The tritone, a highly dissonant interval, spans three whole tones, or six frets on the guitar, such as the distance from B on the open second string to F on the sixth fret of the same string. The tritone is symmetrical. For example, the distance from the sixth-fret F to the octave B on the twelfth fret of the second string is also six frets.

The new way of treating modulation was particularly apparent in the sonata, a form of Italian program music played by the orchestra while the audience found their seats at the beginning of a comic opera. Beginning with Giovanni Battista Sammartini (1700 or 1701 – 1775), the classical composers refined the sonata into a complex, three-part form with an expanded middle act (the development section), which was filled with adventurous excursions into foreign keys. The bridge section of a modern pop song plays a similar role on a much more modest scale.

Though their symphonies were bigger and more ambitious than anything that had come before, the classical composers honored simplicity and elegance by anchoring their symphonic works in melodies that audiences could hum on the way out of the concert hall.

In the late 1700s and early 1800s, composers began to turn toward Romanticism for inspiration. The new movement, which affected all the arts, sought truth in passionate emotion and a reverent awe at the forces of nature. They found their musical language in the use of motifs (melodic fragments), rather than memorable melodies, and chromatic harmony, which makes liberal use of tones outside the key.

Chromaticism first appeared in Bach and Mozart, and arguably as early as the Renaissance madrigals of Carlo Gesualdo (1566 – 1613) and certain lute pieces by John Dowland, a contemporary of William Shakespeare at the court of Queen Elizabeth, but it reached new heights in the Romantic works of Beethoven, Schubert, Schumann, Brahms, Chopin, and Wagner.

By pushing harmony to its outer limits, chromaticism began to dissolve the foundations of tonality. Romanticism was succeeded by Impressionism (Debussy), polytonality (Stravinsky), cross-cultural tonality (Bartók), and the harshly dissonant *atonality* (Arnold Schoenberg), an artificial system that rejects the whole concept of a tonal center. In the late nineteenth and early twentieth century, mechanized warfare, aerial bombing, weapons of mass destruction, and the omnipresent threat of global destruction gave birth to the Age of Anxiety.[3] Composers found musical metaphors for the atmosphere of impending doom by weakening, undermining, and even jettisoning tonality. But there was a price to be paid. The more tonality was left behind, the more audiences for serious music began to shrink.

While some composers explored the outer fringes of tonality, pop artists embraced it, and audiences loved it. At the turn of the twentieth century, Scott Joplin wrote classically-inspired piano rags. Tin Pan Alley—an area of New York with a high concentration of music publishers—cranked out tune after tune, all of them tonal. Jazz was born, then swing, and then rock 'n' roll, rock, and all the other forms of popular music that make up the soundtrack of our lives. Pop employs colorful chords and bends the tones of the scale with abandon, but it almost never challenges the sense of a key center.

The moral is that far from being exhausted, tonality is as lively now as it ever was, and that's why we'll focus on the basics of tonal grammar here. This will make chromatic harmony and counterpoint more understandable when you decide to study them, and it will prepare you to compose and improvise in popular styles with confidence.

---

3 The term comes from the title of a 1947 poem by W.H. Auden.

Intervals

Dyads—two tones played together or one after the other—make a natural starting point for harmony. An *interval* is the distance in pitch between the two tones of a dyad. A *harmonic* interval occurs between two tones played at the same time. A *melodic* interval occurs between two tones played one after the other.

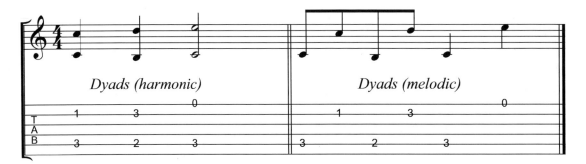

I-2. Harmonic and melodic intervals

The mood of an interval is instantly apparent to all listeners, regardless of musical training, which is why intervals are one of the most important vehicles of musical communication. Harmonic intervals influence the mood of chords. Melodic intervals influence the mood of melody. The difference—and it's an important one—is that *harmonic* intervals communicate a mood without delay, while *melodic* intervals unfold, revealing harmonic relationships one note at a time, which is why a melody (a line of notes in succession) seems to tell a story.

Just as an English sentence is a meaningful sequence of words, a melody is a meaningful sequence of *melodic words*, whose meaning depends on the mood of melodic intervals, rhythm, and tempo. As a melody unfolds, it traces out intervals. These intervals, plus connecting tones and rhythm, form melodic words. Melodic words are easy to create—one can hardly avoid it—the trick is to choose one's words wisely. A logical sequence of melodic words creates a meaningful melody. *Lesson 3 – The Heart of Melody* covers this subject in more detail.

Perfect Pitch and Relative Pitch

As creative musicians, we must become fluent in the language of intervals, which means that we must learn to recognize them instantly when they are played. We must also be capable of imagining how they will sound *before* we play them, and develop a refined awareness of their emotional implications. This naturally leads to the question of pitch perception. How do we perceive intervals? How can we improve our perception and imagination of them?

There are two kinds of pitch perception: *perfect* (or *absolute*) and *relative*. Perfect pitch means the ability to recognize or sing any tone on the basis of its intrinsic quality, without hearing a reference pitch. If you have perfect pitch, the tone C is as plain as the color red, which makes it much easier to identify musical notes and manipulate them in your imagination. But perfect pitch is rare—roughly one in ten thousand has it—so most composers and improvisers rely on relative pitch, which is a perception of the spatial relationships between tones.

To experience relative pitch perception, just play or think of the first two notes of *Over the Rainbow*, the song Judy Garland made famous in *Wizard of Oz*. The second note is higher than the first, but the two tones sound almost identical, like "red" and "light red." If you had perfect pitch, you'd be able to name the two notes. With relative pitch, you can name their relationship (an octave), but not the notes themselves without referring to an instrument. Someone with a well-developed sense of relative pitch can track the intervals in chords and melody while the music is streaming by at full speed.

While perfect pitch is unquestionably a prize asset for any musician, a keen sense of relative pitch is at least as valuable. If perfect pitch were necessary in order to hear the beauty in music, only a fraction of the population would have the musical experience. But music is universally popular. Only relative pitch, which is accessible to all, can explain why. This has important implications for you as a creative musician. It is your sensitivity to the moods of intervals and chords, as well as an intellectual understanding of them, that will enable you to use the musical language. For this, a well-developed sense of relative pitch is not just useful, it is *essential*.

The good news is that virtually anyone can acquire relative pitch through training. Most musicians hone their sense of relative pitch through *ear training*, a series of drills and exercises in singing, listening, and analyzing what you hear. Ear training is beyond the scope of this course, but it deserves a high place on your to-do list, because it is essential to realizing your full Musical I.Q.[4]

For a simple example of the power of relative pitch to create mood, compare the feeling you get from a *major* third and a *minor* third (see next page):

I-3. Major and minor thirds have dramatically different moods.

---

4 Perfectpitch.com offers a unique and highly effective course in relative pitch developed by music educator David Lucas Burge. The course can be self-taught, which makes it a good fit for students who don't have time for school. A perfect-pitch course is also offered. Citing his personal experience, university studies of the course's success, and enthusiastic testimony from students, Burge contends that perfect pitch *can* be learned, even by adults. I have not had an opportunity to evaluate the perfect pitch course, but the relative pitch course is without equal, and far superior to software-based training methods.

Almost everyone immediately recognizes the positive, warm, happy quality of the major third and the somber, sad, melancholy quality of the minor third. Major and minor thirds transfer their moods to major and minor chords:

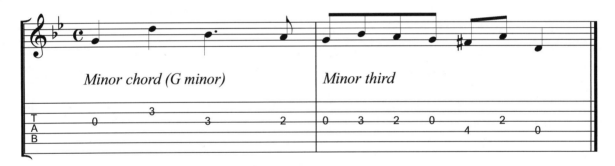

I-4. Major and minor thirds alter the moods of major and minor chords.

The same effect occurs in melody:

I-5. Theme from Little Fugue in G Minor *by J.S. Bach, BWV 578 (written between 1703 and 1707). Bach called this the "little" fugue in order to distinguish it from a bigger one in the same key (BWV 542). It is by no means little in its effect. Incidentally, note the melodic rhyme between the minor thirds on beats 1 and 3 of measure 2, and the descending major third, F♯-D.*

Your reaction to major and minor thirds is predictable, and has little or nothing to do with the absolute pitch of the notes. This is good news, because it implies that you can be a creative musician whether or not you have perfect pitch. While most of the great composers have had perfect pitch, some, such as Richard Wagner, did not. Many singers, songwriters, and instrumentalists do quite well without it, and of the two people I've known who unquestionably had it, one had no interest in music (he was nine years old and wanted to be an astronaut), and the other, a software engineer, liked Baroque music, but had no interest in learning an instrument. Both of them thought that perfect pitch was trivial and could not understand why the rest of the world was "blind" to the obvious color of tones, from a piano note to a squeaky door hinge.

Octaves

Remember the soaring melodic leap in the first two notes of *Over the Rainbow*? Ever since musicians have been making music, the "Over-the-Rainbow interval"—an octave—has been recognized as supremely important. The term *octave*, which has the same Greek root as *October*, *octopus*, or *octagon*, is the interval between the first and eighth step of a scale.

The upper and lower tones of an octave have the same name—"C" and "C", "D" and "D", etc.—because they sound alike. Any two tones whose frequencies differ by a factor of two are an octave apart. For example, a tone with a frequency of 440 Hz (cycles per second) is called "A." The tone A-880 is an octave above it, and A-220 is an octave below it.

Tones with the same name, regardless of register (highness or lowness), are said to belong to the same *pitch class*. An electric guitar in standard tuning (EADGBE), for example, may produce up to fourteen different tones in the pitch class "E":

- String 6, frets 0, 12, 24
- String 5, frets 7, 19
- String 4, frets 2, 14
- String 3, frets 9, 21
- String 2, frets 5, 17
- String 1, frets 0, 12, 24

Octaves are spatial organizers in music. The top and bottom tones of the octave make convenient boundaries, partly because everyone—musically trained or not—can hear the identical character of tones that are an octave apart, and partly because a scale or chord in one octave is structurally the same in all octaves:

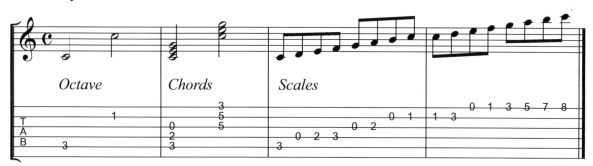

I-6. Octaves are spatial organizers because chords, scales, and other musical materials repeat themselves in cookie-cutter patterns from one octave to the next.

Half Steps

Western music divides the octave into twelve equal intervals called *half steps*. A twelve-tone scale comprising all the half steps in an octave is called a *chromatic scale*. The frets on a guitar or the keys on a piano (including black keys) form a chromatic scale because adjacent piano keys or adjacent guitar frets are a half step apart.

The tones B-C and E-F are on adjacent white keys of the piano with no black key between them. This is because the white keys form the C major scale, and the tones B-C and E-F are a half step apart in that scale. Since the C major scale makes up the so-called *natural tones*, the intervals between B-C and E-F are called *natural half steps*. Similarly, B-C and E-F are on adjacent frets of the guitar. Guitarists just have to memorize the locations of the natural half steps.

When we pair the lower tone of an octave with all twelve tones of the chromatic scale, we get thirteen intervals, from a *unison* (the lower tone of the octave paired with itself) to an octave (the twelfth step of the chromatic scale, which is the same as the first step of a new scale).

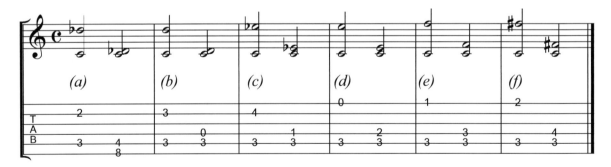

I-7. Numbers in the illustration refer to the number of half steps between the two tones in the interval. (0) Unison, (1) minor 2nd, (2) major 2nd, (3) minor 3rd, (4) major 3rd, (5) perfect 4th, (6) diminished 5th, (7) perfect 5th, (8) minor 6th, (9) major 6th, (10) minor 7th, (11) major 7th, (12) perfect octave. (Interval names will be explained shortly.)

Intervals that exceed an octave are called *compound* intervals. A compound interval sounds similar to the smaller interval that results if the octave is subtracted. For example, a major tenth minus an octave is a major third:

I-8. Subtract "7" from a compound interval to reduce it by an octave: (a) minor 9th becomes a minor 2nd, (b) major 9th, major 2nd, (c) minor 10th, minor 3rd, (d) major 10th, major 3rd, (e) perfect 11th, perfect 4th, (f) augmented 11th, augmented 4th.

Whole Steps

Two half steps make up a *whole step*. With few exceptions, scales are exclusively made up of whole steps and half steps, which means that *steps* (half and whole) are the meat and potatoes of melody. The next larger interval than a whole step is a minor third. Any melodic interval a minor third or larger is called a *skip* or *leap*. Skips tend to detract from linear melodic movement because they are heard as harmony. Too many skips can disrupt the melodic line.

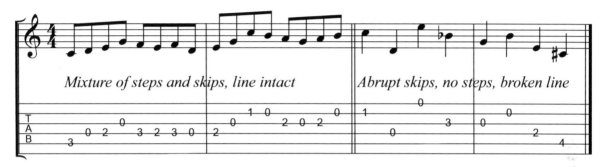

I-9. Half steps and whole steps make for horizontally unfolding melodic lines. Larger intervals tend to disrupt the line. Too many skips will fragment a melodic line.

Whole steps are also called *major seconds*, and half steps are called *minor seconds*. A "second" is the interval between two adjacent scale steps, such as A and B, C and D, and so forth. On the guitar, a whole step is two frets. Consider, for example, the tones G-A-B, which cover the first four frets on the third string. The tone G is on the open string. The tone A is on the second fret, which makes it a whole step (a major second) higher than G. The tone B is two frets higher than A, on the fourth fret of the G string, so B is a whole step (a major second) higher than A. Frets one and three on the third string correspond to black keys on the piano (G♯ and A♯ or A♭ and B♭).

On the piano, a whole step is two adjacent keys from a given starting key. Always include black keys, if any, in the count. For example, two keys above G, counting the black key between them, is A. Two keys above A, counting the black key between them, is B. This involves a total of four keys from G to B, which is the equivalent of four frets on the guitar.

The Major Scale Formula

Major and minor scales are made up of patterns of whole steps and half steps. The pattern for a major scale, for example, is "whole-whole-half-whole-whole-whole-half" (1-1-½-1-1-1-½). It is easier to think of this as a pair of 1-1-½ units separated by a whole step [1-1-½]-1-[1-1-½]. Each 1-1-½ unit is called a *tetrachord* because it encompasses four tones. All major scales conform to this intervallic pattern, no matter what their key signature.

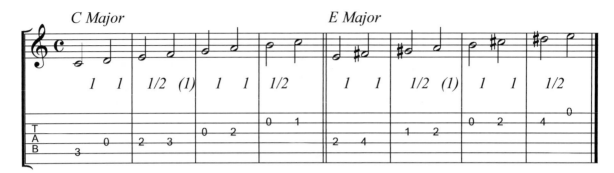

First tetrachord | Second tetrachord || First tetrachord | Second tetrachord ||

I-10. Two major scales: C major and E major. Each has two tetrachords, and each tetrachord has the same intervallic formula, (whole step)-(whole step)-(half step).

Naming Intervals

Intervals have two characteristics: *number* and *quality*. An interval such as a perfect fifth, for example, has a number (a "fifth") and a quality ("perfect").

To find the number, just count the alphabetical steps from the bottom tone to the top tone on your fingers. C and E, for example, are a third apart because it takes three fingers to get from C to E (C-D-E). The tones C and G are a fifth apart because it takes five fingers to get from C to G (C-D-E-F-G). Remember that the musical alphabet starts over after G, which means that G and B are a third apart (three steps, G-A-B), G and D are a fifth apart (five steps, G-A-B-C-D), E and A are a fourth apart (E-F-G-A), and so on.

Finding the quality of an interval is a bit more complicated. There are five choices: *major*, *minor*, *perfect*, *augmented*, and *diminished*. There are two steps in identifying the quality of an interval:

- Step 1: Think of the bottom tone as the first tone in a major scale, and determine whether the top tone belongs to that scale. (To do this, you have to know the key signatures of the major and minor keys or refer to an online source, such as Wikipedia or a book on music fundamentals.)

I-11. (1) B is the lower note. (2) Does G♯ fit with a B major key signature? Yes! (3) C♯ is the lower note. (4) Does B♯ fit the key of C♯? Yes! (5) G♭ is the lower note. (6) Does C♭ fit the key of G♭? Yes!

- Step 2: If the top tone fits in a major scale based on the bottom tone, then the interval is *major* or *perfect*, depending on the number of scale steps: unisons (identical scale steps), fourths, fifths, and octaves that fit are *perfect*. Seconds, thirds, sixths, and sevenths that fit are *major*.

For example, if we play a D major scale over the bass tone D, the intervals will be major or perfect, depending on the scale step:

I-12. If the top tone belongs to a major scale based on the bottom tone, unisons, fourths, fifths, and octaves are perfect, and seconds, thirds, sixths, and sevenths are major. Numbers 1-8 refer to intervals based on scale step of the top note. (1) Perfect unison, (2) major second, (3) major third, (4) perfect fourth, (5) perfect fifth, (6) major sixth, (7) major seventh, (8) perfect octave.

We now know how to name major and perfect intervals. The rest of the interval qualities—minor, diminished, augmented—concern the *exceptions*, that is, the cases when the top tones do *not* fit a major scale based on the bottom tone. To put it another way, minor, diminished, and augmented intervals result from *adding or subtracting a half step to a* major or perfect interval:

• A *major interval* *minus a half step* becomes *minor* (M = Major, m = minor):

I-13. (a) M3, (b) m3, (c) M3, (d) m3, (e) M6, (f) m6, (g) M10, (h) m10, (i) M10, (j) m10, (k) M6, (l) m6, (m) M2, (n) m2, (o) M7, (p) m7

• Conversely, a *minor interval* *plus a half step* becomes *major*:

I-14. (a) m2, (b) M2, (c) m3, (d) M3, (e) m6, (f) M6, (g) m7, (h) M7, (i) m9, (j) M9, (k) m6, (l) M6, (m) m10, (n) M10, (o) m6, (p) M6

• A major interval *plus a half step* becomes *augmented.*

I-15. M = major, aug = augmented. (a) M2, (b) aug2, (c) M6, (d) aug6, (e) M9, (f) aug9, (g) M2, (h) aug2, (i) M6, (j) aug6, (k) M6, (l) aug6, (m) M9, (n) aug9, (o) M6, (p) aug6

• A *perfect* interval *plus a half step* also becomes *augmented*.

I-16. (a) P4, (b) aug4, (c) P5, (d) aug5, (e) P8, (f) aug8, (g) P5, (h) aug5, (i) P5, (j) aug5, (k) P4, (l) aug4, (m) P4, (n) aug4, (o) P5, (p) aug5

• A *perfect* interval *minus a half step* becomes *diminished*.

I-17. (a) P5, (b) dim5, (c) P5, (d) dim5, (e) P5, (f) dim5, (g) P5, (h) dim5, (i) P5, (j) dim 5, (k) P5, (l) dim5, (m) perfect octave, (n) dim8, (o) P4, (p) dim4

• A *minor* interval *minus a half step* also becomes *diminished*.

I-18. (a) m3, (b) dim3, (c) m6, (d) dim6, (e) m3, (f) dim3, (g) m6, (h) dim6 (G is sharped)

This may have been a lot to absorb, so let's summarize the rules for naming intervals:

- If the top tone belongs to a major scale based on the bottom tone, the interval is *perfect* or *major*. Unisons (identical tones), fourths (such as C to F), fifths (such as C to G), and octaves (such as the interval between C and C') are perfect. Seconds, thirds, sixths, and sevenths are major.

Alterations to the interval qualities are summarized in *Table I-1* below. *Memorize this table!*

Table I-1 – Half-Step Alterations to Intervals		
Interval Quality	Subtract a Half Step	Add a Half Step
Major	Major becomes minor	Major becomes augmented
Minor	Minor becomes diminished	Minor becomes major
Perfect	Perfect becomes diminished	Perfect becomes augmented
Diminished	Diminished becomes doubly diminished	Diminished becomes minor or perfect
Augmented	Augmented becomes major or perfect	Augmented becomes doubly augmented

Enharmonic Equivalents

Identical pitches, intervals, scales, and keys may sometimes be designated by two names. These musical homonyms (same sounds, different names) are called *enharmonic equivalents*. Here are a few examples:

I-19. Enharmonically equivalent pitches: (a) F-sharp and G-flat, (b) E-sharp and F-natural. Enharmonically equivalent intervals: (c) augmented second and minor third, (d) augmented fourth and diminished fifth. Enharmonically equivalent scales or keys: (e) C-sharp major and (f) D-flat major.

Are enharmonic equivalents really necessary? Wouldn't it be simpler to give things one name and be done with it? This bold move has been considered and rejected because it would create other problems. Enharmonically equivalents are necessary because the same tones have different functions in different contexts.

Consider *I-19(c)* above. The minor third F – A♭ is found between the root and 3rd of an F minor chord.[5] The augmented second F – G♯, however, is found between the sixth and seventh steps of an A harmonic minor scale. If we rename the G♯ in the A harmonic minor scale "A♭," then the scale would have two tones named "A," which would imply a scale with two different tonics. And, if we rename A♭ in the F minor chord G♯, we must respell it F – G♯ – C, which implies a chord with no 3rd.

In short, enharmonic equivalents may be a bit of a hassle, but not much when compared with the alternative.

---

5 Arabic numerals identify component members of chords, such as 3rd, 5th, and 7th.

Inversions

Intervals may be inverted (flipped) by raising the bottom tone an octave. For example, when the C in the major third C-E is raised an octave, the interval becomes the minor sixth E-C.

I-20. Intervals and their inversions: (a) M3, (b) m6, (c) P5, (d) P4, (e) P5, (f) P4, (g) m6, (h) M3, (i) M6, (j) m3, (k) aug4, (l) dim5, (m) M6, (n) m3, (o) M2, (p) m7

An interval and its inversion always add up to nine. That is, an inverted second becomes a seventh (2 + 7 = 9); an inverted third becomes a sixth (3 + 6 = 9), and so on. Interval qualities reverse, too: minor becomes major, major becomes minor, diminished becomes augmented, and augmented becomes diminished. Perfect intervals, however, remain perfect when they are inverted, which is one reason they are called "perfect." As shown above, the inversion of a perfect fourth is a perfect fifth and vice versa; the inversion of a perfect unison is a perfect octave and vice versa (1 + 8 = 9).

Another reason that a perfect interval and its inversion are both perfect is because of their unchanging tonal quality, which might be described as a stark hollowness. Early church music, such as Gregorian chant, was restricted to perfect intervals, because its aim was to inspire solemn contemplation, and it was felt that thirds and sixths, not to mention sevenths and seconds, let alone a grating tritone,[6] were far too sensual. Incidentally, it is ironic that perfect intervals have now become the basis of the hedonistic "power chords" beloved by rock and metal guitarists. Power chords get their power from a heavy envelope of distortion (the Tyrannosaurus-like roar of overdriven speakers) and bone-rattling high volume.

Ex. I-21 on the following page shows all the inversions of the intervals shown in *Ex. I-12*.

---

6 A *tritone* (also see footnote 2, page 22 above) is an interval spanning three whole tones, reaching the exact midpoint between the top and bottom tones of an octave. For example, the tones B and F form a tritone (B is on the open second string, F is found at the sixth fret of the same string, halfway to the octave on the twelfth fret). The intensely dissonant tritone was called *diabolus in musica*—the Devil in music—by early theorists, and was banned by papal decree. Nowadays it is as common as salt and pepper.

I-21. Inversions of the intervals in a one-octave major scale (see I-12): (a) P8, (b) m7, (c) m6, (d) P5, (e) P4, (f) m3, (g) m2, (h) perfect unison.

Chord Construction

The study of chords begins with the *triad*, a tonal sandwich of three notes at intervals of a third. The thirds between the bottom and middle tones and the middle and top tones add up to a fifth between the top and bottom tones. Visually, triads are easily recognized because the three tones are stacked like pancakes on adjacent lines or spaces on the staff.

I-22. A triad is always named for its bottom tone, which is called the root. *(a) C major, (b) A minor, (c) E major, (d) B♭ major, (e) F major, (f) C major, (g) D major, (h) A♭ major.*

From lowest to highest, the three tones of a triad are called the *root*, *3rd*, and *5th*. The C major triad, for example, is spelled *C-E-G*: C is the root, E is the 3rd, and G is the 5th. The two adjacent thirds in a C major triad are *C-E* and *E-G*. Notice that C, E, and G are the first, third, and fifth tones in the scale C-D-E-F-G. This makes triad fingerings easy to find on piano: just use the thumb, middle, and pinky fingers of either hand (designated *1-3-5* in piano notation).

Doubling any tone of the triad has no effect on the name or function of the triad. For example, a C major chord with two Cs is still C major. The tones of a triad can also be placed anywhere on the staff without changing the triad's identity. Since we think of each note in a chord as representing a human voice, we call the spacing of the notes the *voicing*. In a *close* voicing, the tones are as close together as possible. An *open* voicing has gaps where another chord tone could be inserted, as shown in *I-23* on the following page.

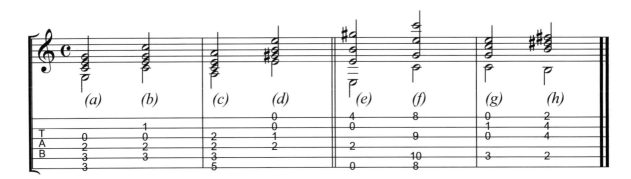

I-23. Close voicings (a-d), have no gaps: (a) C major, (b) C major, (c) A minor, (d) E major. Open voicings (e-h), have gaps: (e) E major, (f) C major, (g) C major, (h) B major.

The Overtone Series

Triads are so familiar that we seldom give any thought to where they come from, but they are modeled on a natural phenomenon called the *overtone series*, which is an array of tones given off by all vibrating bodies. Like the colors of a rainbow, the overtone series is a natural constant, which is why it is sometimes called the *Chord of Nature*. This is more than a mere curiosity. The overtone series is arguably the big bang of the musical universe, as it provides models for scales and chords, as well as a potent hint at the mechanics of tonal harmony. If you understand the overtone series, it will help you understand the musical language.

The lowest, most audible tone generated by a vibrating body is called the *fundamental*. A guitar string tuned to C, for example, emits a fundamental tone of C. The fundamental results from the entire string whipping back and forth in a bow-shaped arc between two stationary points (nodes), which causes it to emit sound waves of a certain frequency. (The stationary nodes on the guitar are the nut and bridge.)

The overtone series occurs because the vibrating string also shivers in fractions of its length—halves, thirds, fourths, fifths, and so on—while the fundamental is ringing. Overtones always occur in the same pattern of intervals above the fundamental. When the fundamental changes, the overtones change, too, preserving the intervallic pattern, as shown below (notice bass clef):

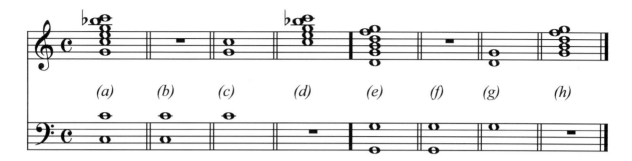

I-24. The overtone series for C (a-d) and G (e-h). Different fundamentals give rise to different overtones, but the intervallic pattern stays the same. The first interval is an octave (compare b and f). The second octave (compare c and g) includes one new tone a perfect fifth above the octave of the fundamental. The third octave (compare d and h) contains a major triad and a dominant 7th tetrad.

The strongest overtones sound "good" (consonant or harmonious) with the fundamental. As mentioned in the *Historical Overview of Harmony*, Pythagoras discovered that consonant intervals can be expressed in simple ratios. The most consonant intervals—the octave (2:1), the perfect fifth (3:2), and the major third (5:4)—make up the first four overtones of the series. The more complex the ratio between top and bottom tones, the more dissonant (harsh and clashing) the interval becomes. The highly dissonant diminished fifth (tritone), for example, is based on the complex ratio 64:45.

In the book *Aural Harmony* (see *Recommended Reading*, no. 21), Dr. Franklin W. Robinson describes the overtone series as a living source of tonal musical materials. Octaves, scales, chords, and some of the basic principles of harmony can be inferred from the overtones in the first five octaves. Whether or not these musical materials were actually *derived* from the overtone series isn't as important as the easily observed fact that the overtone series provides a natural palette of stable, consonant tone colors. Just as the overtone series is everywhere the same in nature, so is the human response to it. Without the universal perception of consonance (stability) and dissonance (instability), composers would not be able to compose, because they would have no idea what effect their tone choices would have on audiences.

How the Major Scale Echoes the Chord of Nature

In Pythagoras's time, music consisted primarily of melodies played to the accompaniment of a drone (a single, monotonously repeated pitch). Harmony as we know it was evidently all but nonexistent. The melodies were based on exotic scales called *modes*, which Plato (428 – 348 BC) called Ionian, Dorian, Phrygian, Lydian, Mixolydian, Aeolian, and Locrian, after geographic regions of Greece. The modes can be constructed by playing an octave scale on each degree of the familiar major scale (see I-25 on the following page):

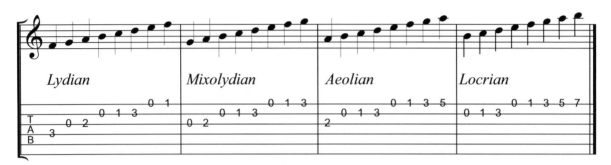

I-25. To replicate the Greek modes, simply play one-octave scales on each tone of a major scale, as shown above.

The major scale, which we know today by the syllables "Do-Re-Mi-Fa-Sol-La-Ti-Do," is identical in sound to the Ionian mode. All of the tones of the Ionian mode can be derived by a method suggested by the second octave of the overtone series, which contains one new tone—the first in the overtone series with a different name—a perfect fifth above the fundamental. Similarly, we can generate a series of new scale tones by taking the perfect fifth of the perfect fifth of the perfect fifth, and so on. Starting with C as the tonic, for example, we find the following series of scale tones generated by an ascending series of perfect fifths:

- A fifth above C is G (scale tone 5)
- A fifth above G is D (scale tone 2)
- A fifth above D is A (scale tone 6)
- A fifth above A is E (scale tone 3)
- A fifth above E is B (scale tone 7)

All five new tones—G, D, A, E, B—are harmonic children and grandchildren of the tonic C (see *I-26* on the following page):

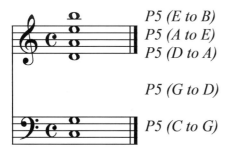

P5 (E to B)
P5 (A to E)
P5 (D to A)

P5 (G to D)

P5 (C to G)

I-26. Six out of seven scale tones can be generated by repeated application of the perfect fifth.

If we try to generate the seventh member of the scale family in the same manner, we run into a problem. A perfect fifth above B♮ is F♯, which unfortunately is an augmented fourth above the tonic, C. The dissonance of the augmented fourth calls C's role as the tonic into question. First, the two tones are a tritone apart, a harsh dissonance. Second, the F♯ is like a leading tone rising upward toward G, implying that G, rather than C, is the tonic. This competition undermines tonality because G is the dominant—the fifth tone of the scale and the strongest overtone of C other than the octave—which makes it the most likely candidate for promotion to a new tonic (modulation to the dominant is common in tonal music). In other words, F♯ implies a second harmonic vanishing point, which destroys harmonic perspective.

Because the ♯4 scale degree (F♯ in the key of C) undermines tonality, it must be discarded. The sharp fourth scale degree sounds good in Lydian mode, but modes were designed primarily for melody, not harmony. While Lydian mode produces some wonderful exotic harmonies, it isn't well-suited for creating a stable tonal solar system. Plato himself disparaged the pure Lydian mode as "convivial," that is, sensual.

The ancients solved the problem of the sharp fourth scale step by substituting F♮ for F♯, which makes the fourth scale step a perfect fifth below the tonic C and a perfect fourth above it. The corrected fourth step is called the *subdominant* because it is the same interval *below* the tonic as the dominant is *above* the tonic (a perfect fifth).

The new fourth step (F in the key of C) does have a slight flaw: it is not an overtone of the tonic. Rather, the tonic is an overtone of the subdominant (C is a perfect fifth above F), which undermines the supremacy of the tonic, but only in a subtle way that can easily be overlooked. Harmonically, the corrected fourth step forms a perfect fourth or fifth with the tonic. Melodically, it yearns to fall a half step into the harmonious major 3rd of the tonic triad.

Together, scale tone 7 (the leading tone) and scale tone 4 (scale tones B and F in the key of C) make up a dynamic duo that reinforces the tonic harmonically and melodically. Their dissonant interval leads by half steps in opposite directions to the root and 3rd of the tonic chord:

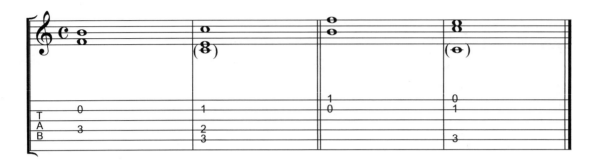

I-27. The tritone between scale steps 4 and 7 generates a restless urge for movement that reinforces the tonic chord both harmonically and melodically.

We now have seven tones that divide the octave evenly into half steps and whole steps.

Fig. 1 – Major Scale Whole-Step, Half-Step Pattern

C	D	E	F	G	A	B	C
whole — whole — half (whole) whole — whole — half							
Lower tetrachord				Upper tetrachord			

Note the symmetry of the major scale: The tetrachords C-D-E-F and G-A-B-C are separated by a neutral whole step, and have the same intervallic structure: 1-1-½ (whole-whole-half) steps.

Whole steps and half steps make for good melody. First, they are small enough to be heard as melodic stepping stones rather than harmonic leaps. Second, the half steps 3-4 and 7-8 in the major scale support the supremacy of the tonic because they converge on the root and 3rd of the tonic chord. All seven tones belong to one harmonic family, because all are related to the tonic by intervals of a perfect fifth. This helps explain why the scale tones, which function well in melody, can also be combined vertically in chords, and why triads based on the scale tones (melodic material) work well in chord progressions, which are primarily based on root movement by a perfect fifth.

The first tone in each of the Greek modes is a tonic—a master tone, a home base for melodic movement—but the modes lack the most important harmonic ingredient for tonality: a dominant 7th chord. The dominant 7th chord, which appears only in the Ionian mode, thoroughly reinforces the egocentricity of the tonic tone and the tonic chord. So rich and powerful is this reinforcement that all twelve tones of the chromatic scale and all kinds of chords foreign to the scale can appear in a tonal composition without overwhelming the primacy of the tonic chord. We will see how this works in *Lesson 2*.

Model for Triads in the Chord of Nature

The third octave of the overtone series contains a major triad. Notice that the root of the triad is an octave of the fundamental, while the 3rd and the 5th are strong overtones.

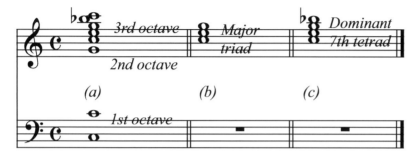

I-28. The third octave of the overtone series (a) provides a model for (b) triads and (c) tetrads (7th chords). Also see example I-24.

All major triads have a stable, balanced, warm, and "happy" quality that reflects their kinship with the Chord of Nature. As mentioned earlier, this stability and warmth seems to result from the simple ratios in the intervals between the root and 3rd, and the root and 5th. Whatever the cause, their stability is a psychological fact.

In the tonic chord, and in every major triad, the root resembles a fundamental, and the 3rd and the 5th resemble overtones. In other words, the 3rd and 5th of a major chord "grow" from the root. They are organically connected, in the same way that overtones are connected to the fundamental. Our ears seem to have an innate grasp of the parent-child relationship between the root, 3rd, and 5th of a major chord.

As you've no doubt noticed, the third octave of the overtone series also contains the model for a four-tone chord, the tetrad C-E-G-B♭. The principle difference between them is that a triad is stable and a tetrad is dynamic; the 7th chords (with a minor 7th) want to *go* somewhere.

If we treat all seven tones of the scale as chord roots (fundamentals with their own set of overtones), and fill in the 3rds and 5ths with scale tones, we get seven diatonic triads. *Diatonic* comes from the Greek *diatonikos*, meaning "progressing through tones." The diatonic triads bring two new types of chords into being: *minor* and *diminished*. The Chord of Nature favors a major triad. The minor and diminished triads *resemble* the triadic principle embodied in the overtone series, but they are artificial confections, creatures of diatonic harmony.

I-29. Diatonic triads in the key of C and the key of G.

The Roman numerals I through VII are used to identify the roots of diatonic chords. For example, the chord based on the first tone of the scale is "I," or "the *one* chord." The chord based on the fifth degree of the scale is "V," or "the *five* chord." Uppercase letters (I, IV, V) represent major chords. Lowercase letters (ii, iii, vi) represent minor chords. The diminished triad vii° is minor in character, so it is symbolized with lowercase letters. Roman numeral chord symbols are called *functional notation* because they focus our attention on the *relationships* between chords in a progression. For example, the chord progressions Gmaj > Cmaj (> means "progressing to") is a dominant-to-tonic progression, but the chord names tell us little or nothing about that. Roman numeral notation V > I, however, instantly shows the function of each chord.

Major Triads and Minor Triads

Three of the diatonic triads (I, IV, and V) are major. A major triad has a major third (four half steps) on the bottom and a minor third (three half steps) on top. The same pattern of intervals is found in the third octave of the overtone series.

I-30. In C major, I, IV, and V (the chords based on scale degrees 1, 4, and 5), are major triads.

But in three of the diatonic chords (ii, iii, vi), the pattern of thirds is flipped: the minor third is on the bottom and the major third is on top. This flip-flop transforms the chord into a *minor* triad, a chord that is as sad and forlorn as the major triad is happy and confident:

I-31. In C major, ii, iii, and vi (the triads based on scale degrees 2, 3, and 6) are minor triads. Minor triads have a minor third on the bottom and a major third on top. The perfect fifth between root and 5th is unchanged.

Why does such a "minor" change have such a major effect on the major triad? In a major chord, the 3rd is an overtone of the root and is based on a simple ratio (5:4). In a minor chord, the 3rd is *not* an overtone, and is based on a more complex ratio (6:5). In this sense, minor chords have literally lost their connection to their roots. Composers use minor chords for sad, somber, dramatic, disturbed, and mysterious subjects. Vivaldi's *Winter* from the *Four Seasons* suite, for example, is in C minor. Chopin's *Funeral March* is in the dark and gloomy key of B♭ minor. Beethoven's *Moonlight Sonata* conveys a mood of somber, meditative dreaminess in the sparkly key of C♯ minor. Richard Strauss's *Also Sprach Zarathustra* (the theme from Stanley Kubrick's *2001: A Space Odyssey*), drops dramatically from C major to C minor in the opening theme.

Minor keys aren't as common as major keys in pop music, but examples are not hard to find: *Eleanor Rigby* (Lennon/McCartney, 1966), *Nights in White Satin* (Moody Blues, 1967), *All Along the Watchtower* (Bob Dylan, 1967), *Layla* (Eric Clapton, Jim Gordon, 1970), *Stairway to Heaven* (Led Zeppelin, Jimmy Page, Robert Plant, 1971), *Witchy Woman* (Eagles, 1972), *Voulez Vous* (ABBA, 1979).

Minor Scales, Relative Minor, Parallel Minor

The 3rd of a minor chord is lowered by a half step, as is the third step of a minor scale. Unlike the major scale, which has only one form, the minor scale has three forms, all based on the sliding positions of the sixth and seventh scale degrees:

Natural minor scale (1, 2, ♭3, 4, 5, ♭6, ♭7): The third, sixth, and seventh degrees are lowered by a half step, making this scale identical to the Aeolian mode, which is the mode based on the sixth degree of a major scale. In other words, if you play the notes of a major scale from the sixth degree to the sixth degree, you have played a natural minor scale. The A natural minor scale, for example, has the same tones as the C major scale, but played from A to A, rather than from C to C.

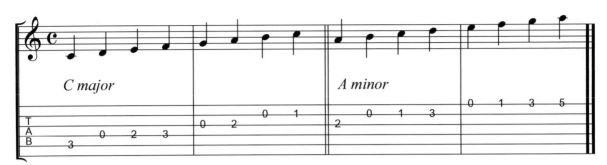

I-32. The A minor scale is the same as the C major scale played from A to A.

The lowered 7th degree of the natural minor scale causes problems in defining the key because it deprives us of a leading tone that points strongly to the tonic. The need for a leading tone is the motivation behind the harmonic and melodic forms of the minor scale, discussed below.

Harmonic minor scale (1, 2, ♭3, 4, 5, ♭6, ♯7): In the natural minor scale, the V chord is minor. The purpose of the harmonic minor scale, with its raised 7th degree, is to create a major V chord whose 3rd is a leading tone to the tonic. Compare the progressions below to hear how the major V or V7 establishes A minor as the tonic chord.

I-33. (a) The A harmonic minor scale sharps the 7th degree to obtain a leading tone. (b) In natural minor, the V > i progression is vague. (c) In harmonic minor, V > i and (d) V7 > i support tonality.

The harmonic minor supports harmony, but it is problematic for melody. The augmented second between scale degrees 6 and 7 is difficult to sing and sounds exotic, but the aura of doom, dread, and chaos that it projects makes it popular in heavy metal.

Melodic minor scale: This scale has a flatted 3rd degree and a raised 6 and 7 when ascending (1, 2, ♭3, 4, 5, ♯6, ♯7), but a *lowered* 6 and 7 when descending (1, 2, ♭3, 4, 5, ♭6, ♭7). In ascending melodic lines, the raised 6th and 7th degrees provide a strong thrust to the tonic, which is absent in the natural minor, and they eliminate the augmented second between 6 and 7, which is found in the harmonic minor. In descending melodic lines, the 6th and 7th degrees revert to the flatted, natural minor form because a leading tone is no longer needed.

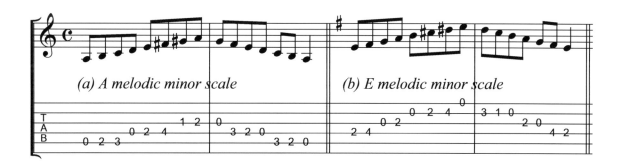

I-34. (a) The A melodic minor and (b) E melodic minor scales. (c) Bach's Bourrée *in E minor (BWV 996) illustrates how to use the sliding sixth and seventh degrees of the melodic minor scale in ascending and descending melodic lines.*

Composers often borrow tones from the minor mode to spice up their melodies. Blues melodies, for example, use the flatted third, sixth, and seventh scale degrees characteristic of natural minor, plus the flatted fifth degree. Interestingly, the blues uses I7, IV7, and V7 chords, which are all based on major triads. The minor, bluesy intervals in melody suggest sorrow, loss, and hard times, while the restless dominant 7ths, with their underlying major harmony, show resilience in the face of trouble.

Relative minor and parallel minor keys: Since every major scale can become a natural minor scale if played from the sixth degree to the sixth degree (A to A in the key of C, for example), each key signature stands for two keys: a major key and its *relative minor* key, which is based on the sixth degree of the major scale. Conversely, every minor key signature stands for a relative major key. For example, A minor is the relative minor key of C major, and C major is the relative major key of A minor. The key signature of G major (one sharp) also represents the key of E minor, since "E" is the sixth step of the G major scale, and E to E forms the E natural minor scale. The relative minor key is easier to find by counting three steps down from the tonic of the major key (C-B-A, for example, or G-F♯-E).

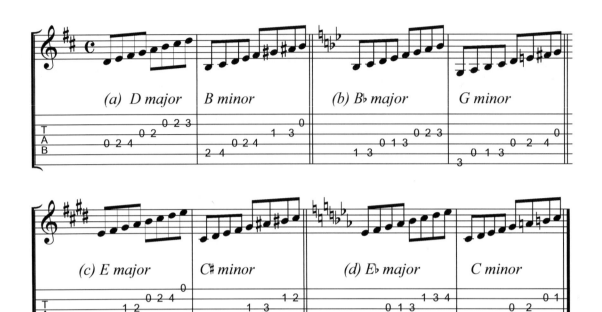

I-35. Four major keys and their relative minors (a-d). A major key and its relative minor have the same key signature, but different tonics.

The *parallel minor* scale or key is based on the same tonic as the major scale or key. For example, the parallel minor of C major is C minor. The key signature for C major has no sharps or flats, while the key signature for C minor has three flats (C minor is the relative minor of E♭ major, which also has three flats).

I-36. Parallel major and minor keys have the same tonic but different key signatures.

How to Determine Key

Every key signature stands for a major and a minor key, so look at the first and last notes and chords of the piece. Pay special attention to the dominant 7th (discussed later in the lesson). If you're in the key of A minor, the key signature will have no sharps or flats, the first and last notes will probably be "A," the first and last chords will probably be A minor, and the chord just before the final A minor will probably be E7, the dominant 7th of A minor. If you're in the key of C (the relative major to A minor), the key signature will be the same as A minor, but the first and last notes will probably be C, the first and last chords will probably be C major, and the chord just before the final C major will probably be the dominant 7th chord of the key, G7.

Diminished and Augmented Triads

As you now know, major and minor triads consist of three tones, an interval sandwich with thirds between root and 3rd, and 3rd and 5th, and a perfect fifth between the root and 5th. A major chord has a major third between root and 3rd and a minor third between 3rd and 5th. In a minor chord, the thirds are flip-flopped: a minor third on the bottom and a major third on the top. *Diminished* triads are made up of minor thirds between root and 3rd, and 3rd and 5th, and a *diminished* fifth between the root and 5th. *Augmented* triads are made up of a major thirds between root and 3rd and 3rd and 5th, and an augmented fifth between the root and 5th.

I-37. Diminished triads are made up of two minor thirds, such as the minor thirds between B and D and D and F in the B diminished triad (first triad). Augmented triads are made up of two major thirds, such as the major thirds between C and E and E and G♯ in C augmented (the first triad in the augmented group above).

Warping the perfect fifth that is the structural backbone of major and minor triads upsets the stability of the chord. Any resemblance to the Chord of Nature is lost. In this sense, diminished and augmented triads are artificial, unnatural, disturbing, eerie, and strange. For example, consider the theme from the 1960 TV show *Twilight Zone*. Written by avant garde French composer Marius Constant for two guitars and bongos, the signature lick (played by Howard Roberts) outlines a diminished fifth (E to B♭). Constant's title for the famous piece was *Etrange No. 3* (*etrange* is French for *strange, peculiar, odd, weird*).

The triad based on the seventh degree of a major scale (vii°) is diminished. The diminished fifth between the root and 5th destabilizes the triad by making it impossible to hear the bottom tone as a root. In diatonic progressions, the root of the vii° chord would normally move down a perfect fifth to the iii chord, but this isn't practical with vii° because it has no root and its tones are drawn inexorably by half step toward the root and 3rd of the I chord.

The III triad in the harmonic minor scale is augmented, symbolized III+. The capital letters "III" indicate the major character of the chord. The "+" sign is added to indicate the augmented fifth that distinguishes augmented chords from major chords.

As with the diminished chord, the alteration of the perfect fifth destroys the stability of the triad by making it impossible to hear the bottom tone as a root.

Augmented and diminished chords can't function as points of rest in a phrase, but they are useful as transitional chords between stable triads.

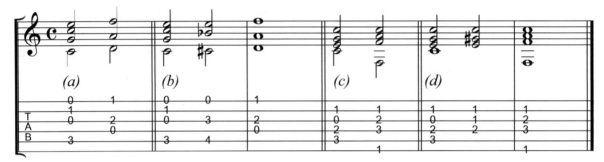

I-38. Augmented and diminished chords typically function as transitional chords between stable triads: (a) C > Dm, (b) C > C♯° > Dm, (c) C > F, (d) C > C+ > F (the > sign means "progresses to").

Seventh Chords (Tetrads)

The third octave of the overtone series provides a model of a four-tone chord (tetrad) made up of *three* adjacent thirds. Chords of this type are called *7th chords* because the fourth tone in the tetrad is a seventh above the root. When we use each scale tone as the root of a tetrad, we get six types of 7th chords: major 7th (Imaj7 and IVmaj7), dominant 7th (V7), minor 7th (ii7, iii7, vi7), minor/major 7th (i+7 in a minor key), half-diminished 7th (vii°7 in major and ii°7 in minor), diminished 7th (diminished triad with a diminished 7th, ii°7 in minor). A degree symbol with a slash through it (°) symbolizes a *half-diminished* 7th chord, which is a diminished triad with a minor seventh. The tetrad based on the seventh step of a major scale, such as B-D-F-A in the key of C major, has a diminished triad (B-D-F) and a minor seventh (B to A), so it is a half-diminished 7 chord (symbol: vii°7).

A full diminished seventh chord is composed of all minor thirds. B diminished 7 (B°7 or Bdim7), for example, would be spelled B-D-F-A♭. The interval B to A♭ is a diminished seventh, and sounds just like a minor sixth (they are enharmonically equivalent intervals). The diminished 7th chord occurs on the seventh degree of the harmonic minor scale. Composers also alter the ii7 chord in minor to a fully diminished chord for a dramatic introduction to the V7 chord.

I-39 below illustrates the gamut of 7th chords and some common voicings for them.

I-39. (a) C major 7th, (b) C dominant 7th, (c) a common voicing for C7 (d) C minor 7th, (e) a common voicing for Cmin7, (f) C minor with major 7th, (g) a common voicing for Cmin+7, (h) C half-diminished 7th, (i) a common voicing, (j) C diminished 7th, (k) a common voicing.

In a major scale, the diatonic 7th chords include two major 7ths (Imaj7, IVmaj7), three minor 7ths (ii7, iii7, vi7), a dominant 7th (V7), and a half-diminished 7th chord (vii°7):

I-40. The dominant 7th, V7, is "dominant" because it is based on the fifth degree of the scale, which has a strong harmonic relationship with the tonic. The dominant triad leads firmly to the tonic chord. The dominant 7th virtually demands a tonic chord to come next.

Most of the chords encountered in classical and pop music belong to three groups: major and minor triads, and the dominant 7th. Major 7th and minor 7th chords are common in jazz.

The Engine of Harmony

Because the dominant 7th (V7) contains so many active tones, it has a unique ability to herald the arrival of the tonic chord (I). If we simply swing back and forth between V (or V7) and I, the cycle of tension and release propels us forward in time, like pushing and pulling the pedals of a harmonic bicycle (see the following page):

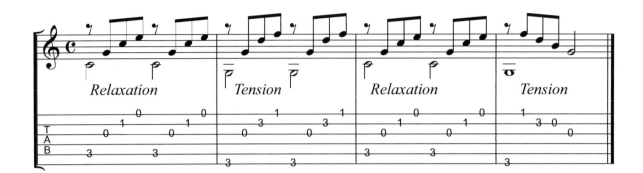

I-41. Alternating between the tonic and dominant chords fuels forward movement with a cycle of tension and relaxation.

In the age of counterpoint, the dominant 7th chord occurred as a byproduct of interwoven melodies. As soon as composers caught on to the dramatic power of dominant harmony, counterpoint (interwoven melody) receded in importance and harmony moved to the fore. The power of the dominant 7th chord to reinforce the tonic chord gave birth to tonality. Once the chord progression V7 > I (dominant 7th to tonic) is heard, the tonic becomes the aural vanishing point, the great attractor of all the rays of melody and harmony. We'll explore this idea more thoroughly in the next lesson.

Project: Cracking the Interval Code

Like colors, intervals suggest moods. Even if you can already identify all twelve intervals by ear, that is only part of what you need to know. You must dive deeply into the emotional character of each interval and bring the feelings it touches to the surface. These associations will be subjective—yours and yours alone—but that's the way it should be. Ultimately only *you* can write the dictionary of music. Trust your intuition, and rely on the knowledge that your responses will be similar to those of others.

To crack the interval code, sing each interval four ways, as described below. Then do it again and list the adjectives and images that come to mind for each of the four steps:

- Harmonically (play the lower tone and sing the upper tone at the same time)
- Harmonically (play the upper tone and sing the lower tone at the same time)
- Melodically, ascending (sing the lower tone first, then the upper tone)
- Melodically, descending (sing the higher tone first, then the lower one)

Your list should have at least three words in each category. Less than three is a sign that you have not meditated deeply enough. For example, have you noticed the way an *ascending* melodic major third differs from a *descending* major third? All ascending and descending intervals convey different moods. Also notice the effects of singing the intervals quickly or slowly, loudly or softly, or softly then loudly (or the reverse), or in a high register versus a low register.

A worksheet is provided below and continued on the following page. A list of descriptive words and song examples begins on page 56. It is important *not* to look at pages 56-62 before you make an effort to define interval moods yourself. If you skip ahead, looking for the "answers," you will deny yourself a unique opportunity to enhance your musical imagination.

Table I-2 – Cracking the Interval Code				
Name, no. of half steps	Example	Harmonic Interval Adjectives	Melodic Interval Adjectives	
			Ascending	Descending
Unison (0)	C > C		(Direction does not apply to unisons)	
Minor 2nd (1)	C > D♭			
Major 2nd (2)	C > D			
Minor 3rd (3)	C > E♭			
Major 3rd (4)	C > E			
Perfect 4th (5)	C > F			
Augmented 4th, Diminished 5th (6 half steps)	C > F♯ C > G♭			

Table I-2 – Cracking the Interval Code				
Name, no. of half steps	Example	Harmonic interval adjectives	Melodic ascending adjectives	Melodic descending adjectives
Perfect 5th (7)	C > G			
Minor 6th (8)	C > A♭			
Major 6th (9)	C > A			
Minor 7th (10)	C > B♭			
Major 7th (11)	C > B			
Octave (12)	C > C'			

Descriptive Words for Intervals

If you have made an effort to find words to describe the feelings associated with intervals in *Table I-2*, then you should find the list that follows thought-provoking. Whether or not you agree with the terms used, simply comparing your ideas with those listed below will add depth to your understanding of the rainbow of emotional color inside every interval.

Some well-known songs have been cited for each interval, including historical information on the songs that will help you find an online performance. Try to listen to *all* of the songs, since they are only a few quick clicks away. Listening to each ascending or descending interval in an artistic context will allow you to hear similarities in mood that transcend the different styles of music.

When you consider the emotions generated by melodic intervals, it's helpful to imagine the gesture that an actor or dancer might make to dramatize them. As you listen to the example songs, listen for proof of the suggested adjectives, and for further adjectives that might apply.

The list includes adjectives for ascending and descending melodic intervals only, since these are most relevant to the upcoming lessons.

Ascending and Descending Melodic Intervals in General

Gravity-defying, ascending melodic intervals often indicate a burst of emotional energy, such as happiness, exuberance, joy, or ecstasy. Think of *Beyond the Sea, My Bonnie Lies Over the Ocean, Over the Rainbow*, or *O Mio Babbino Caro.* Rhythm and tempo affect the message. Transient upward leaps occur in the styles of some contemporary female vocalists, such as Joni Mitchell and Avril Lavigne. Context determines meaning, but the flash of emotional color and intensity comes through clearly.

Descending intervals often indicate sad, droopy, introspective emotional states, but they may also indicate a heightened sense of resolve and purposefulness.

If the melody falls by a half-step in the opposite direction after a leap, the effect is tragic, like crying, and often expresses pangs of sorrow or, in minor keys, grief. Chopin's *Etude, Opus 10, No. 3*, for example, is in the key of E major, but it uses the "upward leap, falling-step" pattern repeatedly to communicate nostalgic, tender sorrow, in spite of the major key setting. The entire tragic middle section of the *Etude* is based on the same idea. The melody makes a shocking leap upward more than an octave and falls, weepingly, half-step by half-step, through a shattering series of tonally chaotic diminished seventh chords until it recovers its ground in the original key. The return to the original theme is more than just a "ray of sunlight." It expresses the ultimate consolation and solace amidst grief: a rebirth of hope and faith through eternal love.

Over the Rainbow shows descending scalar lines in another light: an increasing sense of strength, determination, hope, faith, belief, and resolve. This is because the descending melody traces a path through the warm 5th and 3rd of the tonic chord, developing anticipation and inevitable momentum on its path to the root (the tonic of the key). The first two notes of *Over the Rainbow*—an octave leap followed by a half step down to the leading tone in a major key—dramatize Dorothy's pangs of longing for home and a happier place (the tonic). The melody then descends, traversing, and in a sense recovering, all the warm harmonic points of the tonic chord that were bypassed in the octave leap. The same pattern is heard in Beethoven's *Ode to Joy*, notes 5 through 9.

In *White Christmas* (Irving Berlin) the melody accompanying the line "Just like the ones I used to know" traces an arc, half the notes rising, half the notes falling, expressing joy on the ascending side of the arc and nostalgia on the descending side.

0 Half Steps: Perfect Unison (Identical Tones)

Melodic unison adjectives: (a melodic unison is a repeated note, so no ascending or descending version is possible): Affirmation, insistence, belief, steadfastness, hypnotic drumming, echoing, winding up for an explosion, lingering, droning, stuttering, pent-up energy, buzzing, humming, emotionally neutral attention-getting

Examples: The first **two** notes of Brahms's *Lullaby* (1868) and the *Happy Birthday* song (melody by Patty Hill, Mildred J. Hill, 1893), first **three** notes of *I Can't Help Myself (Sugar Pie, Honey Bunch)* (Four Tops, Lamont Dozier, Brian Holland, Edward Holland Jr., 1965), the Fate theme from the *Fifth Symphony* (Beethoven, 1808), *O Mio Babbino Caro* (Puccini, 1918), first **four** notes of *Nine to Five* (Dolly Parton, 1980), *Deep in the Heart of Texas* (on "Deep in the heart"; Don Swander, 1941), first **five** notes of *All My Rowdy Friends (Have Settled Down)* (Hank Williams Jr., 1981), first **six** notes of *Freeze Frame* (J. Geils Band; Seth Justman and Peter Wolf, 1981), first **seven** notes of *Blackbird* (Beatles, Lennon/McCartney, 1968), the *William Tell Overture* (Rossini, 1829), first **nine** notes of *Rock Around the Clock* (Bill Haley and His Comets, Max C. Freedman, Jimmy DeKnight, 1954), first **ten** notes of *Trumpet Tune* (Jeremiah Clarke, attributed to Purcell, 1878), first **twelve** notes of *Funeral March* (*Piano Sonata No. 2, Op. 35*, Chopin, 1839), *Gentle on My Mind* (John Hartford, 1968), **multiple repeated notes** in the droning bass intro to *Eight Miles High* (Byrds; Gene Clark, Jim McGuinn, David Crosby, 1966), and *Toccata y Lamento* (classical guitar solo by Roberto Sierra, b. 1953)

1 Half Step: Minor Second

Ascending minor second adjectives: Gliding, sliding, mutating, oozing, creeping, sneaking, stealthy, undulating, or—when moving from nonharmonic tone to harmonic tone, such as leading tone to tonic—fulfilling, completing, ecstatic, sensual, or suave

Examples: *Dancing Queen* (on the word "Dan-cing"; ABBA, 1976), *A Hard Day's Night* (Lennon/McCartney, 1964), *I Left My Heart in San Francisco* (music, George Cory, lyrics, Douglass Cross, 1954), *I'm Getting Sentimental Over You* (music, George Bassman, lyrics, Ned Washington, 1932), *Insensatez* (*How Insensitive*, Jobim, 1963), *Isn't She Lovely* (Stevie Wonder, 1976), *Jaws* theme (John Williams, 1975); *New World Symphony, Fourth Movement* (Dvořák, 1893), *Nice Work If You Can Get It* (music, Gershwin, lyrics, Berlin, 1937), *Pink Panther* theme (Henry Mancini, 1963), *Stormy Weather* (Harold Arlen, Ted Koehler, 1933), *White Christmas* (Bing Crosby, singer, composed by Irving Berlin, 1940)

Descending minor second adjectives: Crying, sighing, loss, fractured, tragic, ratcheting, leaking, oozing, creeping, sliding, slipping, shruggingly dismissive, or, contrastingly, fulfilling or relieving (when dropping from a non-harmonic point to a harmonic point)

Examples: *Blue Bayou* (chorus, on "back some day"; Roy Orbison and Joe Melson, 1963), *Boléro* (Maurice Ravel, 1928), *Le Cygne* (*The Swan*, Camille Saint-Saëns, 1886), *Für Elise*

(Beethoven, 1810), *Flight of the Bumble Bee* (Rimsky-Korsakov, 1900), *Happy Trails* (Dale Evans, 1940?), *Joy to the World* (Christmas carol, 1719), *Jurassic Park* theme (John Williams, 1993), *O Little Town of Bethlehem* (Phillips Brooks, Lewis Redner, 1868), *Solar* (Miles Davis, 1963), *Sophisticated Lady* (Duke Ellington, Irving Mills, 1932), *Stella by Starlight* (Victor Young, 1944), *Symphony No. 40 in G Minor, K. 550* (Mozart, 1788)

2 Half Steps: Major Second (One Whole Step)

Ascending major second adjectives: Confident, deliberate, dignified striding, restrained or modest (but justifiable) rise in emotion, going forward toward a goal, emotional neutrality, neutral connection, linking, reaching, rolling, moving, floating upward, airy indifference, pensive

Examples: *Body and Soul* (Coleman Hawkins, performer; written by Heyman, Sour, Eyton, Green, 1939), *Do-Re-Mi* song from *Sound of Music* (Rodgers/Hammerstein, 1959), first two notes of major or minor scale, *Frère Jacques* (French nursery rhyme, 1600s), *Happy Birthday* song (melody by Patty Hill, Mildred J. Hill, 1893), *My Funny Valentine* (from *Babes in Arms*, Rodgers/Hart, 1937), *Never Gonna Give You Up* (Rick Astley, singer; written by Stock, Aitken, Waterman, 1987), *Rudolph the Red-Nosed Reindeer* (Johnny Marks, 1948), *Silent Night* (Franz Gruber, 1819), *Sleeping Sun* (Nightwish, 2005), *Strangers in the Night* (Frank Sinatra, singer; written by Charles Singleton, Eddie Snyder, 1966), *There Will Never Be Another You* (Frank Sinatra, singer; Harry Warren, lyrics by Mack Gordon, 1942)

Descending major second adjectives: Yielding ground or reaching a harmonic goal with confident, deliberate, dignified steps, neutral connection, linking, easy steps

Examples: *Eight Days a Week* (Lennon/McCartney, 1964), *The First Noel* (English Christmas carol, 1700s), *Freddie Freeloader* (Miles Davis, 1959), *M*A*S*H* theme (music by Johnny Mandel, lyrics by Mike Altman, 1970), *Mary Had a Little Lamb* (American nursery rhyme, Sara J. Hale, 1830), *Three Blind Mice* (English nursery rhyme, 1609), *Satin Doll* (music, Duke Ellington and Billy Strayhorn, lyrics, Johnny Mercer, 1953), *Whistle While You Work* (from Disney's *Snow White and the Seven Dwarfs*, music, Frank Churchill, lyrics, Larry Morey, 1937), *Yesterday* (Lennon/McCartney, 1965)

3 Half Steps: Minor Third

Ascending minor third adjectives: Wistful, sadly yearning, melancholy but hopeful, dreamy, disturbed, sorrowful, angry, unnatural, or, when rising from the 3rd to the 5th of a major chord, sweet, affectionate, sentimental, tender, dear, tenderly hopeful

Examples: *Bad* (Michael Jackson, 1987), *Brahms's Lullaby* (Johannes Brahms, 1868), *Cowboys From Hell* (Pantera, 1990), *A Foggy Day* (George Gershwin, lyrics by Ira Gershwin, 1937), *Galveston* (Glen Campbell, singer; Jimmy Webb, 1969), *Georgia on My Mind* (Ray Charles or Willie Nelson, singer; Hoagy Carmichael, 1930), *Greensleeves* (traditional English folk song, composed before 1580), *Happiness Is a Warm Gun* (Lennon/McCartney, 1968), *I Still Haven't Found What I'm Looking For* (U2, 1987), *The Impossible Dream* (from *Man of La Mancha*; Mitch Leigh, music, Joe Darion, lyrics, 1965), *Minor Swing* (Django Reinhardt and Stéphane Grappelli, 1937), *O Canada* (national anthem of Canada, Calixa Lavallée, 1880), *Oh Where, Oh Where Has My Little Dog Gone* (Septimus Winner, set to a German folk song, 1864), *Smoke on the Water* (Deep Purple, 1972), *Somewhere My Love* or *Lara's Theme* (from *Dr. Zhivago*, Maurice Jarre, 1965), *A Time for Us* (theme from Zeffirelli's *Romeo and Juliet*; Nino Rota, 1968), *Voulez-Vous* (on "Vou-lez"; ABBA, 1979), *Yellow Rose of Texas* (on "yellow," traditional Texas song, 1836)

Descending minor third adjectives: Melancholy, brooding, tenderly loving, dreamy, dark, disturbed, sad, tragic, longing, wicked, unnatural, threatening

Examples: *Claire de Lune*, (Debussy, 1890), *Fantasia No. 7* (*No. 1* in Poulton, John Dowland, 1597), *Frosty the Snowman* (Jack Rollins, Steve Nelson, 1950), *Hey Jude* (Lennon/McCartney, 1968), *Hook* theme (John Williams, 1991), *Back in the Saddle Again* (Gene Autry, Ray Whitley, 1939), *Just Call Me Angel of the Morning* (on "An-gel"; Chip Taylor, 1968), *Misty* (Erroll Garner, 1954), *The Star Spangled Banner* (U.S. national anthem, lyrics by Francis Scott Key, music by John Stafford Smith, 1812), *This Old Man* (nursery rhyme, 1870s or earlier), *They Don't Care About Us* (Michael Jackson, 1996), *What Hurts the Most* (Steve Robson, Jeffrey Steele, 2005), *What Is This Thing Called Love* (Cole Porter, 1929)

4 Half Steps: Major Third

Ascending major third adjectives: Warm, joyful, happy, bold, brave, positive, fearless, exuberant, trusting, swelling with emotion, sensual, warmly tender, loving

Examples: *Bo Diddley* (Bo Diddley, performer, by Elias McDaniel, 1955), *Marines' Hymn* (1891), *I Could Have Danced All Night* (*My Fair Lady*, Lerner/Loewe, 1956), *I'm So Lonesome I Could Cry* (Hank Williams, 1949), *Kumbaya* (spiritual), *Michael Row the Boat Ashore* (African-American spiritual, early 1800s), *Morning Has Broken* (Cat Stevens, singer, Christian hymn, 1931), *When the Saints Go Marching In* (Louis Armstrong, singer, New Orleans traditional)

Descending major third adjectives: Happy, joyful, warm, confirming, declaring, proving, secure, homecoming, positive, heavenly, faithful, true

Examples: *Fifth Symphony* (the Fate motif, Beethoven, 1808), *Good Night, Ladies* (anon., earlier than 1917), *Shoo Fly, Don't Bother Me* (children's song, 1860s), *Summertime* (*Porgy and Bess*, Gershwin, 1935), *Swing Low Sweet Chariot* (Negro spiritual, earlier than 1909), *Westminster Quarters* (traditional clock bell melody used to chime the third quarter hour)

5 Half Steps: Perfect Fourth

Ascending perfect fourth adjectives: Bold, energetic, leaping, confident, resolute, declarative, assertive, fearless, compelled, immune to doubt, announcing, trumpeting, slamming, ramming, jamming, driving, vigorous, forceful, unified, disciplined

Examples: *All the Things You Are* (music, Jerome Kern, lyrics, Oscar Hammerstein II, 1939), *Amazing Grace* (Christian hymn, John Newton, 1779), *Apache* (chart-topping instrumental, Jerry Lordan, 1960), *Auld Lang Syne* (traditional Scottish song, poem by Robert Burns, 1788), *Beyond the Sea* (Bobby Darin hit, 1959; original French version, Charles Trenet, Albert Lasry, 1943; U.S. version, Jack Lawrence), *El Cóndor Pasa (If I Could)* (Simon & Garfunkel hit, 1970; composed by Peruvian Daniel Alomía, 1913), *Hark, the Herald Angels Sing* (Christmas carol, Charles Wesley, 1739), *La Marseillaise* (French national anthem, Claude Joseph Rouget de Lisle, 1792), *Love Me Tender* (Elvis Presley hit, 1956, adapted from Civil War song, *Aura Lee*, music, George R. Poulton, lyrics, W.W. Fosdick), *Mamma Mia* (on "I've been…," ABBA, 1975), *O Tannenbaum* (Christmas carol, adapted from folk song by Ernst Anschütz, 1824), *Someday My Prince Will Come* (Disney/*Snow White*), *Taps*, (Civil War General Daniel Butterfield, 1862), *We Wish You a Merry Christmas* (English Christmas carol, 1500s), *Wedding March* (*Bridal Chorus* from *Lohengrin*, Wagner, 1850), *You Are My Sunshine* (Jimmie Davis, Charles Mitchell, 1939), *Your Cheatin' Heart* (Hank Williams, 1952)

Descending perfect fourth adjectives: Bracing, calling forth, announcing, boldly faithful, assertive, demanding, summoning strength, steadying, winding up, reaching deep

Examples: *A Mighty Fortress Is Our God* (Martin Luther, 1527), *Adeste Fideles* (*O Come All Ye Faithful*) (John Francis Wade, 1751), *All Shook Up* (Elvis Presley, singer, Chris Blackwell, composer, 1957), *Born Free* (movie theme, John Barry, 1966), *Eine Kleine Nachtmusik* (Mozart, 1787), *I've Been Working on the Railroad* (American folk song, 1894), *Shave and a Haircut* (anon., 1899), *Star Trek (Next Generation) Theme Music* (slow introduction, first two notes, Alexander Courage, Jerry Goldsmith, 1987), *Yardbird Suite* (Charlie Parker, 1946)

6 Half Steps: Augmented Fourth or Diminished Fifth

Ascending adjectives: Alarming, troubled, mysterious, strained, false, disturbed, wanton, wicked, wild, evil, threatening, distressed, lustful, chaotic, out of control, careening

Examples: *Maria* (Leonard Bernstein, 1957), *The Saint* (movie theme, Orbital, Edwin Astley, 1997), *The Simpsons Theme* (Danny Elfman, 1989)

Descending adjectives: Ominous, evil, menacing, strained, alarming, troubled, false, wicked, disturbed, deliberately wanton, threatening, distressed, lustful, chaotic, possessed

Examples: *Black Sabbath* (Ozzy Ozbourne and Black Sabbath, 1969), *Blue 7* (Sonny Rollins, 1956), *YYZ* (Rush, Geddy Lee, Neil Peart, 1981), *Turn Back, O Man* (*Godspell*, Stephen Schwartz, 1971)

7 Half Steps: Perfect Fifth

Ascending perfect fifth adjectives: Elevating, noble, regal, heavenly, principled, bare, bold, hollow, soaring, strong, hopeful, reaching outward

Ascending perfect fifth examples: *The Alphabet Song* (similar to *Twinkle, Twinkle, Little Star*), *Alfie* (on "Al-fie?"; sung by Cher, written by Hal David, Burt Bacharach, 1966), *Also sprach Zarathustra* (theme from 1968 film *2001 : A Space Odyssey*; Richard Strauss, 1896), *Baa Baa Black Sheep* (English nursery rhyme, sung to a variant of the 1761 French melody *Ah! vous dirai-je, Maman*), *Bags' Groove* (performed by Miles Davis; vibraphonist Milt Jackson, 1954), *Blackbird* (Lennon/McCartney, 1968), *Can't Help Falling in Love* (Elvis Presley hit, 1961; written by Weiss, Peretti, Creatore), *Lavender Blue* (English folk song and nursery rhyme, 1600s), *My Favorite Things* (*Sound of Music*, Rodgers/Hammerstein, 1959), *One* (Metallica, 1989), *Star Wars Episode IV: A New Hope* (theme, John Williams, 1977), *Scarborough Fair* (Simon & Garfunkel, 1968; English ballad, 1600s), *Twinkle, Twinkle, Little Star* (English nursery rhyme based on French song, *Ah! Vous dirai-je, Maman*, 1700s), *X-Files Theme* (Mark Snow, 1996)

Descending perfect fifth adjectives: Thoughtful, conclusive, reaching inward, deep, rooted, anchored, complete, resonant, profound, noble

Examples: *Bring a Torch, Jeanette, Isabella* (French Christmas carol, 1500s), *Carmen* (Bizet, 1845), *Donna, Donna* (sung by Joan Baez, Donovan, Chad & Jeremy, Theodore Bikel, and others; composed by Sholom Secunda, lyrics, Aaron Zeitlin, 1940s), *Feelings* (soft rock sung by Ella Fitzgerald, Frank Sinatra, Johnny Mathis, and others; credited to Morris Albert, 1975; original music attributed to Loulou Gasté, 1957), *Flintstones Theme* (Hoyt Curtin, 1960), *Have You Met Miss Jones* (Rodgers/Hart, 1937), *It Don't Mean a Thing (If It Ain't Got That Swing)* (music, Duke Ellington, lyrics, Irving Mills, 1931), *Seven Steps to Heaven* (Miles Davis, 1963), *Swan Lake* (Tchaikovsky, 1876), *The Way You Look Tonight* (sung by Frank Sinatra; music, Jerome Kern, lyrics, Dorothy Fields, 1936), *What Should We Do With the Drunken Sailor* (sea shanty, before 1824)

8 Half Steps: Minor Sixth

Ascending minor sixth adjectives: Painful, wistful, tragic, sentimental, sad, lost, pining, torn, melancholy, fated, languidly sensual

Examples: *1492: Conquest of Paradise* (movie theme, Vangelis, 1992), *Because* (Lennon/McCartney, 1969), *Don't Worry Baby* (on "Oh, I don't know"; Beach Boys hit, Brian Wilson, Roger Christian, 1964), *In My Life* (instrumental riff that begins the song, Lennon/McCartney, 1965), *Makes Me Wonder* (Maroon 5, 2007), *Manhã de Carnaval* (from the film *Black Orpheus*; Luiz Bonfa, Antonio Maria, 1959), *She's a Woman* (on "My love…," Lennon/McCartney, 1964), *Waltz in C-sharp Minor* (*Opus 64, No. 2*, Chopin, 1847)

Descending minor sixth adjectives: Sad, coy, sensual, sentimental

Examples: *100 Years* (Five for Fighting/John Ondrasik, 2003), *(Where Do I Begin?) Love Story Theme* (music, Francis Lai, lyrics, Carl Sigman, 1970), *Misty* (between the first and third notes, Erroll Garner, 1954), *Please Don't Talk About Me When I'm Gone* (Dean Martin singer, music, Sam H. Stept, lyrics, Sidney Clare, 1930), *You're Everything* (Chick Corea, 1972)

9 Half Steps: Major Sixth

Ascending major sixth adjectives: Flight, journey, soaring joy, confident hope, call to adventure, lush, florid, exotic, sensual, awakened longing, alluring mystery, forbidden delight

Examples: *For He's a Jolly Good Fellow* (also *The Bear Went Over the Mountain*, based on a French song, 1709), *Hi-Lili, Hi-Lo* (from the movie *Lili*, with Leslie Caron, music, Bronislau Kaper, words, Helen Deutsch, 1952), *Hush Little Baby* (American lullaby, dates unknown), *I Have a Dream* (ABBA hit, 1979), *It Came Upon a Midnight Clear* (Christmas carol), *Marion's Theme* (*Raiders of the Lost Ark*, John Williams, 1981), *My Bonnie Lies Over the Ocean* (Scottish folk song, date unknown), *My Way* (on "And now…," sung by Frank Sinatra, written by Paul Anka, based on a French song by François and Revaux, 1969), *NBC Theme Music*, *Nocturne* (*Opus 9 No. 2*, Chopin, 1830-32), *Princess Leia's Theme* (*Star Wars Episode IV*, John Williams, 1977), *Sloop John B* (Beach Boys, 1966, based on West Indies folk song)

Descending major sixth adjectives: Lovingly confiding, testifying, admitting, confessing, warmly affirming, bursting with joy and confidence, sensually caressing, cradling, comforting

Examples: *Crazy* (Willie Nelson, 1962), *Down by the Riverside* (African American spiritual, on the words "lay down"), *Nobody Knows the Trouble I've Seen* (spiritual), *The Music of The Night* (*Phantom of The Opera*, Andrew Lloyd Webber, lyrics by Charles Hart, 1986), *The NeverEnding Story Theme* (Giorgio Moroder, Keith Forsey, 1984), *Over There* (George M. Cohan, 1917), *Sweet Caroline* (Neil Diamond, 1969), *Take the "A" Train* (Duke Ellington signature song, Billy Strayhorn, 1939), *A Weaver of Dreams* (music, Victor Young, lyrics, Jack Elliott, 1952)

10 Half Steps: Minor Seventh

Ascending minor seventh adjectives: Call to adventure, hope bravely bracing against uncertainty, masculine, anticipating, strengthening resolve, mystery

Examples: *Somewhere* (*West Side Story*, Leonard Bernstein, 1957), *Star Trek: The Original Theme* (Alexander Courage, 1966), *"The Take Over, the Breaks Over"* (Fall Out Boy, 2007, quotes appear in the original title)

Descending minor seventh adjectives: Clumsy, blue, lost, awkward, full of reservations, alarmed, disjointed, off-balance, broken, elephantine, goofy, stalled, honking, ironic

Examples: *An American in Paris* (George Gershwin, 1928), *Lady Jane* (on the refrain, Rolling Stones, Jagger/Richards, 1966), *Watermelon Man* (Herbie Hancock, 1962)

11 Half Steps: Major Seventh

Ascending major seventh adjectives: Dreamy, magical, yearning, dreamily desiring, bitter-sweet, otherworldly, transporting, celestial, heavenly, supernal

Examples: *Bali Ha'i* (*South Pacific*, music, Richard Rodgers, lyrics, Oscar Hammerstein II, 1949; melody leaps an octave, then falls a half step to the major seventh), *Don't Know Why* (Norah Jones, singer, by Jesse Harris, 2002), *Fantasy Island Theme* (Laurence Rosenthal, 1978), *Popular* (Nada Surf, 1996), *Pure Imagination* (on "a world," song from *Willie Wonka & the Chocolate Factory*; sung by Gene Wilder, written by Leslie Bricusse, Anthony Newley, 1971), *Over the Rainbow* (*Wizard of Oz*, music, Harold Arlen, lyrics, E.Y. Harburg, 1939; like *Bali Ha'i*, the melody leaps an octave and descends to the major 7th on the third note), *Take on Me* (a-ha, 1985)

Descending major seventh adjectives: Tautly yearning, aching, wishing, hoping, turned inside out with desire, broken, shattered, honking, urgently needy

Examples: A difficult interval to sing, which makes examples hard to find. *I Love You* (Cole Porter, 1944)

12 Half Steps: Perfect Octave

Ascending octave adjectives: Soaring, leaping, spirited, whole, complete, fulfilled, perfect, sparkling

Examples: *Over the Rainbow* (from *Wizard of Oz*, music, Harold Arlen, lyrics, E.Y. Harburg, 1939; first two notes), *Bali Ha'i* (South Pacific; music, Richard Rodgers, lyrics, Oscar Hammerstein II, 1949; first two notes), *Singin' in the Rain* (music Nacio Herb Brown, lyrics, Arthur Freed, 1952), *Let It Snow! Let It Snow! Let It Snow!* (Christmas song, music by Jule Styne, lyrics by Sammy Cahn, 1945), *Blue Bossa* (Kenny Dorham, 1963)

Descending octave adjectives: Rooted, resolved, resolute, completed, perfect, closed, hollow, fixed, mechanistic

Examples: *Willow Weep for Me* (Ann Ronell, 1932), *Doogie Howser, M.D. Theme* (TV series; Mike Post, 1989)

Outro

The *Interlude* has a lot of history behind it, some of it dating back to ancient Greece, the Middle Ages, and the Renaissance, and some of it dating back to my childhood.

When I was thirteen or so, I found out that scales had seven tones. It was the 1960s in the San Francisco Bay Area. Astrology, numerology, and other mystical concepts were in vogue, which gave the number *seven* a magical aura. When I heard that the mysterious Pythagoras— patron saint of mathematics, Greek philosopher, cult leader—was somehow behind it, I was sure there must be more to the story. The perfection of triads bothered me as well. I could imagine one or two triads in a key working, but all of them on all seven scale degrees? Nothing in life came that close to perfection except mathematics. But scales were *real*. For that reason, music and music theory seemed like a gateway between worlds. Then Laura Weber, a folk guitar instructor on public television, said that if you knew the chords to a song, you could generally find the notes of the melody nearby. *Why?* I felt there must be some kind of profound meaning in that statement, but she never went further in explaining it, and I never forgot it.

Obviously my thinking was naïve, but basic questions such as these continued to bother me throughout my years as a music student. Somehow it seemed hollow to use the materials of music without understanding their history or the motivations of their creators. The answers were a long time in coming, partly because of the diversity of opinion on the subject, and partly because we musicians were the fish, and tonality was the water. *Our* job was to swim, and not to reason why. Nevertheless, everything I learned about music theory and its history helped. While it would take a book in itself to do justice to the evolution of harmony, I hope that the historical background given here has provided a few practical insights.

To summarize the *Interlude*, the universal responses produced by intervals are what make music a universal medium of communication. The first step in learning to use this language is to learn to recognize these intervals and the moods they create. The final project in meditating on the moods of intervals was a start in this direction, but only a start. It is vital to continue ear training through classes or an ear training program such as the relative pitch ear training course found at PerfectPitch.com (see footnote, p. 25).

Part of the mood of an interval stems from its consonance (restfulness) or dissonance (restlessness). Like painters creating passages of light and dark, composers weave restless and restful tones together to create emotional effects. The history of music is in some ways a history of the evolution of techniques for handling dissonance.

Nowhere is the dynamic cycle of tension and release more audible than in the chord progression V7 > I. The dominant 7th chord is packed with restless tones with an urge to resolve to nearby tones of the restful, stable tonic chord. The V7 chord changed the course of music history by ushering in the practice of tonality, which is comparable to the use of the vanishing point in visual art.

We'll explore the perspective analogy in depth in *Lesson 2 – The Harmonic Journey.*

Lesson 2 – The Harmonic Journey

It is good to have an end to journey toward;
but it is the journey that matters, in the end.

– Ursula K. LeGuin, American science-fiction writer

Intro

To cover all of harmony in one easy lesson would be impossible, so we'll narrow our focus down to a question of craftsmanship: *How do we create a meaningful chord progression?* Whether you're writing a country-and-western song or composing a rock anthem, "meaningful" suggests that a chord progression should *communicate something*: a feeling of logical movement, a mood, or maybe even a story.

To acquire this art, one must acquire an ear for harmonic perspective[1] and practice juggling harmonic perspective with the rhythmic forms of time (sections, phrases, and periods). This is what *Lesson 2* will show you, and your Musical I.Q. will take a giant leap forward as a result.

If any of the terms used in *Lesson 2* are unfamiliar, please refer to the *Interlude*.

The Harmonic Journey

Aristotle said that stories have three parts: a beginning, middle, and an end. The same might be said of chord progressions, which resemble a harmonic journey:

- Beginning: *Home Sweet Home*
- Middle: *Leaving Home*
- End: *Returning Home*

---

1 See *Tonality and Perspective*, p. 21.

The time span of a harmonic journey may be a couple of measures or an entire composition, such as a classical sonata, but for now we're interested in short, simple journeys that fill sections, phrases, or periods. These are the most common units of musical composition, the stuff that songs are made on.

In the harmonic journey, "home" is the tonic chord. The tonic embodies rest, repose, inactivity, balance, contentment, and completeness. The tonic chord may be major or minor. The major mode is capable of expressing many shades of emotion, but in general it is reserved for positive, outgoing themes. The minor mode expresses somberness, introspection, melancholy, sorrow, grief, and other variations on emotionally dramatic or disturbed themes.

Act I of the Harmonic Journey, *Home Sweet Home*, is easy—the tonic and dominant chords alone suffice to establish a tonal center. Acts II and III are where the drama begins. The possibilities seem endless. Some routes for leaving and returning are rarely taken, while others have become musical clichés. How do we decide which way to go?

Fortunately, harmonic perspective provides an answer. In the hands of the classical masters, harmonic perspective can be enormously complex and sophisticated. In the hands of a pop musician, it is simpler, but still clever. Once you understand how it works, you'll be able to make up your own progressions with ease.

Tonic and Dominant Fuel Forward Movement

The simplest, most direct round-trip of all is from the tonic (I) to the dominant (V) and back: I > V > I. This cycle of tension and relaxation creates a pumping action that moves us forward in time, like a pair of pistons cranking 'round and 'round, or every breath you take:[2]

2-1. The power of I > V > I to energize forward movement. In the key of C, the C chord is I, the G chord is V.

As pointed out by Dr. Franklin W. Robinson in *Aural Harmony* (*Recommended Reading*, No. 21), written music suggests that this movement resembles the written word: left to right and

---

2 *Voice leading*, the art of graceful chord connection according to tonal principles, is not covered in *Compose Yourself*, and voice-leading rules, such as the prohibition against parallel fifths and octaves, have been relaxed for examples.

down the page. But this is misleading. A chord progression moves forward in time, but it also moves *spatially*, away from the tonic and back, as shown in the diagram below:

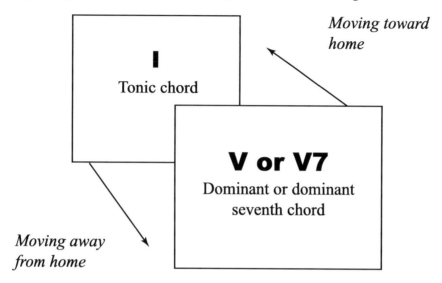

Fig. 2-1. The progression I > V > I is movement back and forth in space.

The figure above illustrates the common ground between harmonic and visual perspective. In the first part of the journey, I > V (lower arrow), we leave home, which moves off into the distance (recedes into memory). While the V chord occupies the foreground, the I chord lingers in the background, generating anticipation of a homecoming. Every tone of the V chord promises that the return is right around the corner. With a flip of the fingers on fretboard or keyboard, we deliver on that promise and return home (upper arrow). V disappears, I takes its place.

Play I > V > I a few times and imagine that you are moving away from the tonic and back, as shown in the diagram above. After a few repetitions you should begin to experience harmonic perspective. Once you've felt it, you'll never hear music quite the same way again. The i > V > i progression in minor has much the same effect:

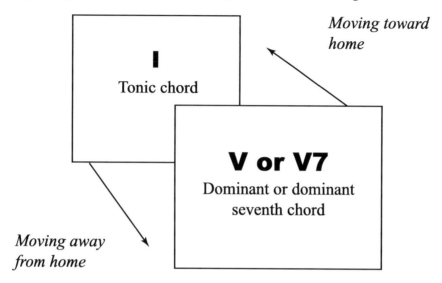

2-2. i > V > i in A minor

In major keys, the tonic chord expresses rest, contentment, calm, peace. In minor keys, it expresses sorrow, melancholy, depression, loss. In either case, the tonic is a stable chord, while the dominant is a restless, active chord with a desire to return to the tonic. The mood of the dominant is ecstatic, elated, as if you were starving and suddenly the doors to a banquet were flung open before you. The build section on V7 in *Twist and Shout* (Beatles cover version, 1964; also see *Ferris Bueller's Day Off*, the downtown Chicago parade scene) is a perfect example. Other chords may suggest desire, but they are restrained in comparison to the dominant, which positively revels at the prospect of rejoining the tonic.

Cadences, Questions, and Answers

The first half of the I > V > I round-trip is I > V. As soon as the dominant sounds, it raises the question, "When do we go home?" The second half, V > I, provides the answer: "Now we're home." In the case of a minor key, "home" may be moody, but it's home all the same.

The progressions I > V and V > I are useful punctuation marks for phrase endings. We call harmonic formulas such as these *cadences* (from the Latin *cadentia*, "a falling"). The progression I > V is termed a *half cadence* because it half-completes the I > V > I round-trip, leaving us in suspense. The progression V > I is called a *full cadence* because it finishes the cycle, bringing the flow of musical thought to a pause or a full stop.

The English language has six punctuation marks (period, comma, colon, semi-colon, exclamation mark, question mark). *Cadences*, which are the equivalent of musical punctuation marks, are far more numerous and nuanced. A long note or a rest can form a *rhythmic* cadence. An accented tension tone or rest tone[3] can form a *melodic* cadence. Most of the time, however, *cadence* refers to a formulaic chord progression. Cadence types include full, half, perfect, imperfect, authentic, inauthentic, plagal, feminine, masculine, deceptive, and variations of these. But in essence, all cadences are either *open* or *closed*. An *open* cadence is inconclusive; it implies more music will follow. A *closed* cadence is conclusive; it implies that the thought is complete. Either no music will follow, or a new idea, or an old idea will begin to repeat.

The full cadence, V > I, is a closed cadence. A closed cadence is a musical answer. It functions like a period or exclamation mark.

---

3 Essentially, the root, 3rd and 5th of the tonic chord (C, E, and G in the key of C major, for example) are rest tones and function as melodic "answers." Every other tone is a restless tension tone and functions as a melodic "question." We will discuss subtle differences between the tones in *Lesson 3*.

2-3. A full cadence. With the tonic as accented top note in the I chord, it signals the conclusion of an idea.

The *half* cadence, I > V, is an *open* cadence. An open cadence is a musical question mark because it leaves us in suspense, implying "more music to come."

2-4. A half cadence is an unanswered question.

Focused Listening – Questions and Answers

Listen to some of your favorite music and try to identify phrases. Open and closed cadences are one clue to phrase endings, but also listen for long notes, pauses, repetition of melodic ideas, or the introduction of a new melodic idea in conjunction with cadences.

Tap your foot and count downbeats on your fingers. You will find that most phrases are two to four measures long. You will also find that the majority of phrases are questions. In other words, the majority of phrases end with open cadences.

You will often hear a chain of question phrases linked together to prolong the drama before the composer uses a decisive, closed cadence (Q > Q > Q > A). You can hear this pattern in Bob Dylan's folk-rock classic *Love Minus Zero/No Limit* (1965). Seven out of the first eight sections are questions of varying intensity. The eighth section is an answer because it ends with a decisive, closed cadence (V > I) with the tonic (scale tone 1) as the final note.

Sometimes a piece ends with a question hanging in the air as a poetic device (*Seis por Derecho*, by Venezuelan composer Antonio Lauro, for example, ends on a plaintive V7 chord).

Sometimes the final cadence is vague, as when the tonic chord mingles question tones with the basic triad. All of these thought patterns are familiar in everyday language, but in music they are symbolized by harmonic progressions, rather than words.

2-5. (a) A decisive, unequivocal closed cadence. (b) A less decisive closed cadence. (c) A tantalizingly ambiguous closed cadence.

Some cadences may confuse you because they seem like a question *and* an answer. This is often because the music has changed keys (modulated). In order to effect a convincing key change, composers use a strong, closed cadence in the new key. This sounds like an answer, but in the context of the original key, it is not a cadence on the tonal center. Ambiguities like these make music interesting. Just accept them and do the best you can to sort out the cadences.

Suffice it to say that the tonal system is subtle and flexible. Composers prolong the drama of a piece of music by ending phrases with open cadences or not-quite-conclusive cadences, reserving the strongly conclusive closed cadences for breaking points in the flow of musical thought or the fully committed endings.

Improvising Questions and Answers

In *Lesson 1*, you improvised sections, phrases, and periods with rhythm alone. Now we'll add harmony, giving you a chance to juggle two musical balls at once. For example, play this half cadence in A minor.

2-6. Half cadence in the key of A minor

This is an open cadence, such as you might find in the final measures of a question phrase. By adding different rhythms to the given chords, you can alter its mood:

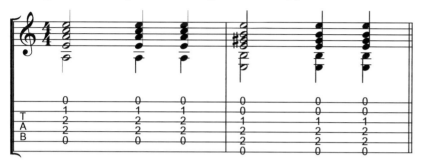

2-7a. A plodding, heel-stompin', martial rhythm

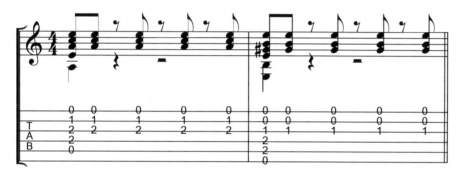

2-7b. An upbeat, slightly syncopated rhythm

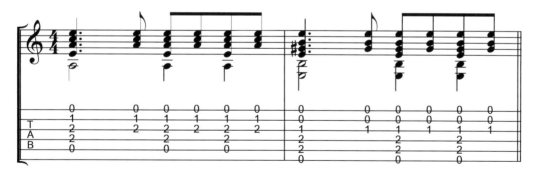

2-7c. A folky, possibly pop rock rhythm, depending on the tempo and the strength of the beat

Questions (Sections Ending With V or V7)

Improvise harmonic questions with the following two-measure I > V chord progressions. Just add rhythm, as shown above in *2-6* and *2-7(a-c)*. The progressions below are written for guitar, but may be adapted for piano. Feel free to change the meter from 4/4 to 2/4, 3/4, or 6/8, and add pickup beats for variety.

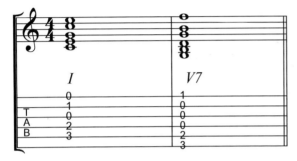

2-8.

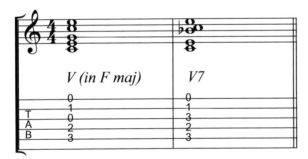

2-9.

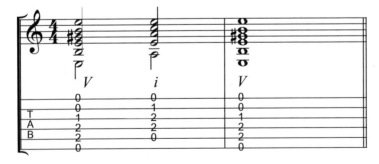

2-10.

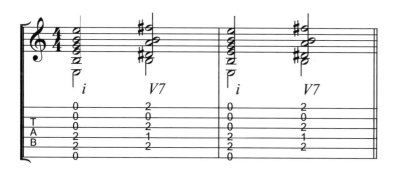

2-11.

Answers (Sections Ending With I)

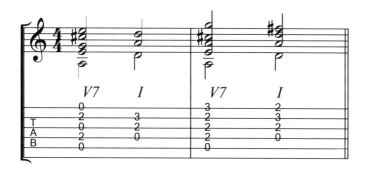

2-12.

2-13.

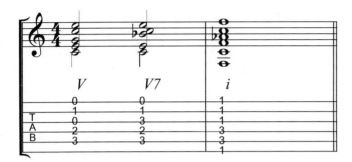

2-14.

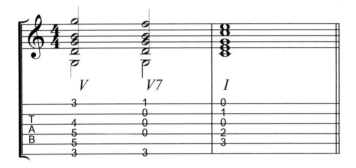

2-15.

Harmonic Rhythm

The pattern of accent and duration in a chord progression makes up the *harmonic rhythm* of a phrase. Generally speaking, harmonic rhythm is slower and more predictable than melodic rhythm. The improvisation exercises above have shown that chord changes tend to occur on accented beats, especially the downbeat. Unaccented beats and offbeats—the "ands" in "One-and-two-and-three-and-four-and"—are less likely sites for a chord change. This doesn't mean you have to change chords on the first beat of every measure. Composers often extend one chord for two or more measures, especially at faster tempi:

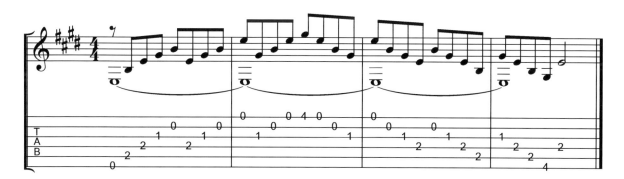

2-16. Four measures on one chord (E major), adapted from Toccata V *for harpsichord by Alessandro Scarlatti (1660 – 1725; original in G major). A "toccata" (literally "touch piece") is a virtuosic instrumental composition.*

At slower tempi, changes are often more frequent, as in the choral music of J.S. Bach.

2-17. Bach uses eight chords in nine beats. Adapted from Der Tag, der ist so freudenreich *(no. 158, original in G major).*

If two chords occur in a single measure of 4/4 time, the second chord usually comes on beat three, as in many of the examples above. This is a natural spot because a measure of 4/4 is typically divided into two groups of two beats, and beat three, which begins the second group, is accented.

A chord change that occurs on the fourth beat becomes rhythmically linked to the chord on the downbeat of the next measure, like the pickup beat at the beginning of *Ex. 2-17* and *2-18* below.

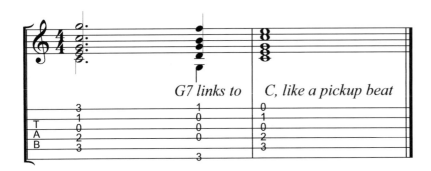

2-18. In 4/4 time, a chord on the fourth beat acts like a pickup beat to the following measure.

In a measure of 3/4 time, the second chord will usually come on the third beat, where it links rhythmically to the downbeat of the next measure:

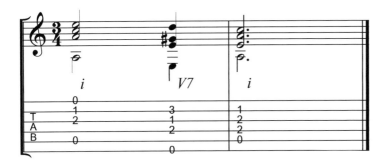

2-19.

These are only general guidelines. Ultimately, harmonic rhythm is a matter of taste. For example, Billie Joe Armstrong of Green Day often changes chords on the final eighth note of a measure, which gives his songs a quirky, "offbeat" quality. For Green Day, it works. In other words, anything goes, as long as your harmonic rhythm fits what you want to express.

Getting to Know the Getaway Chords (ii, iii, IV, and vi)

The dominant and dominant 7th are heralds of the tonic chord, ever ready to cheer for its imminent arrival. The flip side of this mutual attraction society is that V and V7 never take us far from home. That is the role of the *getaway chords*, which open up the third dimension in harmonic perspective. The getaway chords provide escape, departure, or digression from the ping-pong back-and-forth between V and I. In taking us farther from home than the tonic-friendly dominant, they leave multiple routes back home again. They can fall back to I without visiting V, which tends to prolong the drama by delaying the arrival of a conclusive cadence. *Or* they can lead into the dominant, which is why they are sometimes called *pre-dominant* chords.

The getaway chords are made up of the remaining diatonic chords—ii, iii, IV, and vi—as well as chords borrowed from the minor mode. In major mode, the vii° chord requires special handling, so we will set it aside for now. In the key of C major, the getaway chords include D minor (ii), E minor (iii), F major (IV), A minor (vi), and chords from the key of C minor, including F minor (iv), A♭ major (♭VI), and B♭ major (♭VII), as well as colorful forms of the dominant 7th, such as G7♭9. C minor might be considered a getaway chord, if it is part of a digression into the minor mode, and vice versa (C major often appears in the key of C minor).

If you have built a mental wall between major mode and minor mode, it would be a good idea to tear it down. The artificial division usually comes about because of the way harmony is taught: major mode first, minor mode second, with a distinct set of rules for each. In the real world, composers mix and mingle chords from both modes all the time.

Next, we'll get to know the mood of the diatonic getaway chords by improvising rhythms with I > GC > I progressions ("GC" stands for "getaway chord"). Each progression has a unique feeling, but none have the assertive power of V > I. Before you read the discussion that follows each example, improvise three different rhythms (slow, medium, and fast), and try to describe the mood of the progression in your own words:

Getaway Progression 1: I > IV > I

2-20.

Discussion: In a major key, I, IV, and V form a family. Like the V chord, the IV chord has the ability to herald the coming of the tonic. The relationship is strong enough to earn the IV > I progression its own title: *plagal cadence*. While the V chord expresses an active, assertive desire for the tonic, the IV chord expresses a gentle yearning. There are several reasons for the air of surrender and yearning that accompany this progression, which is also called the *amen cadence* because of its use as a tagline in hymns.

First, there is the relationship between the roots of IV and I. The root of IV (F in the key of C) is a perfect fifth below the tonic (C), just as the dominant (G) is a perfect fifth above it. This is why the IV chord is called the *subdominant*. But the dominant relationship between the IV and I is the reverse of the relationship between V and I. Since the I chord is the dominant of the IV chord, IV undermines the supremacy of the tonic. This undermining lends IV a reflective, sentimental quality that slows the momentum of chord progressions.

Second, in the IV > I progression, the root (F) rises a perfect fifth to the tonic, (C). This is the reverse of the natural flow of root progressions down by a fifth (or up a fourth). Movement down by a fifth retraces the path of an overtone to its fundamental, which resolves tension, like folding up a telescope. Rising by a fifth runs contrary to the natural flow, hence it is called *retrograde motion*. The IV > I progression has the backward flow of a retrograde progression, but it reinstates the tonic on the throne, which gives it an air of homage, affection, and humility.

In melodies based on IV > I, the root of IV (F in the key of C) falls a half step to the 3rd of the tonic chord (see *Ex. 2-22* below). The falling half step is classically a "crying" or "sighing" sound, associated with sorrow, surrender, or yearning. The 3rd of the tonic chord (E in the key of C) is the most emotionally sensitive tone of the scale, since it defines the character of the key. This gives the melodic movement F > E (scale tone 4 > 3) a warm, melting feeling suggestive of religious devotion or loving surrender.

In the IV > I progression, the I chord seems to emerge like the sun from behind a cloud. This is because the tonic, the first tone in the scale, is found in both IV and I, but in the IV chord, the tonic is temporarily frozen as the 5th of the chord. When the harmony changes to I, the tonic becomes the root again, thawing it out of its supporting role as the 5th of the IV chord.

The IV > I progression is gentle when compared to the magnetism of V > I, but this gentleness is useful. For example, the progression IVmaj7 > I (or Imaj7) often appears in hip folk, jazz, bossa nova, and pop music. Improvise a few rhythms in slow, medium, and fast tempi for the following progression:

2-21.

In the minor mode, the IV chord is minor (iv). In C minor, for example, iv is F minor. The flatted 3rd of iv (A♭ in F minor) intensifies the yearning quality of the chord, since it only a half step above the 5th of the tonic chord. The shift from IV major to iv minor appears on the word "senses" in *Desperado* by the Eagles (Glenn Frey, Don Henley, 1973), a song chosen as No. 494 in *Rolling Stone* magazine's "500 Greatest Songs of All Time" list (2004). The Beatles use the minor iv chord to intensify the sad aura of memories of things loved and lost in the song *In My Life* (Lennon/McCartney, 1965), which *Mojo* magazine rated the best song of all time in 2000. Clearly, the minor IV chord has a track record of success in pop music.

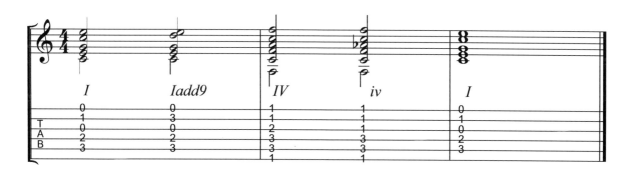

2-22.

Getaway Progression 2: I > ii > I

2-23. Improvise some rhythms for this progression. Describe the feeling it conveys.

Discussion: The ii chord is called the *supertonic* because its root is one step above the tonic. All of the tones of the ii chord are one step away from tones of the tonic chord, which gives the I > ii > I progression a gentle, rocking, floating feeling, like going over gentle waves in a rowboat. The alternation between the major I chord and the minor ii chord gives the progression an emotionally cool, wistful quality. The I > ii > I progression appears in *Groovin'* by the Young Rascals (Felix Cavaliere, Eddie Brigati, 1967), *Blackbird* (Lennon/McCartney, 1968), and *Don't Let Me Down* (Lennon/McCartney, 1969).

Getaway Progression 3: I > iii > I

2-24. Improvise some rhythms for this progression. Describe the feeling it conveys.

Discussion: The iii chord is called the *mediant* because its root is midway between the tonic and the dominant: I-II-III-IV-V. The iii chord is harmonically distant from the tonic, more so than any diatonic chord other than vii. As we'll see, this makes it useful in longer harmonic journeys, but here we are considering only the back and forth movement between I and iii.

The first half of the progression, I > iii has a mysterious quality well-suited to wan moods of melancholy and mystery. This is partly because the 5th of the iii chord is the leading tone (scale tone 7), the most passionately yearning tone of all, but its natural rising energy is all but nullified by its harmonic position as the stable 5th of the iii chord. The return movement, iii > I, is similar to V > I because it descends from an overtone of the tonic to the fundamental (E > C), while the leading tone rises to the tonic, but it lacks the decisiveness of a full cadence.

Elvis Presley uses I > iii in his 1960 hit, *Are You Lonesome Tonight?* (music, Lou Handman, lyrics, Roy Turk, 1926). The I > iii change comes on the word "to-night." French impressionist composer Claude Debussy (1862-1918) uses I > iii in his masterpiece *Clair de Lune*, where it expresses a mood of mystery and intensely sad, sensitive, delicate emotion—like backlit clouds drifting in front of a chilly full moon. This may be because the root of iii is the most emotionally sensitive scale degree, and the root movement I > iii is retrograde (outward bound from the tonic to an overtone), rather than resolving, like V > I (falling from an overtone to the tonic).

Getaway Progression 4: I > vi > I

2-25. Improvise some rhythms for this progression. Describe the feeling it conveys.

Discussion: The vi chord (Am in the example) is called the *submediant* because it is midway between the tonic and the subdominant, or a similar distance below the tonic as the mediant is above it. The I > vi progression casts a restless chill over the stable tonic (C) by transforming it into the emotionally sensitive 3rd of a somber minor chord.

A root progression that moves down by a third, as in C to Am, is a resolving progression (it mimics the descent from an overtone toward a fundamental), which relieves the monotony of downward movement by a fifth. The side-slipping, downward-by-a-third progression is an interesting way to enter new harmonic territory. Sometimes the side-slipping movement continues, as in the progression I > vi > IV (C > Am > F).

2-26.

In the minor mode, the progression i > ♭VI > i (e.g. Em > C > Em) has a portentous, mystical quality, as evidenced in the song poems *Sand and Foam* (1966) and *Isle of Islay* (1968) by Donovan.

Expanded Harmonic Perspective

The diagram below shows how getaway chords open up the third dimension in harmonic perspective by taking us farther away from the tonal vanishing point (the tonic chord):

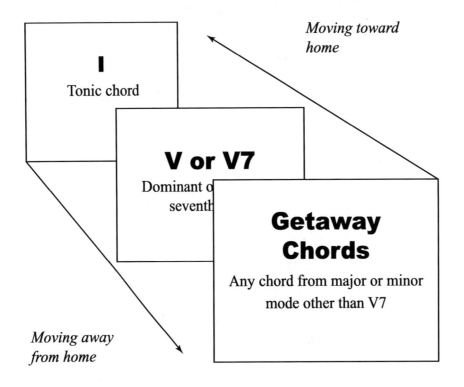

Fig. 2-2. Getaway chords telescope harmony into the third dimension. They take us farther away from the tonic than the dominant, opening many new pathways back home.

As we've seen, the getaway chords are also effective when they return directly to the tonic without passing through the dominant. But, as mentioned above, they are so effective at introducing the dominant chord that they are sometimes called *pre-dominant* chords:

2-27. Just as the dominant introduces the tonic, getaway chords introduce the dominant.

Table 2-1 below shows the tonic, dominant, and getaway chords in easy keys for guitar. This will be a useful reference for the upcoming exercises in improvising chord progressions for pop-song phrases. Pianists should review the same chords in the easy keys for piano.[4] If you're not already familiar with these chords, concentrate on just one or two keys where you feel comfortable. Single letters, such as "E," stand for major chords; "m" means *minor*, ° means *diminished*, and *ø* means *half-diminished*.

Table 2-1 – Tonic, Dominant, and Getaway Chords in Easy Guitar Keys						
Chord type	Tonic	Getaway Chords			Dominant	Getaway (vi)
	I	ii	iii	IV	V or V7	vi
Easy Guitar Keys	C	Dm	Em	F	G, G7	Am
	A	Bm	C♯m	D	E, E7	F♯m
	G	Am	Bm	C	D, D7	Em
	E	F♯m	G♯m	A	B, B7	C♯m
	D	E	F♯m	G	A, A7	Bm
	Am	B°, B°7, Bø7	C	Dm	E, E7	F
	Em	F♯°, F♯°7, F♯ø7	G	Am	B, B7	C
	Dm	E°, E°7, Eø7	F	Gm	A, A7	B♭

Improvising Three-Chord Pop Song Progressions

When Nashville songwriter Harlan Howard (1927-2002) said, "All you need to write a country song is three chords and the truth," he was probably thinking of I, IV, and V—the workhorse harmonies of pop music throughout the '50s and early '60s. The Beatles expanded the harmonic vocabulary of popular music far beyond this holy trinity, but thousands of songs have been written and continue to be written with just three chords: I, V, and a getaway chord.

---

4 No chord charts for guitar or piano are given, because it is assumed that readers have a basic chord vocabulary (see the *Prelude*). However, chord charts can easily be found online, if necessary.

The following exercise puts Howard's three-chords-and-the-truth maxim into action. The goal is to juggle rhythm and harmony in improvised phrases consisting of I, V, and a getaway chord. The exercise is broken down into steps below. After you follow the steps a few times, they will merge together. If you do the exercise once a day for a couple of weeks, you will be able to improvise pop song progressions in sections and phrases with ease.

- Memorize the chord progression blueprint. A blueprint is a plan, such as "I > GC (getaway chord) > V". Ten blueprints are shown below. Notice that they are categorized as questions or answers, depending on the final chord (I makes the progression an answer, any other chord makes it a question).

- Choose three chords—I, V, getaway chord—from *Table 2-1* above. Use major, minor, or dominant 7th chords anywhere. You can recycle the same three chords in different blueprints.

- Practice the three chords until you can play them smoothly. Rhythm doesn't matter.

- Add a rhythmic structure. This is the heart of the exercise. Place the three chords in a two-measure section or a four-measure phrase, one or two chords per measure. It is okay to repeat a chord from one measure to the next.

- Add rhythmic personality and ornamentation: Work up the tempo, insert offbeats, rests, and so on until you're making a "statement." Add some ornamentation (hammer-ons, pull-offs) as desired.

Example Improvisation Based on Blueprint 1

1) **Memorize the blueprint**: Blueprint 1 is "I > GC > V."

2) **Choose three chords**: Let's try the key of G. Referring to *Table 2-1*, we see that the I chord is G, the V chord is D or D7, and the getaway chord can be Am, Bm, C, or Em. We'll choose Em just because the change from G major to E minor feels good on the guitar. This is a straightforward set of garden variety chords. If you're into jazz, you might want to try some 7ths, such as Gmaj7, Am7, D7♭9. When converted to functional notation, it's easy to see that this chord progression still follows the I > GC > V blueprint: Imaj7 (the tonic chord) > ii7 (the getaway chord) > V7♭9 (the dominant).

.

2-28. Both chord progressions follow the I > GC > V blueprint.

3) **Practice**: Play through the chord progression G > Em > D7 until you're able to change chords smoothly and quickly while thinking about the I > GC > V question form.

4) **Add a rhythmic structure**: Use only whole notes or half notes to express the harmonic rhythm. Notice where the changes occur, and how the rhythmic placement affects the mood of the phrase. When you perform, count the beats vigorously in order to exaggerate the rhythmic framework. The importance of counting aloud and accenting the downbeat strongly can't be overemphasized, as we are now juggling two balls at once (harmony and rhythm) and it is easy to drop one of them:

2-29.

5) **Add rhythmic personality and ornamentation**: By repeating a two-measure section, we get a four-measure phrase, or double section. The rhythm is reggae. Use string damping on the rests by relaxing the left-hand fingers and smacking the strings with the edge of the right palm for a cymbal effect.

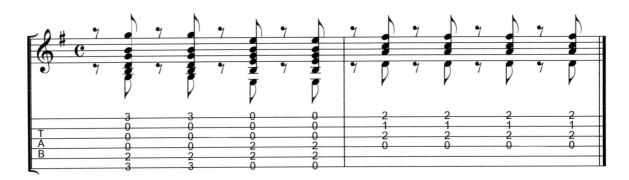

2-30. Rhythm has been added to the progression in Ex. 2-29.

Blueprints for Improvisation

1) I > GC > V

Type of progression: Question
Example (key of G):   G > Em > D7. See *Ex. 2-30* above.

2) I > V > GC

Type of progression: Question
Example (key of C):   C > G7 > Am

Discussion: This is a deceptive cadence: V goes to a different chord than the anticipated I chord, postponing or denying a decisive V > I cadence.

3) GC > I > GC > V

Type of progression: Question
Example (key of D):   Em > D > Em > A7.

4) V > I > GC > V

Type of progression: Question
Example (key of A):   E > A > D > E7

5) I > GC > I > V

Type of progression: Question
Example (in E minor):   Em > Am > Em > B7

6) I > V > I

Type of progression: Answer
Example (key of C):   C > G7 > C

7) I > GC > V > I

Type of progression: Answer
Example (key of E):   E > C♯m > B7 > E)

8) V > GC > V > I

Type of progression: Answer
Example (key of G):   D > C > D > G

9) V > I > V > I

Type of progression: Answer
Example (key of Am):   E > Am > E > Am

10) GC > I > V > I

Type of progression: Answer
Example (key of D):   G > D > A7 > D

Congratulations! You are now beginning to think like a composer.

True Harmonic Perspective

In order to fine-tune harmonic perspective, we need to know how far each chord is from the tonic. As described in the *Interlude*, harmonic distance is reckoned in intervals of a perfect fifth, rather than scale steps. Using the perfect-fifth system of measurement, the dominant chord (V) is closest to the tonic, because it is a perfect fifth above it. The next closest will be a perfect fifth above the dominant, and so on, giving I > V > ii > vi > iii > vii° > IV. If the sequence is played in reverse, I > IV > vii° > iii > vi > ii > V > I, the progression uses every scale degree as a root and moves in the most typical manner of a resolving chord progression (downward by a perfect fifth, or the inversion: upward by a perfect fourth):

2-31.

As a practical matter, this progression is seldom seen. First, it's longwinded. Second, the root of the IV chord is a diminished fifth above the root of the vii chord. The diminished fifth is as dissonant as fingernails on a blackboard and difficult to sing, so the IV chord does not move smoothly to vii. Third, vii is a diminished chord, which means it has no root in the same sense as the other chords. It is so tense and dissonant that it pulls in another direction, toward the root and 3rd of the tonic chord.

By changing the vii chord to a minor chord, rather than a diminished chord, The Beatles were able to use a I > vii > III > vi progression in the first three measures of *Yesterday* (C, Bm, E7, Am).[5] They continued along more routine lines in the next measure (IV > V > I). Most diatonic harmonic journeys do not venture out beyond iii. Even the I > iii > vi > ii > V > I progression sounds longwinded, but at least its logical:

2-32. *Journeying out to the iii chord and back home again by perfect fifths.*

Since all chords in this progression are connected by perfect fifths, composers break the diatonic monotony by changing one or more of them into a dominant 7th:

5 Original key, F major (guitar tuned down a whole step and played as if in the key of G)

I   V7/vi   vi   V7/ii   ii   V7/V   V   V7   I

2-33. When iii (Em in C) is altered to III7 (E7 in measure 1), it is called a secondary dominant, since it is the dominant 7th of the vi chord (V7/vi). Similarly, VI7 (A7 in measure 2) is the secondary dominant of ii (V7/ii), and II7 (D7 in measure 3) is the secondary dominant of V (V7/V).

But where does IV belong? The progression IV > V > I is undeniably compelling. For one thing, it contains all seven scale degrees, which convincingly defines the key:

IV-V-I: Key of C   Key of A   Key of E   Key of D

2-34. IV > V > I in the keys of C, A, E, and D. Each cadence contains all seven scale tones.

This is a good argument for placing IV closer to V than ii, and yet the great composers, not to mention jazz players, prefer to precede V with ii or ii7, especially ii in the first inversion, that is, with its 3rd in the bass.[6] The 3rd of the ii chord is the fourth scale degree, so this progression blends ii and IV:

---

6 All of the chords discussed so far have had the root in the bass. For example, a root position C major chord (C-E-G) has C in the bass. *Inversions* have the 3rd, 5th, or 7th in the bass. The first inversion of C major has E in the bass. The root moves up an octave, and the chord is spelled E-G-C. The second inversion is G-C-E. A 7th chord, such as Dmi7 (D-F-A-C), has three possible inversions: F-A-C-D, A-C-D-F, and C-D-F-A. In modern notation, the first inversion of Dmi7 would be written *Dmi7/F*.

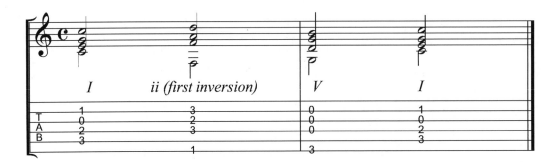

2-35. The first inversion of the ii chord places the 3rd of the chord in the bass. The 3rd is scale degree 4 (F in the example), so we get the same bass line for IV > V and ii > V, but the stronger sounding root progression by a fifth in ii > V.

Based on the practice of the great composers, we'll place IV farther away from the tonic, between ii and vi in the harmonic perspective diagram. When you understand how to use the chart below, you'll find that this placement gives good results. Because ii and IV are closely related, feel free to use them both in any order when it seems right. The same applies to substitutes for ii and IV discussed below.

Fig. 2-3 – True Diatonic Harmonic Perspective

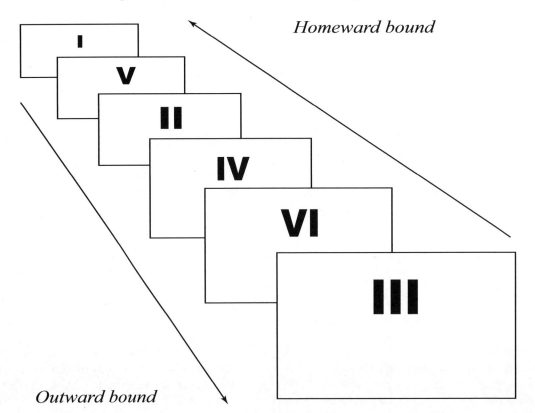

Using the *True Diatonic Harmonic Perspective* diagram is simple and straightforward. There are no "rules," just *common* moves and *less common* moves:

- You may jump outward from the tonic to any other chord.

- Once you're out, the natural flow is back again, either by coming straight back home to the tonic or by stopping at one or more of the intervening stepping stones.

- Once you're away from the tonic, you can step outward again, such as from II to IV, rather than IV to II. Reverse moves sound great on occasion, but they're less common.

- Here are some other points:

- Moving away from the tonic raises a question. By putting the tonic off on the horizon and opening up harmonic space between the chord of the moment and the tonic, you arouse curiosity: "How will we get home again?"

- Moving homeward moves toward a resolution of the question. That is, it increases anticipation of the arrival of V or I.

- Arrival at the tonic resolves the question and completes the harmonic journey. Not all completed journeys are the same, however. Some are weaker than others. For example, if the root is in the soprano and the bass (top and bottom notes), the ending is *conclusive*. If the 3rd is in the soprano, the ending is less conclusive.

- Skipping the dominant chord on the return trip, as in VI > I or II > I, can be useful in prolonging the journey because it postpones a more conclusive V > I cadence.

- Root movement by a fifth down, such as such as II > V or V > I, is the norm. It resolves tension by retracing the path from overtone to fundamental, like folding up a telescope. Movement by a fifth up, such as VI > III or V > II, is called a *retrograde progression*. Retrograde movement is unusual, but it can be useful as a "backing off" tactic before taking another run at the dominant or the tonic, as in the progression II > V, II > V > I. In a sense, any progression that moves from a fundamental to an overtone, such as I > III, is retrograde. Overuse of retrograde movement, or wandering back and forth among the modal degrees (ii, iii, and vi), produces an aimless feeling that weakens the tonic, which is usually undesirable.

- Movement from V to I is expected and anticipated. Movement from V to any chord other than I is called a *deceptive cadence*. Common deceptive cadences include V > IV (in blues, rock, and folk) and V > VI. Both VI and IV include the tonic, but as 3rd and 5th of the chord, rather than the root. Deceptive cadences have surprise value and are useful in prolonging the build-up to the final V > I.

Capital-letter Roman numerals identify the harmonic outposts in the chart because we can use many different types of chords at each harmonic station. The supertonic II, for example, accommodates ii, ii7, II, II7, ♭II, ♭ii7, ii°7, as well as inversions of all of these chords. All substitutes are shown at the end of the lesson. For now, it is better to understand the simple view of the chart before plunging into exotic substitutes for root-position diatonic chords.

The significance of these guidelines won't sink in until you hear how they work in real-life music. That begins on page 93. An *Extended Harmonic Perspective Chart* with many substitute harmonies for I through VI begins on page 122.

Decoding Chord Symbols

The majority of chords you meet in the real world of music will be major, minor, or dominant 7ths. However, a glance at most scores reveals an intimidating array of chord names and symbols that seem to imply otherwise. Just remember that in general these added numbers and symbols have no effect on the function of the chord. For example, in the key of C, the chords C6, C9, and Csus4 still function as a tonic chord, and the chords G7+9, G11, G13 still function as dominant chords. They are just uptown relations of their less sophisticated kinfolk.

Numbers stand for intervals above the root. A G13 chord, for example, is a G7 chord with an added tone a 13th above the root (E, when the root is G). The term "sus" stands for "suspended," which means that the numbered tone is held over or tacked on to the basic triad and is a substitute for the nearest chord tone at that position. For example, the chord "Csus4" is spelled C-F-G, because the 4th tone above the root, F, substitutes for the 3rd of the chord, E. The "+" sign means "augmented," so G7+9 (or G7♯9) is a G7 chord with an augmented 9th. A ninth above G is A, so the augmented 9th above G is A♯. Sometimes, however, "+" means "added," rather than augmented. Unfortunately, pop chord symbols are not as consistent as Roman numeral notation, which has had a couple of hundred years to settle.

2-36. C6 has an added tone a sixth above the root. Cadd9 adds D, the ninth above the root. Dsus4 substitutes G, a tone a fourth above the root for the chord 3rd. G9 is a dominant chord with an added ninth. The C in G11 substitutes for B, the 3rd of the chord.

The Nashville system—another alternative to Roman numeral notation—uses Arabic numerals to represent scale degrees of chord roots. For example, I > IV > V > vi becomes "1 ma > 4 ma > 5 ma > 6 min." Since this could lead to some confusion between scale degrees, chord roots, and chord elements, such as 3rds and 5ths, we will stick with the Roman numeral system, which is also what you will encounter college harmony courses.

Harmonic Perspective in the Real World

The fifteen chord progressions below occur and reoccur in countless songs and instrumental pieces, as shown by the example titles. Each is shown in three easy keys and described in terms of the *True Diatonic Harmonic Perspective Chart* shown above. Read the discussion and improvise rhythms for each one. Most important, *listen to the examples*; they are only a few clicks away. For extra credit, transpose each progression to additional keys.

Progression 1: I > IV > V > I

IV-V-I: *Key of C*   *Key of D*   *Key of G*

2-37.

Examples: A classic rock-and-roll progression found in thousands of songs, including *La Bamba* (Ritchie Valens, 1958), *Do You Love Me* (Berry Gordy, Jr., recorded by The Contours, 1962), *Twist and Shout* (recorded by The Beatles, 1963; Phil Medley and Bert Russell, also recorded by the Top Notes and the Isley Brothers), *Like a Rolling Stone* (Bob Dylan, 1965), *Here Comes the Sun* (George Harrison, The Beatles, 1969; verse), *Come and Get It* (Paul McCartney, popularized by Badfinger, 1969 and 1978), *Born to Run* (Bruce Springsteen, 1975), *Rock and Roll All Nite* (Kiss, 1975; chorus), *Mr. Jones* (Counting Crows, 1993; chorus).

The variation I > IV > I > V > I is found in *Teach Your Children* (Graham Nash, Crosby, Stills, Nash & Young, 1970), among other songs. The insertion of I between IV and V prolongs the build up to the V chord.

In a two-measure section, the I chord can occupy the first measure, and IV and V can occupy the second measure. In a four-measure phrase, I > IV > V can be expanded to I > I > IV > V (one chord to each measure), as in *My Boy Lollipop* (sung by Millie Small, 1964).

Harmonic perspective: Progression 1 conforms perfectly to harmonic perspective. From the tonic, it jumps outward beyond the dominant to getaway chord IV, then returns home triumphantly via the dominant V or V7. The progression IV > V (or V7) thrusts upward by a whole step, which has the strength and logic of a rising scale step, but gains added momentum from root movement by a fifth: the subdominant IV is a fifth below the tonic, and the dominant V is a fifth above the tonic, so IV > V swings to the left and to the right of the tonic chord before coming home. The progression contains all seven notes of the scale, so it defines the key with utmost certainty. All of these elements combine to make the mood of the I > IV > V > I progression exuberantly positive.

Improvise some of your own rhythms to the examples above and perhaps you'll be the next songwriter to compose a page in rock history.

Progression 2: V > IV > I

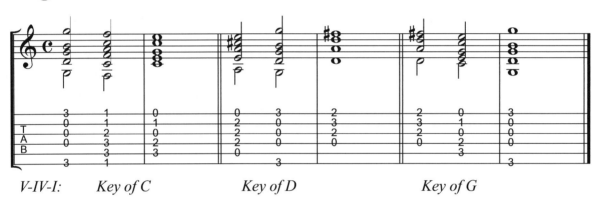

V-IV-I: *Key of C*   *Key of D*   *Key of G*

2-38.

Improvise a few rhythms in four-measure phrases.

Examples: *Brimful of Asha* (Tjinder Singh, 1997), *If Not for You, Knockin' on Heaven's Door* (Bob Dylan, 1970, 1973), *Maggie May* (Rod Stewart, Martin Quittenton, 1971), *Mary's Song (Oh My My My)* (Taylor Swift, 2006), *Peaceful Easy Feeling* (Jack Tempchin, recorded by the Eagles, 1972).

Harmonic perspective: Progression 2 contains a V > IV deceptive cadence, which is found in measures 7 through 11 of a twelve-bar blues, and in folk and rock music. The V chord promises to return to the tonic, but backs away from that promise by moving to IV, which then melts into I with the feeling of surrender characteristic of the plagal cadence.

The nearness of the V chord to the tonic adds strength to the plagal cadence, because the arrival of I was delayed, but not denied.

In the blues, the message of I7 > V7 > IV7 > I7 is "strength and endurance in the face of frustration and denial." Harmonically, the blues literally tells how it feels to have no home, because even the I chord (home) is a restless, unstable dominant tetrad, not a stable tonic triad. The I, IV, and V are all dominant 7th chords in the blues, which adds a minor 3rd and minor 7th degree to the blues scale. Due to their conflict with the major I, IV, and V, these minor scale degrees express agitated sadness in melody and harmony.

The use of dominant 7ths for I and IV in the blues shows that tonality is flexible: it welcomes substitute harmonies for the standard diatonic chords. Think of I, II, III, and so forth as positions in harmonic space, rather than specific chords, and you will come closer to thinking like a composer. Each position can accommodate many chords other than routine diatonic chords. A full list of substitutions begins on page122.

Progression 3: ii > V7 > I

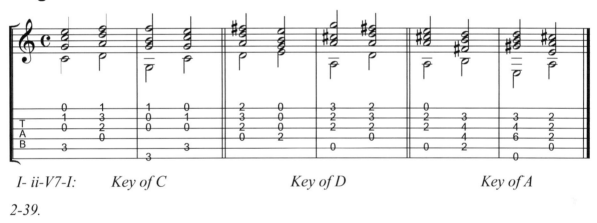

I- ii-V7-I: Key of C   Key of D   Key of A

2-39.

Examples: This progression appears in all genres of music, including classical, jazz, and rock. Listen to *Honeysuckle Rose* (Fats Waller and Andy Razaf, 1928), *Take the "A" Train* (written by Billy Strayhorn in 1933, recorded by Duke Ellington in 1941), *Stella by Starlight* (words and music by Victor Young, Ned Washington, 1944, recorded by Frank Sinatra, among others).

Harmonic perspective: Progression 3 conforms perfectly to harmonic perspective. Classical and jazz composers prefer ii > V > I to IV > V > I as a key-defining cadence because it uses root movement by a fifth, which is always strong, and mingles minor and major sounds, unlike the all-major IV > V > I. However, classical composers generally preferred to use the ii chord in first inversion, with the 3rd of the chord in the bass, because the 3rd (scale tone 4, the subdominant) progresses smoothly to a root position V chord (see *Ex. 2-35*).

Classical composers also substituted ♭II for ii in the ii-V-I cadence. This distinctive chord was known as the Neapolitan 6th because it was popular with a certain group of Italian opera composers, including Alessandro Scarlatti (1660 – 1725). It was also a favorite of Beethoven. The chord almost always appears in its first inversion. For example, in the key of C, the Neapolitan 6th is D♭-F-A♭, and in first inversion, it becomes F-A♭-D♭. The term "6th" refers to the interval of a minor 6th between the bass (F, in this case) and the inverted root above it (D♭). The first inversion resembles a IV > V progression, which gives smooth voice leading. The following progression also uses a I chord in its second inversion as a dramatic introduction for the V chord:

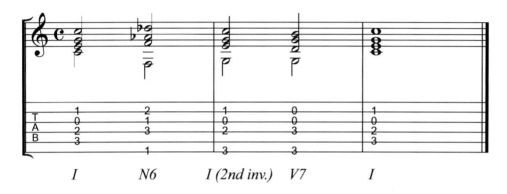

             I   N6   I (2nd inv.)   V7   I

2-40. The Neapolitan sixth ("N6") is the first inversion of a ♭II chord.

The ♭II Neapolitan substitution conforms to the *True Diatonic Harmonic Perspective Chart*, which shows once again that the diatonic chords are only the beginning of the possibilities hidden in the harmonic stepping stones.

    In the following progression, J.S. Bach uses a ii7 chord in its third inversion,[7] which allows him to hold over the tonic in the bass from one chord to the next:

I (root position)	ii7 (third inversion)	V7 (first inversion)	I (root position)

2-41. First four chords from Prelude No. 1, Well-Tempered Clavier, Book 1, *J. S. Bach.*

---

7 In C major, the ii7 chord is spelled D-F-A-C. The first inversion is F-A-C-D (the root is raised by an octave, and the third is in the bass), the second is A-C-D-F, and the third is C-D-F-A. Notice that in the third inversion, the bass note is only a whole step below the root.

In jazz, 7ths are usually added to I and ii. The V7 chord can use every note in the chromatic scale except the major seventh as an added tone:

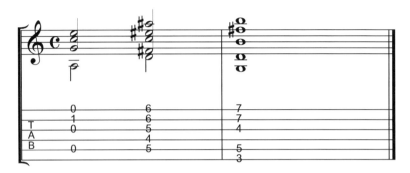

2-42. ii > V7♯5♯9 > Imaj7

II7 may be substituted for ii, as shown below:

2-43. The first chord is D7, II7, or V7 of V, the "dominant of the dominant." The V13 chord is a V7 chord with an added 13th (E). The 5th of both chords has been dropped. As the least of the defining elements of the chord, the 5th is often left out.

The II7 chord is not obligated to resolve to V. In *Yesterday* (Lennon/McCartney, 1965), for example, The Beatles reverse harmonic perspective with the deceptive cadence II7 > IV > I (see *Ex. 2-44* on the following page). Because of the kinship between ii and IV (see *Ex. 2-35*), the effect is soft, like the acceptance of fate implied by the deceptive cadence V > IV in the blues. The V7 chord, which was strongly implied by II7, is almost felt by its *absence* as we skip to a IV > I cadence. As the lyrics say, something is gone.

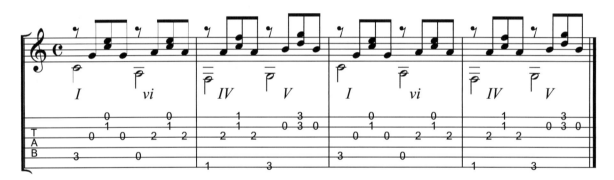

2-44.

This chord progression also appears in *You Won't See Me* (Lennon/McCartney, 1965), and *Sgt. Pepper's Lonely Hearts Club Band* (Lennon/McCartney, 1967).

Progression 4: I > vi > IV > V > I

2-45.

Examples: This progression is familiar from *Heart and Soul* (music by Hoagy Carmichael, lyrics by Frank Loesser, 1938, recorded by the Four Aces in 1952). *Heart and Soul* was also the theme music for the film *Big*, starring Tom Hanks (1988). Many other rock 'n' roll hits of the 1950s and early 1960s feature Progression 4, including *Earth Angel* (Curtis Williams, Jesse Belvin, Gaynel Hodge, 1955), *Blue Moon* (Rodgers and Hart, 1934; sung by Elvis Presley, 1956), *Donna* (Ritchie Valens, 1958), *Poor Little Fool* (Sharon Sheeley, recorded by Ricky Nelson, 1958), *Stand by Me* (Ben E. King, Jerry Leiber, Mike Stoller, 1962), and *Duke of Earl* (Gene Chandler, 1962).

Examples by The Beatles form a category unto themselves: *Please Mr. Postman* ("Dobbins/ Garett/Brianbert," recorded by The Marvelettes, 1961, and The Beatles in 1963, who credit the song to Holland/Bateman/Gordy, according to Wikipedia), *Happiness Is a Warm Gun* (Lennon/ McCartney, chorus, 1968), *A Hard Day's Night* (Lennon/McCartney, bridge, 1964), *I've Just Seen a Face* (Lennon/McCartney, 1965), *Octopus's Garden* (The Beatles, credited to Ringo— Richard Starkey—1969).

Harmonic perspective: Progression 4 conforms to the perspective chart, but there are two other reasons why it works. First, root movement downward by a third is weaker than downward by a fifth, but it is resolving because it resembles a return from an overtone to the fundamental. Second, the vi chord (A-C-E in the key of C) has two tones in common with the I chord (C-E), and the IV chord (F-A-C) has two tones in common with the vi chord (A-C). The resulting sequence is smooth, but dynamic (that is, full of movement).

Progression 5: I > vi > ii > V7 > I

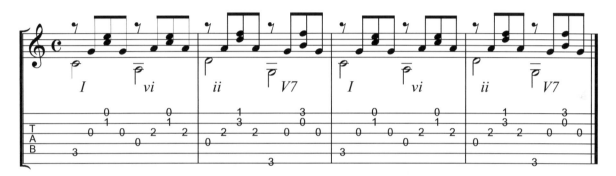

2-46.

Examples: *All I Have to Do Is Dream* (Felice and Boudleaux Bryant, recorded by The Everly Brothers, 1958), *Hungry Heart* (Bruce Springsteen, 1980), *You're Going to Lose That Girl* (Lennon/McCartney, 1965), *This Boy* (Lennon/McCartney, 1963), *I Got Rhythm* (George Gershwin, 1930)

Harmonic perspective: Progression 5 fully conforms to harmonic perspective. The root movement is particularly strong because it is a chain of downward perfect fifths. Classical composers would seek a subtler expression of I > vi > ii > V7 by using inversions to smooth out the bass line with more stepwise, melodic movement.

Progression 6: I > iii > IV > V (or V7) > I

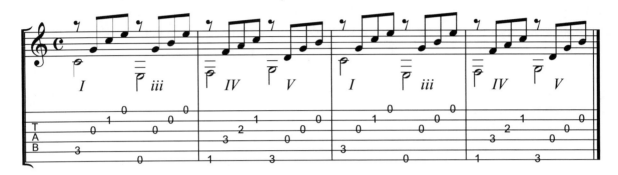

2-47.

Examples: *What a Wonderful World* (music, Bob Thiele, words, George David Weiss, Louis Armstrong recording, 1968), measures 1 and 2. *Voyage of the Moon* (Mary Hopkin on *Postcard*, 1969; Donovan on the *HMS Donovan* album, 1971), between measures 2 and 3.

Harmonic perspective: Progression 6 conforms perfectly to harmonic perspective. The iii chord (E minor in the key of C) has a watery, mysterious sound, but leading it up by a half step into the IV chord energizes IV, lending more drama to the coming V7.

A refreshing variant on I > iii > IV is I > ♭III > IV, used by Lynyrd Skynyrd in *Free Bird*:

2-48.

The I > ♭III > IV progression borrows chords from the Dorian mode, showing once again the flexibility of the tonal system.

Progression 7: I > iii > vi > ii > V > I

2-49.

Examples and harmonic perspective: Even though this progression consists entirely of root movement by a perfect fifth, composers shy away from it, probably because the chain of fifths sounds mechanical and overly drawn out. But if dominant 7ths are substituted for diatonic chords, we get a progression that occurs fairly often in ragtime and blues, such as in the works of seminal jazz pianist Jelly Roll Morton (1885 – 1941):

2-50. The III7 chord (E7) is the dominant of vi (Am), hence the Roman numerals "V7/vi".

A dominant 7th chord that introduces a diatonic chord other than I is called a *secondary dominant* (also see *Secondary dominants*, page 113). *Alice's Restaurant* (Arlo Guthrie, 1967), a Vietnam War protest song written in ragtime guitar style, uses a chain of dominants: I > VI7 > II7 > V > I. At any point in such a progression, the original diatonic chord can appear (see next page):

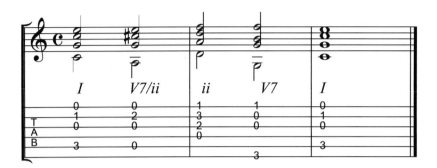

2-51. The secondary dominant A7 introduces the diatonic Dm in measure 2.

Progression 8: I > ♭VII > IV > I

2-52.

Examples: This progression is found in gospel music, as well as in *Orinoco Flow (Sail Away)*, by Enya (co-credited to Roma Ryan, 1988).

Harmonic perspective: Progression 8, also known as a *Mixolydian cadence*, runs contrary to the *Harmonic Perspective Chart*. First, it contains a ♭VII major chord, a harmonic visitor from the Mixolydian mode, which is the same as a major scale played from Sol to Sol (from scale tone 5 to scale tone 5):

2-53. C Mixolydian chords

The ♭VII chord frequently substitutes for the dominant chord, so this progression has something in common with Progression 2, I > V > IV, a deceptive cadence.

Second, the last three chords form a retrograde progression of perfect fifths, which has a solemn, spacey quality, as it advances against the usual downward-by-perfect-fifth flow, yet reaches the tonic all the same, as if by a back door. In effect, it ascends outward and upward to the tonic, instead of downward and backward.

Other Mixolydian songs include *Old Joe Clark* (Kentucky folk ballad), *(I Can't Get No) Satisfaction* (Mick Jagger and Keith Richards, The Rolling Stones, 1965), *Norwegian Wood (This Bird Has Flown)* (Lennon/McCartney, 1965), *Dark Star* (Jerry Garcia and Robert Hunter, The Grateful Dead, 1968), *Dear Prudence* (Lennon/McCartney, 1968), *Sweet Home Alabama* (Ed King, Gary Rossington, Ronnie Van Zant, recorded by Lynyrd Skynyrd, 1974), *Star Trek (The Next Generation) Theme* (Jerry Goldsmith, 1987), *Sweet Child o' Mine* (Axl Rose, Slash, Mikey Wiseman, Guns N' Roses, 1988). (Source: Wikipedia, *Mixolydian mode* article.)

Progression 9: I > IV > v > IV

2-54.

Example: *Louie, Louie* (Richard Berry, 1957)

Harmonic perspective: Progression 9 shows how to add freshness to I > IV > V. The first three chords advance in accord with the guidelines of harmonic perspective, but the dominant chord is minor—a chilly visitor from Aeolian, Dorian, or Mixolydian mode—and the movement from v > IV runs against the natural flow, a deceptive cadence. The up and down movement of Progression 9 generates a rolling-wave or roller-coaster feeling.

Progression 10: I > V > vi > IV

2-55.

Example: *Don't Stop Believin'* (Journey, 1981)

Harmonic perspective: The progression V > vi is a deceptive cadence. Leaving the dominant by the backdoor regains options for the homeward journey. Here, vi sideslips downward by a major third to IV, a refreshing break from movement by a fifth, but a resolving movement (down from overtone to fundamental) all the same. The progression might continue more routinely now by proceeding to V or I.

Progression 11: IV > I > IV > V

2-56. *The sixth string of the guitar is lowered a whole step to D for this example (tuning: DADGBE, from lowest string to highest).*

Harmonic perspective: This ambiguous progression does not begin on the tonic, which undermines harmonic perspective by disguising the tonal center. Progressions such as this often show up in the bridge section of songs. A bridge is to a song what a getaway chord is to the tonic, a digression. The bridge satisfies the need for contrast by wandering around in outer harmonic territory, sometimes even changing keys, which tests the audience's grip on the tonic, but increases the reward of return.

Bridge sections are not as routine a part of song structure as they were in earlier decades, but The Beatles often employed them. For example, *I Want to Hold Your Hand* (Lennon/McCartney,

1963) is in the key of G major, and the bridge is in the key of the subdominant, C. The brief bridge of *A Hard Day's Night* (Lennon/McCartney, 1964) switches from G major to E minor (G major's relative minor). *Girl* (Lennon/McCartney, 1965) is in Cm, and the bridge section is in Fm, the key of the minor subdominant.

Modern songwriters often remain noncommittal about key center by starting a song with a "random" chord progression such as IV > I > IV > V, or a variant, such as vi > IV > I > V, which is popular with The Offspring (formed in 1984), The Cranberries (1989), Linkin Park (1996), and OneRepublic (2002), among others.

Progression 12: I > V > IV > V7

2-57. The sixth string of the guitar is tuned down a whole step to D for this example (DADGBE, from lowest to highest strings).

Harmonic perspective: Progression 12 prolongs the run up to the dominant by backing off and repeating all or part of the approach, a common and important technique, similar to making a trial run to the end of a diving board to measure your steps, then backing off before the final run and dive.

Any of the chord progressions shown so far can be given the same or similar treatment. For example, you could prolong Progression 3, ii > V > I, by repeating ii > V, or you could further elaborate by inserting I > vi prior to the repetition, as shown below:

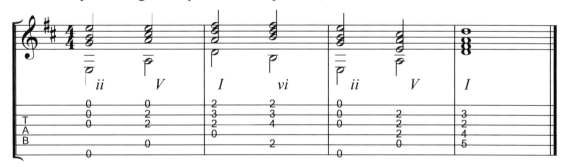

2-58. The guitar is in standard tuning (EADGBE) for this example.

Once you're aware of this teasing device, you'll understand the motivation behind many chord progressions that seem to lack structure. Repetition of the approach to the dominant or the tonic is often linked to a repetition or variation of the melody. (Parroting or playing Q&A with a motive, section, or phrase is a standard way to develop a melody).

Progression 13: I > ii > iii > IV > V7 > I

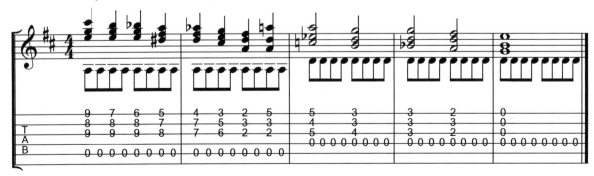

2-59.

Example: Stepwise progressions aren't common in compositions, but they are often used as filler in live performances, such as the proverbial Las Vegas cocktail lounge or a TV game show orchestra, or in jazz (see *Modal Voicing Techniques*, Rick Peckham, DVD, Berklee Press).

Harmonic perspective: Stepwise motion doesn't follow the guidelines of harmonic perspective, but it is often called upon to provide color when one chord must be extended over a few measures. For example, if the sheet music calls for two measures of the tonic chord (let's say C major), the guitar or piano might play C > Dm > Em > Dm > C while the bass drones on the tone C. The droning C is called a *pedal point*, in honor of organ players who hold down one of the bass pedals while playing chords over the droning low note. The tonic or the dominant are the most likely candidates for a pedal point:

Dominant pedal   *Tonic pedal*

2-60. *Pedal point: consonant and clashing chords are played over a single tone.*

A sustained or repeated soprano note may also serve as a pedal point. Chopin (1810 – 1849) uses the technique in the minor middle section of the *Teardrop Prelude (Op. 28, No. 15)*.

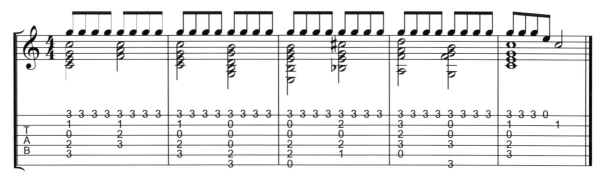

2-61. Dominant soprano pedal tone.

In the *Interlude*, a scale was described as a horizontal version of a tonic chord. Progression 13 is similar, but each scale step has been harmonized. The moral is simply that not everything fits the *Harmonic Perspective Chart*. Two more examples follow.

Progression 14: i > ♭VII > ♭VI > V

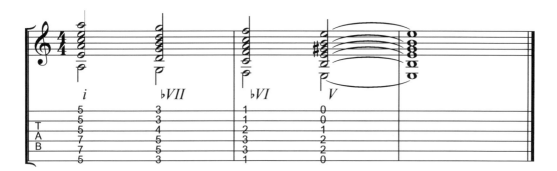

2-62.

Examples: Flamenco guitar, *Toccata and Fugue in D minor* (BWV 565, J.S. Bach, 1703), *Introduction and Fandango* for harpsichord and guitar, Luigi Boccherini (about 1:30 into the *Fandango*), *Anji* (Davey Graham, 1959), *California Dreamin'* (The Mamas & the Papas, John Phillips and Michelle Phillips, 1965), *All Along the Watchtower* (Bob Dylan, 1967, covered by Jimi Hendrix, 1968)

Harmonic perspective: In any of the harmonic perspective charts, the getaway chords generally lead toward the dominant, and the dominant generally leads toward the tonic. Progression 14 shows another way to approach the dominant in the minor mode, by descending stepwise from i to V, using the tones of the natural minor scale as chord roots. In *All Along the Watchtower*, for example, Bob Dylan halts the descent at the ♭VI chord and retraces his steps, i > ♭VII > ♭VI > ♭VII > i. This generates a feeling of pacing in circles while awaiting the arrival of something ominous and decisive (the dominant chord that never comes). All of this tension and waiting is in tune with the ominous, prophetic mood of Dylan's lyrics. A heavy metal bass line descending chromatically by half steps can be achieved with the progression i > ♯vii°7 > ♭VII > IVmajor (first inversion) > IV minor (first inversion) > V. An example would be A minor > G♯°7 > G major > D major with F♯ bass > D minor with F bass > E7.

Descending lines tend to be resolving lines, which explains why flamenco reinterprets the V chord in Progression 14 as a tonic chord. The result is similar to Phrygian mode (Mi to Mi of a major scale). However, in Phrygian, the I chord is minor. In flamenco, it is altered to major.

Like the blues, flamenco treats certain scale degrees as flexible, sometimes raising the third or the seventh of the scale to create a major tonic chord or a major dominant chord. Flamenco uses ♭II (F major) as a dominant chord (a herald of the tonic), but the tonality is ambiguous because E major can also act as the dominant of A minor (iv). Modern flamenco has considerably loosened its harmonic boundaries while preserving its Phrygian mood.

Progression 15: Fighting the Flow

2-63. Running away from the tonic

Example: *Hey Joe* (by folk singer Billy Roberts, 1962; Jimi Hendrix version, 1967).

Harmonic perspective: The progression I > V > II > VI > III > III7 is the reverse of Progression 7 (I > iii > vi > ii > V). The chord roots *ascend* by a perfect fifth, rather than falling back toward the tonic by a perfect fifth, which is a resolving motion. All of the chords in Progression 15 are major, which implies that the tonal center changes with every chord.

This is an expansive, disorienting, rogue progression that runs away from the tonic instead of toward it. *Hey Joe* is about a man who has murdered his lover and become a fugitive. He has no resting place, and never will until he's caught or killed. What better way to dramatize this than to "defy the law" of harmony? *Hey Joe* shows you can break all the rules when it serves a dramatic purpose.

The Circle of Fifths

If the *Hey Joe* progression were to keep marching upward by perfect fifths, it would eventually come full circle, back to C major, as in the progression below. F♯ has been respelled G♭ in order to keep the chord spellings from becoming too complicated. For example, "F" would have to be spelled "E♯" if we were to continue using sharps to name the chords.

2-64. Coming full circle using root movement by perfect fifth. A perfect fifth above F♯ is C♯, which has been enharmonically respelled D♭. A fifth above C♯ is G♯, which has been enharmonically respelled A♭. Eventually progression by fifths leads back to C major.

This parade of perfect fifths uses all twelve tones of the chromatic scale as roots. If we rearrange the twelve chord roots in a circle, like the hours on a watch dial, we have the *circle of fifths*, one of the most important tools in the composer's toolbox (see *Fig. 2-4* below). Moving clockwise, each tone is a perfect fifth above the previous tone. For example, G is a perfect fifth above C.

Counterclockwise movement around the circle gives the most common type of resolving root progression: V > I. For example, C > F (12 o'clock to 11 o'clock) is a dominant-to-tonic progression. Dm > G7 > C (3, 2, 1 o'clock) is also root movement by a fifth.

As described in the *Interlude*, a perfect fourth is the inversion of a perfect fifth and vice versa. Jazz players sometimes call the circle of fifths the *circle of fourths*, because each counterclockwise step is a perfect fourth up (as well as a fifth down) from the last one.

The circle of fifths is a Rosetta stone for key signatures. Moving clockwise from C, the major or relative minor key signature associated with each new tone has one more sharp than the previous key signature: C (A minor is the relative minor) has none, G major (E minor) has one sharp, D major (B minor) has two sharps, and so on. Moving counterclockwise from C, the key signatures acquire one more flat. F major (D minor is the relative minor) has one flat, B♭ major (G minor) has two, and so on, as shown in *Fig. 2-4* and *Ex. 2-65* on the following page:

Fig. 2-4 – The Circle of Fifths

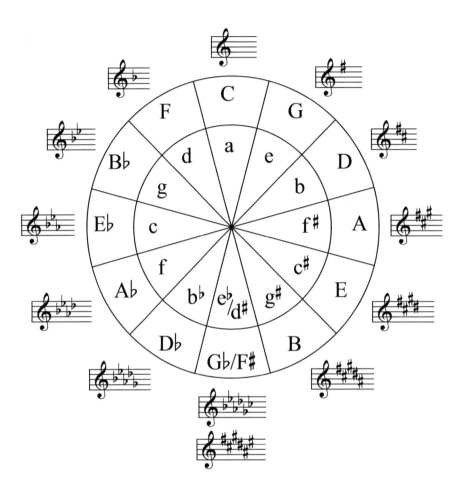

The circle of fifths has the same twelve points as a clock face. Each tick of the clock in a clockwise direction is a perfect fifth above the previous key. Each counterclockwise tick is a fifth down. At the six o'clock position, the keys have six sharps or six flats and are enharmonically equivalent. Capital letters represent major keys, lowercase letters represent relative minor keys. Notice that the word "BEAD" appears on the right and left sides, which aids in memorization. Memorization is important, because chord progressions often match the circle.

Also notice that each new sharp or flat key signature includes all the sharps or flats of the key signature before it, with one addition, which is always the leading tone to the new tonic:

C   G   D   A   E   B   F♯

C   F   B♭   E♭   A♭   D♭   G♭

Ex. 2-65. Sharp and flat key signatures. In the sharp key signatures, the last sharp is the leading tone to the tonic. For example, the last sharp in the key signature of B major is A♯. In the flat key signatures, the second-to-last flat identifies the tonic (except in F major).

The circle of fifths has been around since 1679, when it appeared in a treatise on composition by Ukrainian composer and music theorist Nikolai Diletsky. Why not earlier? Because prior to equal-tempered tuning, which first appeared on lute fretboards in the early 1500s, and was later celebrated in Bach's *Well-Tempered Clavier* (1722), modulation around the circle of fifths was impossible. Only by making perfect fifths slightly out of tune, as they are in equal temperament, is it possible to arrive at C again after traveling completely around the circle by fifths.

Root movement by a fifth, which resembles the return of an overtone to its fundamental, is basic to the grammar of harmony. If you memorize the circle of fifths, you will never again have to stop and calculate a perfect fourth or fifth. The same applies to diatonic progressions, such as ii > V, where one or more of the chords might be minor. For example, Dm7 > G7 > C, a diatonic cadence in C, is essentially D > G > C, three adjacent steps on the circle of fifths.

Finally, whatever key you're in, the IV chord will be one tick to the left on the circle, and the V chord will be one tick to the right. For example, if you're composing in the key of C, the IV chord (F) is one tick to the left, and the V chord (G) is one tick to the right.

Jazz guitar virtuoso Joe Pass, whose harmonic ingenuity is legendary, made frequent use of the circle of fifths in improvisation. At a seminar at the Great American Music Hall in San Francisco in the 1970s, he said, "If you paint yourself into a corner [while improvising], you can always cycle out of there," and humorously played something like this:

E7   A7   D7   G7   C7   F7   B♭7   E♭7♯9♭5

2-66. Joe Pass playing around with the circle of fifths.

The "cycle" he played is simply the circle of fifths with a few added flourishes (those bluesy half-step connecting tones in the bass). The following progression—a series of ii7 > V7 > Imaj7 cadences—also follows the circle of fifths, but with a subtler sound, which results from transforming the Imaj7 into the ii7 of the key center a perfect fifth below:

2-67.

Beyond Harmonic Perspective

Our goal was to show how to put together an interesting chord progression, and what you've learned about harmonic perspective should equip you to do that, especially if you spend some time experimenting with the chord substitutions at the end of the lesson. We could comfortably move on to melody now, but in the interests of total disclosure, we'll touch briefly on seven additional topics that are likely to appear on your musical radar soon, especially if you pursue harmony in college.

1) **Voice leading** is a set of rules and procedures for connecting chords smoothly. Here, for example, is a chord progression with and without the classical style of voice leading:

2-68. The first progression is dramatic, but jerky. The voices have no independence because they move in parallel, equal intervals. The second progression exemplifies good voice leading, with smooth connections between chords and voices that preserve their independence.

Voice leading rules, which are hundreds of years old, are similar to counterpoint, but not as complex. Most readers of *Compose Yourself* are interested in pop music, where the rules for voice leading are relaxed. However, as an aesthetic discipline it has broad applications to instrumental and vocal music, and knowledge of it is useful, even essential. The best way to learn it is to enroll in college-level harmony courses. Also see *Recommended Reading* for *Lesson 2*.

2) **Nonharmonic (nonchord) tones**: These are among the spiciest, most emotionally significant tones at the composer's disposal. Nonharmonic tones are simply melodic tones that are strangers to the chord of the moment. This implies conflict, and conflict implies tension and drama. Because they are so important in melody, we will discuss them in depth in *Lesson 3 – The Heart of Melody*.

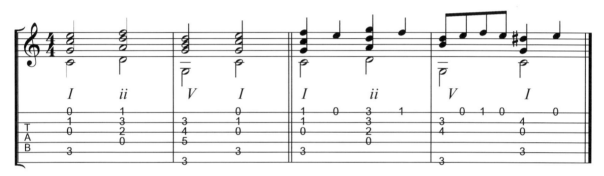

2-69. The progression I > ii > V > I is shown with and without nonharmonic tones.

3) **Secondary dominants:** Just as the tonic may be introduced by the dominant 7th chord (V7), any other diatonic chord may also be introduced by its own dominant 7th chord.

2-70. Four secondary dominants are used in the progression: (a) V7/ii, (b) V7/V, (c) V7/IV, (d) V7/vi

Secondary dominants dramatically accentuate the chords they introduce, but they do not constitute a modulation (a change in key), as they merely serve to briefly introduce diatonic chords in the home key. A convincing modulation requires a full cadence in the new key, such as ii > V7 > I, as well as ongoing harmonic and melodic reinforcement of the new key center.

4) **Diminished and augmented chords**: As mentioned in the *Interlude* (p. 49), any diatonic chord—indeed any chord at all—may be introduced or connected by a diminished or augmented chord wedged in between.

2-71.

The root of a diminished triad may resolve to the root of a major or minor triad a half step up or a whole step down. In the song *Michelle* (Lennon/McCartney, 1965), for example, The Beatles accentuate a dominant triad by approaching it with diminished triads from above and below the root, all in the span of three measures.

An augmented I triad (I+) connects smoothly to the IV chord. An augmented V triad (V+) connects smoothly to the I chord, so it may be used in place of the usual dominant. Listen to the first chord in The Beatles' *Oh! Darling* (Lennon/McCartney, 1969) to hear a melodramatic V+ substituting for V.

The diminished 7th chord has always been a popular choice among composers because of its rich harmony and multiple uses. The four tones of a diminished 7th chord embrace three minor thirds and two tritones. B diminished 7 (B°7), for example, is spelled B-D-F-A♭. The three minor thirds are B-D, D-F, and F-A♭. The two tritones are B-F and D-A♭.

2-72. B diminished 7 combines three minor thirds and two interlocking diminished fifths. A common voicing of the chord is shown last.

Every tone of a diminished 7 chord can act as a leading tone, which makes it ideal for rapid modulation. The diminished 7 chord is also sometimes called a *rootless dominant minor 9th*, because it functions much the same as a dominant chord with a ♭9 degree. B°7, for example, can resolve to four chords (major or minor): C, E♭, G♭ (F♯), and A.

2-73. B°7 has been respelled enharmonically in each example to provide a leading tone to the chord of resolution. Any tone of the diminished 7 chord can be called the root.

In the fourth example in *2-74* above, an A major chord works as a chord of resolution because the 7th of B°7, A♭, can be respelled G♯, making it a leading tone to A. Such a respelling also changes the root. B°7 becomes G♯°7 (G♯-B-D-F). B°7 may also be called a "rootless" G7♭9, since G7♭9 would be spelled G-[B-D-F-A♭]. The tone A♭ is a minor ninth above the chord root G. G♯°7 may be called a rootless E7♭9.

2-74. (a) G7♭9, (b) B°7, (c) common voicing of Bdim7, (d) E7♭9, (e) G♯°7, (f) common voicing of G♯°7 (identical to B°7)

Since diminished 7 chords evenly divide the octave into four minor thirds, the chord duplicates itself every three half steps (every three frets on the guitar), though with a different arrangement of tones:

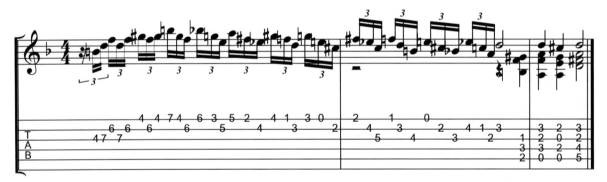

2-75. Because the intervals in a diminished 7 chord equally divide the octave into minor thirds, the chord repeats itself every three half steps. This means there are really only three diminished 7 chords in all of music (the fourth diminished 7 chord would duplicate the third).

J.S. Bach liked the sound of a diminished chord sliding down by half steps. In the following prelude, for example, he uses this device to lead into a standard Baroque cadence, which includes a diminished 7th chord (G♯°7) whose root is the leading tone to A, the root of the dominant. G♯°7 might well be considered a *rootless* E7♭9:

2-76. From Prelude No. VI, Well-Tempered Clavier, *BWV 851, by J.S. Bach. Though the prelude is in D minor, the final chord is D major, a Baroque cliché called the "Tierce de Picardie," or "Picardy third," referring to the major third of the final chord.*

Jef Raskin suggested using the diminished chord for a "Brahms cadence," an unusual deceptive cadence in which the V chord resolves to a diminished or diminished 7 chord based on the root, 3rd, or 5th of the tonic triad (see next page).

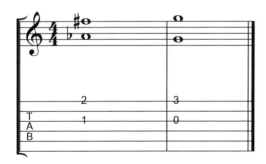

2-77. (a) I > IV > V7 > I in A major, (b) I > IV > V7 > diminished chord based on the root of A major, (c) I > IV > V7 > diminished 7 chord based on the 3rd of A major, (d) I > IV > V7 > diminished 7 chord based on the 5th of A major

A search of libraries and Internet sources failed to disclose any mention of the Brahms cadence. It is possible that Jef learned it from Leonard Bernstein, who was one of his teachers.

5) **Augmented sixth chords**: A favorite of classical and romantic composers, the augmented sixth chord introduces the V chord with a bang. The drama comes from two tones (♭6 and ♯4) that converge on the root of V from a half step above and a half step below. In the key of C, for example, the dominant is G, and the converging tones would be A♭ (♭6) falling a half step to G, and F♯ (♯4) rising a half step to G. The two Gs are at least an octave apart. The chord draws its name from the augmented sixth interval between ♭6 and ♯4 (e.g., A♭-F♯).

2-78. The tones of the augmented sixth converge on the dominant from a half step above and a half step below.

There are four types of augmented sixth chords (see *Ex. 2-79* below): Italian, German, French, and Swiss (the latter name proposed in Walter Piston's respected textbook, *Harmony*, because it combines aspects of French and German). The Italian sixth has three tones: ♯4, ♭6, and 1 (e.g., F♯, A♭, C). The rest have the same three tones plus one more: the German sixth adds the ♭3 of the scale (F♯-A♭-C, E♭), the French adds the 2 (F♯-A♭-C, D), and the Swiss adds ♯2 (F♯-A♭-C, D♯). The Swiss form is also called a *doubly augmented fourth* because of the doubly augmented fourth between A♭ and D♯, but "Swiss" is easier to remember. Indeed the names French, German, and Italian seem to have stuck because of the awkwardness of all the alternatives.

Notice that the Swiss ♯2 is the enharmonic equivalent of the German ♭3. The difference is that the Swiss ♯2 resolves to the second inversion of the tonic chord, whose function is also to provide a dramatic introductory chord to the dominant.

Augmented sixth chords may be tricky in terms of theory, but they sure sound good. As you play the examples below, just listen to the striking drama each of them adds to the arrival of the dominant chord.

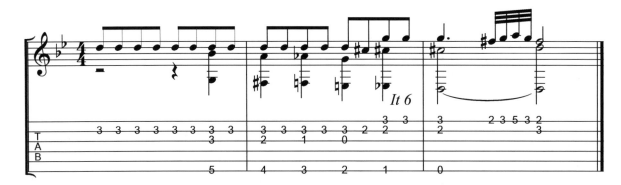

2-79. The four nationalities of augmented sixth chords.

Augmented sixth chords resemble dominant 7th chords, but they resolve differently. The Italian sixth shown above, for example, looks like an A♭7 chord, but resolves to G major rather than D♭ (the chord of resolution for an A♭7). Also, A♭7 has a common tone with D♭ (D-F-A♭), but the Italian sixth has no common tones with G major; every tone is filled with tension.

In *Ex. 2-80* below, Mozart resolves the ♭6 of an Italian sixth first (E♭ > D), while delaying the resolution of the ♯4 (C♯ > D). This causes two chords to overlap, creating even greater tension:

2-80. Mozart, Fantasy in D Minor for Piano, *K. 397. The Italian 6th occurs on the fourth beat of measure 2. The guitar version shown here is close to the original (tune the sixth string to D). Pianists should play the lowest bass notes in octaves. Tempo, 65 bpm.*

Augmented sixth chords are uncommon in today's music. Perhaps they're only awaiting a revival, but we can leave them aside for now and move on to a more common harmonic device.

6) **Flat-five dominant substitutes**: A dominant 7th chord whose root is the flatted 5th degree of a V7 chord is often used in jazz, as the resulting dominant 7th has the same tritone as V7 and is only a half step above the tonic, which allows it to resolve smoothly downward. Take G7 > C, for example. We might substitute D♭9—a dominant chord whose root is the flatted 5th of G7—into this progression and get something like this:

2-81. The first progression is a standard ii7 > V7 > Imaj7. The second uses a flat-five substitute for V7.

The flat-five substitute sounds good because G7 and D♭9 both have the same tritone. The energy core of a G7 chord (G-B-D-F) is the tritone between B and F. The B wants to rise to the tonic C, while the F wants to fall to E, the 3rd of the tonic chord. But the same tritone can be found in a D♭7 chord (D♭-F-A♭-C♭) between F and C♭ (an enharmonic equivalent of B natural). This allows us to substitute D♭7 for G7 and resolve to C. The flat-five substitute has a bluesy sound and sits well on the guitar (see *Exs. 2-66, 2-84a*).

7) **Modulation**: The home key of a composition is like the living room in a house. Modulation is like visiting other rooms, some of them close (one door down), some distant (a couple of doors away), and some remote (upstairs at the end of the hall). We can simplify modulation by sorting the target keys into two groups: *diatonic* and *chromatic*.

The diatonic keys are based on the scale degrees of the home key. They are the most frequent targets for modulation because their tonic chords are already established parts of the harmonic scenery, and their key signatures differ by at most one sharp or flat from the home key. In C major, for example, the diatonic keys for modulation are D minor (ii), E minor (iii), F major (IV), G major (V), and A minor (vi). The three minor keys are simply the relative minors of the three major keys:

Table 2-2 – Diatonic Keys for Modulation in C Major		
Major Key	Relative Minor Key	Key Signature
C major (home key)	A minor	No sharps or flats
F major	D minor	One flat
G major	E minor	One sharp

In minor keys, the most frequent targets for modulation are III, iv, v, VI, and VII. As a diminished triad, ii can not be a tonic chord. From A minor, for example, the most common targets for modulation are C (III), D minor (iv), E minor (v), F major (VI), and G major (VII). All of these keys differ by at most one sharp or one flat from A minor.

Every other target for modulation is *chromatic*. Another way to define chromatic is "any key that differs by two or more sharps or flats from the home key." Six sharps or flats is the theoretical limit. As shown by the circle of fifths, a key that differs by six sharps is the same as a key that differs by six flats, and vice versa.

There are many techniques for modulation, but the most common one is to build a bridge between the home key and target key with a pivot chord that is common to both. For example, Am is the vi chord in C major, and it is *also* the ii chord in G major. If you know your harmonic perspective, then you know that Am is harmonically closer to G than it is to C, which makes it a good pivot chord. Another possibility is the tonic C major itself, which is I in C and IV in G. After the modulation, the new key is confirmed by repetition of the V > I cadence and by organizing all other diatonic chords in harmonic perspective around the new tonic. *Ex. 2-82* below shows two modulations with pivot chords: first, from C major to G major (a diatonic modulation), and second, from C major to E major (a chromatic modulation):

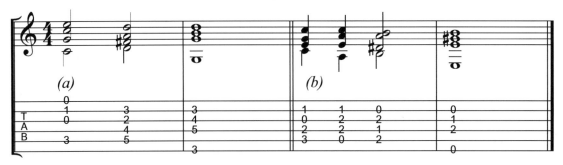

2-82. (a) The pivot chord is the tonic (C major) itself. I > II7 > V in C major becomes IV > V > I in the new key of G major. (b) The pivot chord is Am, which is vi in C major and iv in E major.

With four sharps, the key of E major is harmonically distant from C, and yet a pivot chord was nearby: A minor, which is vi in C major, is also iv (the minor subdominant) in the key of E.

In classical music, the dominant (G major in the key of C, for example) is the most frequent target for modulation because it is as close as possible to the home key in terms of harmonic perspective. Because of the power of the dominant chord to herald the tonic (see the *Interlude*), the dominant key sounds bright, assertive, and extroverted. The same is true of other keys on the clockwise side of the circle of fifths from the tonic. The Beatles take advantage of the vibrant, sunny mood of clockwise keys in the opening measures of *Good Day Sunshine*. The home key is A major, but the melody begins two circle-of-fifths steps up, in the key of B major (A > E > B), and then modulates by dominant 7ths two steps counterclockwise to the home key of A.

Counterclockwise on the circle of fifths, on the subdominant side of the home key, the mood becomes progressively cooler, dreamier, more subjective and introspective. You can hear this effect in this highly simplified version of a section of the *Grand Solo*, by Fernando Sor (1778 – 1839), where he modulates rapidly but smoothly from D major (two sharps) to the remote key of Db major (five flats):[8]

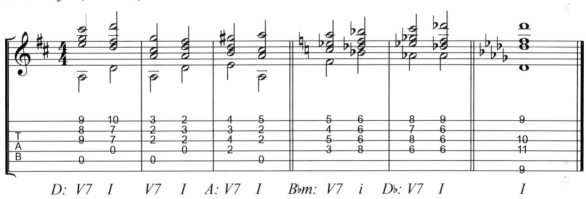

D: V7   I   V7   I   A: V7   I   Bbm: V7   i   Db: V7   I   I

2-83. Harmonic outline of a section of Sor's Grand Solo.

While The Beatles often employed modulation, and it is common in jazz and jazz-influenced songs, such as *The Girl From Ipanema* (Antonio Carlos Jobim, 1962), it is used somewhat sparingly in most pop music. Because of this, and because modulation is outside the scope of *Lesson 2*, we'll leave it aside for now and look forward to a fuller treatment in a future volume.

Extended Harmonic Perspective

Common substitutions for the diatonic chords are listed below, which exponentially increases the possible pathways for a harmonic journey. The best way to present the extended chart would be interactively, with software. Alas, this isn't possible, so we will show a range of substitutes

---

8 For a brilliant interpretation of the *Grand Solo*, listen to Marc Teicholz's 1996 Naxos CD, *Sor: 6 Divertimenti, Op. 13/Cinquieme Fantaisie, Op. 16*, catalog number 8.553354.

for each harmonic station shown in the *True Diatonic Harmonic Perspective Chart* (*Fig. 2-3*), first in Roman numerals, and then in notation. Unfortunately, we won't be able to preserve the perspective effect of the earlier illustrations, but by now the distance of the harmonic stations from the tonic should be ingrained in your thinking.

How to use the extended chart: Take a common progression, such as II > V > I, choose a key, and work out as many alternative chord linkages as you can, using substitute chords from the II, V, and I category.

Only the key of C major is illustrated in *Ex. 2-85* below, but you should learn the substitutions in all keys, beginning with the easiest. Some progressions work better than others, so experimentation is a good idea. Here are five different versions of II > V > I derived from the extended chart:

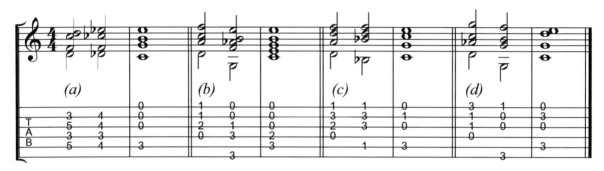

2-84. (a) ii7 > ♭II9 > Imaj7, (b) ii7 > V7♭9add13 > Imaj7, (c) ♭VII substitute for V7, (d) ii°7add9 > V7 > I add 9

Extended Harmonic Perspective Chart

I – The Tonic Chord (Home Base)

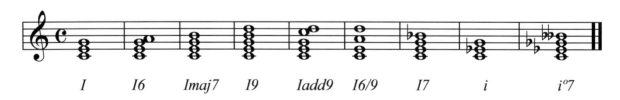

2-85.

Discussion: The restful versions of the tonic triad may serve as the final chord in a phrase or composition. The restless I7 may be the final chord in the blues, or it may be a secondary dominant of the IV chord. The diminished 7th chord is used in deceptive cadences and must resolve to another chord (see *Diminished and augmented chords*, pp. 114-117 above).

V – Dominant (First Harmonic Base Away From I)

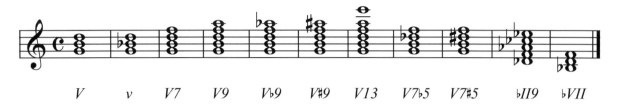

V   *v*   *V7*   *V9*   *V♭9*   *V♯9*   *V13*   *V7♭5*   *V7♯5*   *♭II9*   *♭VII*

2-86.

Discussion: Most of the usual variations on the dominant 7th chord are shown here. If you consult a chord dictionary, you'll find that the 5th is often left out, and sometimes even the root. V minor, which is borrowed from the minor mode, considerably cools the ardor of V and suggests a key change. The ♭II9 chord (also known as a ♭V substitute) resolves downward by half step to I (see *Flat-five dominant substitutes*, p. 119). The ♭VII chord (B♭ above) is modal (Dorian, Mixolydian, Aeolian) and often appears in rock, metal, and gospel. It likes to move up a whole step to I, though it may head toward the dominant via ♭VI or to the IV chord. (See *Progressions 8* and *14* above.)

II – Supertonic (Second Base Away From I)

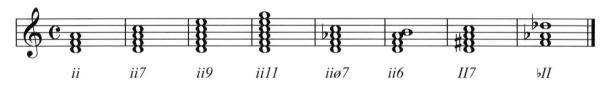

ii   *ii7*   *ii9*   *ii11*   *iiø7*   *ii6*   *II7*   *♭II*

2-87.

Discussion: II7 (D7) is somewhat obligated to resolve to V, but may move sideways to IV because of the near interchangeability of II and IV. The Neapolitan sixth chord (♭II or D♭7, the last chord above) nearly always appears in first inversion (as shown) and resolves to V, V7, or the second inversion of I, which has V in the bass. Chord progressions involving ii and ii7 are discussed above.

IV – Subdominant (Third Base Away From I)

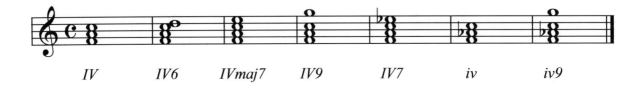

2-88.

Discussion: IV7 (F7 above) is almost always associated with the blues. Otherwise, it would be obligated to resolve to ♭VII (B♭), which may represent a change of modes, such as to parallel minor (C minor in the example), Mixolydian, or Dorian.

VI – Submediant (Fourth Base Away From I)

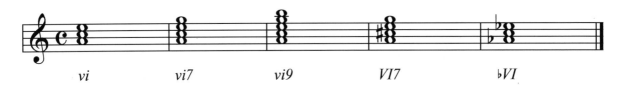

2-89.

Discussion: VI7 (A7) is strongly obligated to resolve to ii or II7 (Dm or D7). The ♭VI chord (A♭ in C major) is borrowed from minor mode. It may move to V or I. The ♭VI7 (A♭7) is a flat-five substitute for II7 and resolves by half step to V (G or G7).

III – Mediant (Fifth and Final Practical Base Away From I)

2-90.

Discussion: The iii7 chord (Emi7 above) is frequently used to soften the stark iii triad (E minor). III7 (E7 in C major) is obligated to resolve to vi (Am), vi7 (Ami7), or VI7 (A7). The ♭III chord (E♭) is an exotic visitor from the minor mode. It fits well with the tonic and other visitors, such as ♭VI (A♭) or ♭VII (B♭). The ♭III7 chord is more or less obligated to resolve to ♭VI.

Games

Continue playing the Parrot game, the Q&A game, and the As If game with your partner. Remember that all cadences are open or closed, Questions or Answers. While you may answer a closed cadence, such as V > I or G7 > C, with another closed cadence, it is more dramatic to reply with an open cadence. Respond to an open cadence with either a closed or an open cadence. Both are effective.

Focused Listening

In *Lesson 1*, you learned how to rise above "beat consciousness" and count measures by counting downbeats. This gave you a new awareness of sections, phrases, and periods. Now focus on open and closed cadences, and you will experience a big gain in your Musical I.Q.

Second, as you no doubt know, the Internet is filled with websites dedicated to song lyrics and chords. Most of them store tens of thousands of songs. Simply take a bunch of your favorite songs, look up the lyrics and chords on one of these sites, and spend a moment analyzing the progression from the standpoint of harmonic perspective.

In order to do this, convert the chord names to Roman numerals. For example, "[G] Happy Birthday to [D7] you," would become "[I] Happy Birthday to [V7] you." The conversion becomes easy after a little practice. Next, listen to the music, read the lyrics, and visualize the *True Diatonic Perspective* chart (*Fig. 2-3*) or the simplified chart (*Fig. 2-2*). Stick to songs with simple chord progressions in the beginning, and broaden your horizons as you get better at classifying the exceptions (the *Extended Harmonic Perspective Chart* can be helpful).

Outro

One summer evening in the mid-1970s, I found myself at an unassuming apartment in North Hollywood, in the company of jazz guitarist Howard Roberts (HR) and HR's publisher, Bob Grebb. We had gotten together to work on a book about Sonic Shapes, one of Howard's favorite concepts. Sonic Shapes links musical elements—chords, arpeggios, intervals, scales—to geometric fretboard shapes, and vice versa.

It was around 11 o'clock at night, and we'd been writing, rewriting, and editing for hours, when Bob asked HR about a musical example. It was just four chords—two measures, all half notes. HR had just strapped on his cherry red, signature model Gibson. Leaning against the counter under the kitchen's fluorescent lights, inscrutable behind his trademark sunglasses, HR looked as if he had just stepped off the stage at a smoky jazz club. He played through the chords slowly. "Oh, I remember that," he said, "I wanted to show how you could expand on a simple chord progression, like this…" and he began to play. Little did I know, but one of the most unforgettable musical experiences of my life was just beginning.

HR made repeated passes through the four chords, each time expanding and elaborating on them with substitute chords, non-chord tones, arpeggios, and melodic motives drawn from his imagination and a lifetime of experience. The pace was leisurely at first; he was savoring every note. But as he entered the eighth-note zone, he stepped on the accelerator into bebop territory. When he hit continuous sixteenth notes, his fingers began darting over the fretboard faster than the flickering fluorescent light could catch, creating an eerie stroboscopic effect that made it seem like he had eight fingers on each hand. I remember thinking to myself that he was changing fully-voiced, four-, five- and six-string chords in *sixteenth notes*, and that no human could possibly go any faster. And then he *did*, breaking another impossible, mindblowing sound barrier. He kept playing at that dizzying pace for several minutes, never repeating a single idea, until finally he wound down the tempo and modulated back to the four chords he had started with. He finished with a bluesy cadenza, a rainbow of artificial harmonics, and one final dissonance on a bent note that was as humorous as it was on target. To say his performance was stunning would be a gross understatement.

"Where did *that* come from?" said Bob.

"I don't know," said HR without hesitation, as if he were as puzzled as we were, and we all laughed.

For years afterward, I wondered what HR had been thinking as he added layer upon layer of complexity and variation to the original four chords. I concluded that a vocabulary of licks and monster technical prowess was only a beginning. Howard could only do what he had done by understanding harmonic principles, not in the textbook sense, but in the sense of a native speaker of the musical language.

Unfortunately, I could never find a good explanation of those principles. The textbooks were full of rules and procedures. The theorists were full of diagrams and generalizations. But no one seemed to have anything useful to say, at least not until I ran across the idea that harmonic movement was spatial movement, which was mentioned briefly in *Aural Harmony* by Dr. Franklin W. Robinson (see *Recommended Reading*, no. 21). Metaphors are powerful, and this metaphor clicked for me. Later, a second book, by Peter Lynn Sessions (my first guitar teacher), also provided genuine, practical insights. Wayne Chase's *How Music Really Works* was also useful and enlightening.[9]

My aim in *Lesson 2* was to seed a consciousness of harmonic perspective in your thinking early in your career as a creative musician. That way, everything you learn from now on will fit into a master framework that you can use to make music, and not just to solve puzzles. Don't despair if you can only put together three-chord songs for now. Just remember what Harlan Howard said (see p. 83).

We turn now to the third and most fascinating element of the musical juggling act: *melody*. Music teachers love harmony and rhythm because explaining them is as straightforward as mathematics or chemistry. But melody is another beast entirely, one that remains wild and untamed to this day. Maybe that's why they say melody can't be taught.

---

9 See *Recommended Reading*, nos. 9, 21, and 32.

Lesson 3 – The Heart of Melody

And smale foweles maken melodye,
That slepen al the nyght with open ye.

– Geoffrey Chaucer (1343 – 1400)

Intro

Melody is the most personal, distinctive, and evocative of the musical elements. It is little surprise, then, that great melody writers—like great poets and novelists—are born, not made. Igor Stravinsky said that the capacity for melody was a gift, and trying to improve it through study was not possible. Yet the same might be said of poetry, and that has never stopped a fifth grader from writing a poem. Too innocent to be overawed by Shakespeare or Yeats, they jump right in and do it, and the results are often strikingly original and entertaining.

A similar phenomenon occurs in music. Never having been discouraged by Stravinsky, kids pick up a guitar and start imitating their guitar heroes. A couple of hundred licks later, they begin making up their own solos, often with great originality, or at least a decent handling of the rhetoric of blues and rock. This isn't unusual; it's *routine*. And that should tell us something.

Melody is the most language-like of the musical elements, and the example set by young rockers shows that you can learn it as you might learn a new language. Just acquire a vocabulary, and then practice changing and rearranging your licks, and keep improving. In essence, that's what improvisation is all about.

Should we aim at building a vocabulary of licks, then, and let nature take its course? Yes, absolutely! If you haven't already done so, you should begin doing that right now. But it still wouldn't ensure what we *really* want: a quantum leap in our Melodic I.Q. Why? Because a deeper, trickier problem lurks beneath the surface.

That problem is *melodic meaning*. Every fifth grader who writes a poem knows the meaning of the words she uses. The same can not be said of music, where we typically learn all the elements of the language *except* their meaning. This question goes to the heart of melody, because without some idea of what we are saying, we won't be able to cope with fundamental problems, such as

- Where to begin?
- What to do next?
- Where to end?

The ability to hear the overtones of meaning in melody and identify them with specific combinations of notes is one of the most important differences between "talented" and "talent challenged" music students. But contrary to popular belief, this talent can be developed. If you have it, you can get more of it, and if you don't, it's probably because no one has shown you how to tap into your natural gifts. The mere fact that you are reading this book shows that you are seriously interested in music, and that could not be true unless you were sensitive to the subtleties we're about to discuss.

Melody and Speech

If our goal was to answer the question of musical meaning once and for all, we'd have an impossible task ahead of us. Fortunately, we're not after an all-encompassing answer, just a practical one, and that's not too hard to find. It starts by noticing the similarities between melody and speech, or more specifically, music and poetry:

- Music and speech both divide thoughts into phrases. Written phrases are set apart by punctuation marks. Musical phrases are set apart by cadences.

- Like spoken phrases, musical phrases unfold logically toward a point.

- A rising line of notes show rising energy, excitement, or emotion.

- A falling line show declining or drooping energy or emotion, or sometimes an increasing sense of resolve, determination, and inevitability.

- *Faster* means more energy and excitement.

- *Slower* means less energy, or a more peaceful, thoughtful mood.

These parallels are good news. They imply that if you can talk, you can design a decent melody. All you need to do is learn some of the special features of the melodic language and then start "speaking" it. Your studies of rhythm and harmony have already paved the way.

Melodic Line

Both melody and poetry have the idea of a "line." A line of poetry is a chain of meaningful words. A melodic line is a chain of meaningful notes. But what is *that*? The notes of a chord played one after the other may be beautiful, but they are not a melody. They fail to generate surprises and twists or to imitate the storytelling power of speech, because our ears automatically restack the notes in a vertical harmony:

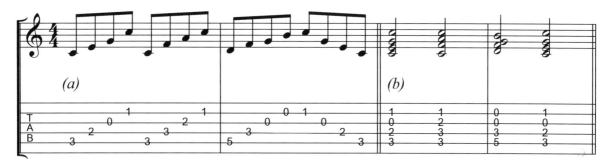

3-1. (a) Arpeggios. (b) The same chords reduced to harmony are relatively static.

This means that you can't make a good melody with chord notes alone. Melody requires *horizontal* relationships between notes. This is accomplished in two ways:

- Mixing scale steps with interval skips
- Creating musical rhymes between groups of notes

Mixing Skips and Steps

Scale steps are made up of half-step and whole-step intervals. *Skips* are melodic intervals of a minor third or larger (see the *Interlude* if these terms are unfamiliar). Some melodies, such as *The Star Spangled Banner*, are rich in skips, most of them borrowed from chords, but most melodies have a more balanced texture, with a majority of steps over skips. Chord outlines (arpeggios) do occur, but usually at the beginning of a phrase, where they state the tonality, or at the end of a phrase, where they announce a cadence (see *3-2* below):

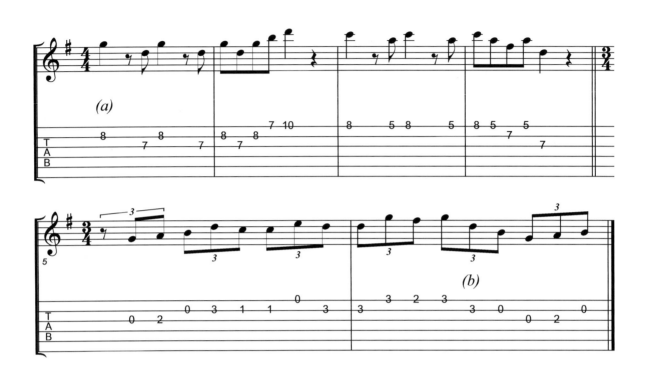

3-2. (a) Mozart, Eine kleine Nachtmusik *(K. 525). A soaring introductory arpeggio such as this was known as the* Mannheim rocket, *after the Mannheim orchestra, which was making waves in the eighteenth century. (b) Bach running an arpeggio at the end of phrase 1 in* Jesu Joy of Man's Desiring *(BWV 147).*

Skips require judicious handling. Composers are wary of breaking the melodic line, so they often fill in the gap opened up by a skip with a run of scale notes in the opposite direction, as if to say "here's what was left out." The gap-fill technique appears in the melodious *Minuet in G* from Bach's *Anna Magdalena Notebook* (see *3-3* below). This minuet was formerly attributed to Bach, but is now regarded as the work of Dresden organist Christian Petzold. In 1965, it was used as the basis of the pop song *A Lover's Concerto*, by The Toys. It has also been recorded by Sarah Brightman and others. Minuets are in 3/4 time. The version by The Toys reworks the melody in 4/4 time, which makes it more danceable for a modern audience.

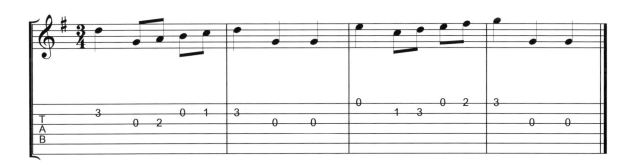

3-3. Minuet in G *(BWV Anh. 114). The melody skips a perfect fifth down, then fills in the gap with a run of scale notes in the opposite direction. This, and the repetition of the downward perfect fifth in measure 2, outlines the tonic chord, announcing the G major tonality of the piece. In measure 3, the pattern repeats, creating a melodic rhyme (see next page), and further confirming the tonality with a passing reference to the IV > V > I progression.*

In the following melody, made famous by the film *Elvira Madigan*, Mozart uses the gap-fill technique to round off a series of skips.

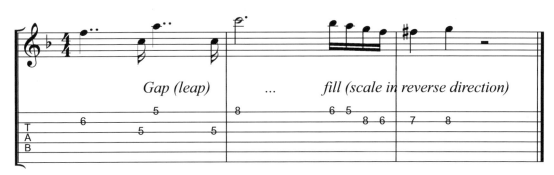

3-4. Mozart, Piano Concerto No. 21 in C major, K. 467, excerpt from the second movement.

Melodic Rhyme

Melodic rhymes occur between similar groups of notes. Similarities may include rhythm, pitch patterns, or both.

  Rhymes of reversal are also possible. For example, one group of notes goes up and the next goes down, or one group is shaped like a rainbow and the next is shaped like a bucket:

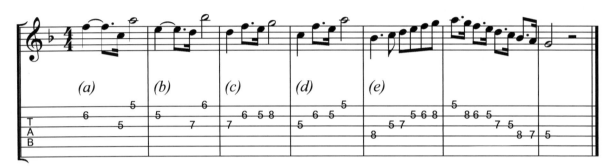

3-5. (a-d) Rhymes of similarity. (e) A rhyme of contrast bridging two measures. The up-down rhyme has its counterparts in ordinary speech in such words and phrases as seesaw, teeter-totter, yin-yang, warp and woof, or "Click it or ticket."

Rhyming groups of notes are like rhyming words: they connect ideas (coded in sound) across the linear dimension of time, overlapping their meanings. Like flint and steel, overlapping ideas generate sparks. In other words, rhymes generate meaning in melody.

  Because they bridge separate points in time, melodic rhymes form the basis of the horizontal, storytelling character of melody. In contrast, a chord or an arpeggio is a vertical, harmonic structure. Chord progressions move back and forth in harmonic perspective, and harmonic rhythm is generally regular and simple. These general characteristics of harmony mute the importance of linear connections that characterize melody. In the hands of the great composers, rhyming is a subtle art, but even the subtlest of rhymes are still based on the Parrot Game (imitation) or the Q&A Game (contrast).

  To play the Parrot game with a group of notes, just repeat the group note for note or with a slight variation, such as a change in starting pitch (see *3-6* below):

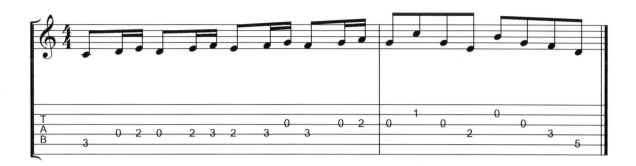

3-6. The first measure contains a sequence, *a scale (C-D-E-F), each step of which has been decorated with a brief melodic pattern. Sequences apply the Parrot Game to a beat-length idea (a* figure*). Measure 2 abandons the sequence and changes to arpeggios based on I and V, allowing the melody to breathe. The phrase might continue to unfold via melodic rhyming, aiming toward a cadence in the fourth measure.*

To play the Q&A game with a group of notes, improvise a contrasting group of notes. Contrast can be accomplished by going up instead of down, fast instead of slow, changing the contour, altering rhythmic values, changing the harmony suggested by the accented notes—the possibilities are unlimited. The Q&A may encompass

- One beat of Q and one beat of A
- One measure of Q and one measure of A
- One section of Q and one section of A
- One phrase of Q and one phrase of A
- One period of Q and one phrase or one period of A

It is important to experiment with *all* the possibilities, but here's an example:

3-7. Measure 2 contrasts with measure 1 in harmony and rhythm (Q&A game). Sections 1 and 2 contrast by using scale steps rather than an arpeggio (measure 1 versus measure 3), thirds rather than scale steps (measure 2 versus measure 4), and by ending with a closed, rather than an open cadence (measures 1-2 versus measures 3-4), an example of Q&A.

When applied to melody, the Parrot game and the Q&A game result in melodic rhymes. The criteria for a rhyme are simple: If one group of notes reminds you of another, it's a rhyme. Rhyming has to be this simple at heart, or else music would not be a universal language. Never underestimate your audience's sensitivity to rhyme. Groups of notes may be separated by many measures, but people will still hear the similarity.

The music of every century is full of melodic rhymes, but for an example close at hand, listen to *Moon River* (lyrics by Johnny Mercer, music by Henry Mancini, 1961), an award-winning hit from the movie *Breakfast at Tiffany's*. If you go to the Wikipedia article (http:// en.wikipedia.org/wiki/Moon_River), you will find some interesting history and a sound file. Play the song and listen for the melodic rhymes in the first verse.

Moon River illustrates the crossover between melodic rhyme and poetic rhyme. A poetic rhyme links lines of verse, which brings about new layers of meaning between them that transcend words. A melodic rhyme links groups of notes, overlapping them in our consciousness and evoking complex layers of emotion. At its best, songwriting brings both forms of poetry together in a single art form.

Focused Listening

Listen to a couple of your favorite songs or instrumentals and mentally note all the rhymes. To put it another way, note all the parts of the melody that fit the Parrot game or the Q&A game (same, similar, or contrasting groups of notes). Listen a second time and see how many more rhymes you can hear. This will open your ears to how much of the fabric of music is based on repetitions or variations of scraps of melody, sections, phrases, and larger units of time.

How to Make a Point with a Melodic Line

In *Lesson 2*, you learned how to make a point with a chord progression:

- Ask a question, such as a section or phrase based on I > V.
- Reply with an answer, such as a phrase based on V > I.

You also learned how to expand Q&A phrase form (Question phrase + Answer phrase = period). For example, you can string together a series of question phrases, and then close with an answer phrase ending in a conclusive cadence (Question + Question + Question + Answer). You can also cadence in a new key at the end of a question phrase, and work your way back to the home key in the answer phrase (or phrases).

It comes as little surprise that melody makes a point in the same way as chord progressions: by accentuating restless chord tones in question phrases, and restful tones in answer phrases. The following melody does that in an obvious way. First, the underlying chord progression:

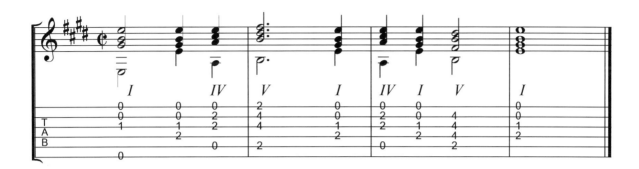

3-8. A phrase-length progression made of Harlan Howard's workhorse I, IV, and V chords.

And here's the melody that flows over these chords:

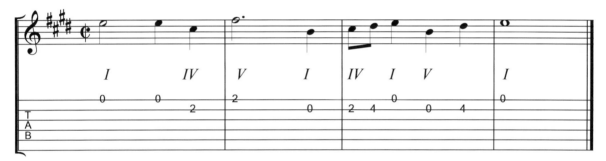

3-9. Monsieur's Almain, *by Daniel Bacheler (1572 – 1619), lutenist and groom of the privy chamber for Queen Anne of Denmark, consort of King James I.*

A second way to make a point with a melody is to weave it together with an obvious scale pattern in the background. Let's build a tune this way. We'll start with a simple melody, *Mi-Re-Do.*

Key of D: Mi   Re   Do

3-10. Mi-Re-Do (shown here in D major) is a melodization of the descending major third, Mi-Do, a resolving cadence. The predictability of Mi-Re-Do makes it uninteresting as a melody. However, the same predictability is a useful tool of structural unity when it stays hidden in the background.

In the next step, we expand the simple Mi-Re-Do melody into eight measures. Part of the trick to this is to duplicate the middle tone, Re, in Sections 2 and 3. This expands the harmonic journey I > V > I into two parts: I > V (question), V > I (answer), as shown on the following page:

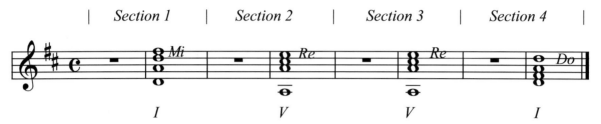

3-11. Now we have the rhythmic and harmonic underpinnings of a full-fledged, eight-measure tune in period form. A period consists of two rhyming phrases, the first of which ends in an inconclusive, open cadence (measure 4), and the second of which ends with a conclusive, closed cadence (measure 8). Phrases vary in length, so not all periods have eight measures. Period form can be extended by multiplying the number of question phrases preceding the Answer.

Finally, we decorate this solid, easily perceived framework with a melody that rhymes from section to section. The result is a familiar folk song:

3-12. Tom Dooley *(Thomas C. Land, 1868). In 1958, The Kingston Trio scored a hit with this ballad, which told the story of Tom Dula, a Civil War veteran who was hanged for the murder of his fiancé Laura Foster, but may have taken the rap for his other girlfriend, Anne Melton, who went insane after Tom's death and died a few years later. The song was a triple hit, appearing at #1 in* Billboard, *the* Cashbox *country music top 20, and the* Billboard R&B *listing. It was also selected as one of the Songs of the Century by the RIAA (Recording Industry Association of America), the NEA (National Endowment for the Arts), and Scholastic Inc. Why mention this? Because it demonstrates the power of Mi-Re-Do, which still has ten thousand songs in it.*

Notice that the long range melody, Mi-Re-Do, gives the song a sense of a storyline and unity over a span of eight measures. Also notice the difference between the melody of *Tom Dooley* and a sequence, discussed earlier (see *Ex. 3-6*). Sequences are made of cookie-cutter patterns repeated from beat to beat, like the famous Hanon exercises for piano. *Tom Dooley* resembles a sequence because it uses scale steps to provide a sense of structure and forward movement, but the scale steps are separated by several measures, and the melodic material between them is varied and complicated enough to mute the supporting scale structure. A prolonged, disguised scale-pattern such as found in *Tom Dooley* is called a *step progression*.

Tom Dooley is but one example among thousands of step progressions in melody. Dowland's *Fantasie* (*Ex. 3-28*) is another. But a scale also represents an arpeggio. The descending scale underlying Dowland's *Fantasie*, Sol-Fa-Mi-Re-Do (5-4-3-2-1), is a melodic expression of the descending tonic arpeggio, Sol-Mi-Do (5-3-1). It comes as little surprise, then, that composers often decorate arpeggios, as well as scales, with melody notes (see *Ex. 3-3* by Bach, *3-4* by Mozart, and *3-35* by Bach). A descending arpeggio is similar to a scale in predictability, which makes it a good framework for melody.

The harmonic journey, step progressions, and melodically ornamented arpeggios may help a melody achieve structural unity and storytelling power, but we all know that a good melody is more than an exercise in *logic*—it's pure *magic*. So how do we become magicians?

Charm

In the 1990s, I was lucky enough to spend over a year arranging the most memorable parts of over two thousand Top-Ten tunes for a software game. It was an ideal opportunity to research what these hit tunes had in common. One conspicuous similarity was that moment of melodic magic, which was like falling in love. Lesser tunes did not. Call it the "hook," if you like, but that just begs the question. How can so few notes trigger such a profound emotional response? That was the riddle of the musical Sphinx.

While working on the project, I was too concerned with weekly quotas to pursue an answer, but in May, 2007, I sat down at a wooden table in a coffee shop in Oregon with my memories, a double shot of espresso, and little else to do but meditate on that all-important question one more time. The first catchy melody that came to mind was not from the 1960s, but the *1760s*.

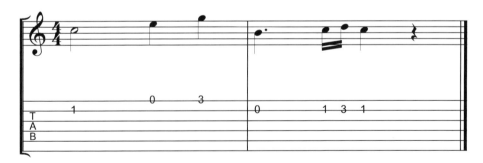

3-13. *Mozart's* Piano Sonata No. 16 in C Major *(K. 545)*

Mozart's melody isn't pop, but it's one of those tunes, the kind that instantly charms an audience. And yet it is disarmingly simple and unpretentious. Then I started thinking about another melody, a similar one by the great guitarist-composer Fernando Sor (1778 – 1839).

3-14. Fernando Sor, Study in C (Opus 35, No. 13)

Sor admired Mozart, and this melody may have been inspired by K. 545. It, too, is charming, but not quite as charming as Mozart's. Why? How can one quantify an intangible like charm?

That's when it hit me: None of the sophisticated music theories I had studied even had a word for "charm," even though it was obviously one of the most important qualities of a good melody, from Mozart's greatest hits to the two thousand Top-Ten tunes I had arranged. Even *Twinkle, Twinkle, Little Star* had charm, but no one had defined it, let alone found its source.

Since the theory books had nothing to say about charm, I decided to let the composers themselves tell me more. After all, the answers weren't hidden; they were out in the open, as plain as the printed notes. I began by playing K. 545 slowly, one note at a time, while asking myself which note was the first to flash with charm. If I could identify the moment it happened, then maybe I could figure out how it worked.

Why not try it yourself?

Play the first note, C. Feel anything yet? The key signature as well as the harmony (C major) indicates that this is the tonic. It's a start, but the melody has no personality yet.

Play the second note, E. Now we have a relationship. This note is a major third above C, and the second note of the tonic triad. Major thirds sound positive, warm, and joyful. We're accumulating a sense of where we're going, but there's no magic yet. In general, two notes are too few to transmit a well-defined feeling.

Play the third note, G. The joyful, gravity-defying trend continues. The rising notes C-E-G outline the tonic chord, C major. The notes E and G come quickly, as a pair. Anticipation grows over what will come on the downbeat of measure 2. Whatever this note is, the downbeat will accentuate its effect.

Play the fourth note, B:

3-15. The fourth note: as poignant as they come.

Feel it? *That* is charm. This single note magically generates a ticklish aura of suspense that is happy and sad at the same time.

What startled me was the distinct boundary between "charm" and "no charm." Over and over, it came down to one magic note. That seemed significant. By the time I had repeated the experiment with fifty or so melodies, I felt like I had uncovered most of the sources of charm. But before my opinions get in the way of yours, why not try a little charm research for yourself?

Find at least five other melodies you like and play them slowly, one note at a time, until you hear the first magical note. Then simply write down the number of notes it took to get there.

Don't skip the opportunity to do your own research! The best composers have something to tell you, and it is best to let them tell you their own way.

Sources of Charm

As you probably found, charm materializes within the first eight notes or so, which hints at a design goal for your own melodies. But how do composers pull off the charm trick so quickly?

The magic is usually in the unexpected twists and turns of the melodic line, specifically rhymes, reversals, and dramatic introduction of tension tones. Let's take a closer look at the fourth note of the Mozart melody:

- **Direction reversal**: The first three notes (C-E-G) rise upward, outlining a C major triad. If the pattern were to continue, the fourth note would also rise joyfully upward. Instead, the fourth note (B) skips downward by the sad interval of a minor sixth. Remember that rising lines express rising emotions, and falling lines indicate falling emotions. In this case, the change in direction is dramatic and sudden, which instantly captures our attention, laying an emotional emphasis on the leading tone B, the most yearning tone of all.

- **Interval reversal**: The first two skips (C to E, and E to G) rise upward by thirds, a smooth, harmonious sound that echoes the overtone series. The fourth note skips downward by a much larger interval, a minor sixth (G down to B). In contrast to the joyful major chord tones, the downward minor sixth is painfully sad, a rootless, unnatural interval from the standpoint of overtone series psychology.

- **Harmonic reversal**: The first three notes outline a merry tonic chord (C-E-G). But note four (B) belongs to the dominant chord. This adds forward thrust, the familiar pedal pumping action of the tonic-to-dominant progression.

- **Dramatic introduction of a tension tone**: Everything up until the fourth note was harmonious, but B is the leading tone of the C scale, a tension-laden note that yearns to glide upward to the tonic C.

- **Dramatic rhythmic accent**: The arrival of B on the downbeat of measure two intensifies all the effects of the reversals noted above, such as the inherent tension of the leading tone and the heart-tugging quality of the descending minor sixth.

Mozart tosses these notes off casually, but a lot is going on below the surface. He sets us up with a simple pattern (the rising C-E-G of a tonic chord), then spins us around with a bunch of reversals in one well-timed note (B). The downward-leaping minor sixth from G to B is markedly wider than the evenly ascending thirds of the tonic chord. The descending minor sixth is also associated with emotional pain (see the *Interlude*), which contrasts sharply with the joyful tonic chord. Harmonically, E-G-B suggests the chilly, lunar mediant chord (E minor) as well as the restless dominant (G major).

The sheer number of reversals packed into a single note helps us understand how charm can strike suddenly, with such electrifying intensity. While Sor's melody is charming, too, none of its notes contains as many layers of reversal or tension as Mozart's fourth note, B. This may explain the greater depth and fascination of Mozart's melody. It also suggests a deeper reason for the often repeated remark that Mozart's music is too easy for children and too difficult for adults. Mozart's melodic moves may sound simple, but they are never accidental, as they are found over and over again in all of his works.

As for rhyming, that is evident in the abrupt reversal of direction and harmony, but it is most conspicuous in the second phrase, which parrots the first, but ends with a gentler cadence:

(a)   *(b)*

3-16. (a) The first phrase cadences on the tonic, but the cadence occurs on the second beat of measure 2, which weakens the sense of closure. (b) The second phrase parrots the first phrase at a higher pitch level, heightening the emotional intensity. However, the cadence is softened by occurring on the weak second beat, and on the sentimental 3rd of the tonic chord.

A hundred years before Mozart, Baroque lutenist Sylvius Leopold Weiss—who was reputedly the equal of his friend J.S. Bach at improvisation—began a fugue with the same three notes, then generated charm of another kind with a different set of reversals:

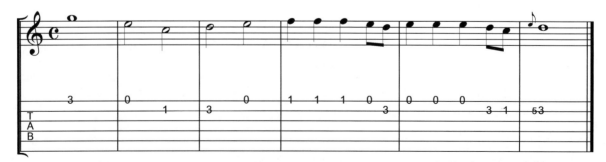

3-17. Fugue in C Major, *opening theme (the* subject*), by Sylvius Leopold Weiss (1686 – 1750).*

Once again, the first three notes outline the tonic triad, and once again charm arrives on the fourth note, but Weiss's meaning is entirely different from Mozart's.

Weiss *descends* to the root of the tonic chord (G > E > C), rather than rising from it, like Mozart (C > E > G). The long pause on the noble dominant (G) and the deliberate downward march to the inevitable goal (the tonic C) lends a determination to the first three notes, which contrasts sharply with the lighthearted playfulness of Mozart's ascending melody. Weiss reverses direction in notes four, five, and six, climbing resolutely upward by step, rather than leaping, as did Mozart. The melody sighs as it falls from F to E, which is repeated three times before the melody line settles firmly on a suspense tone, D. Weiss's melody is resolute and extroverted, similar to trumpet fanfares and military marches. Mozart's melody is coy, playful, and childlike. This is partly communicated by the Alberti bass accompaniment (a rippling arpeggio on close-position chords), but more by the intense, yet playful emotional tug of the downward leaping minor sixth.

Experiment: Compose or improvise reversals such as those described above. All you need to do is improvise a pattern of three or four notes based on a I, IV, or V chord, then systematically reverse direction, interval size, or harmony in the next one, two, or three notes. To generate patterns, simply accentuate two tones from the chord—such as the root and 3rd, 3rd and 5th, or root and 5th—and use one or more scale tones to connect them.

It is important to imagine your reversals before you play them! If you improvise them on your instrument, muscle reflex will override musical thought. Aikido master Koichi Tohei often used to say, "Mind leads body." As creative musicians, we should practice "Mind leads instrument." All too often we do the opposite, allowing the instrument to tell us what to do, which places us in the performing mindset, rather than the creative mindset.

Melodic Words

The riddle of charm is intertwined with another riddle: *melodic meaning*. Mozart, Sor, and Weiss all use similar notes in their melodies, but what they "say" is different. Why?

In ordinary speech, our meaning is conveyed by our words. The same is true of music. Melodic meaning is communicated by *melodic words*, which are the smallest meaningful segments of melody. Each melodic word is based on an interval and has *energy* and *mood*.

- *Energy* arises from rhythm, tempo, and contour of the line (rising or falling, rainbow, bucket, or zig-zag).

- Any interval can form the basis of a word, from a unison to an octave or more. As you learned in the *Interlude*, every interval has a distinctive mood.

- Individual scale steps—Do, Re, Mi—also have a mood (this will be discussed later in the lesson).

- Harmonic mood is generated by the interaction between melody and harmony.

A melodic word can also be formed from an arpeggio, as in *Exs. 3-2, 3-4*, and *3-13* (Mozart), *3-14* (Sor), and *3-17* (Weiss). In the case of arpeggios, the high and low notes will be particularly significant.

Repeated notes (unisons) accentuate a particular tone, but they don't form words unless the harmony changes. Scale steps ornament the tones of the interval. Steps do not usually constitute words unless the harmony changes.

Two to four measures of melody typically contain three to six melodic words. This means they go by quickly, usually in an unbroken chain. We absorb the meanings of melodic words instantaneously because all of their elements—intervals, harmony, rhythm, tempo—bypass the conscious mind and produce an instantaneous emotional response, whether or not we have musical training. The purpose of dividing a melody up into melodic words is simply to slow down this stunningly fast and subconscious process enough to make it conscious.

Essential Tones and Helper Tones

The tones that outline the interval of a melodic word are called *essential* because they carry the *essence* of the word, its general mood. The supporting notes that connect essential tones are called *helper* tones. "Supporting" does not imply "less important." Helper tones are important because they add specific character to the general mood of an interval or arpeggio.

In notating melodic words in text, every tone must be represented. Essential tones are shown in uppercase letters, such as C > D. Helper tones are shown in lowercase letters, such as C > d > E. Repeated tones are lowercase. For example, the first melodic word in Beethoven's *Ode to Joy* is notated E-e > f > g-G (see *Ex. 3-24*). Capital letters indicate accented tones. Examples appear below:

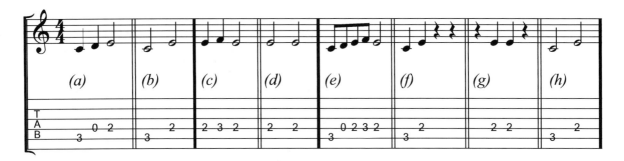

3-18. (a) *C > d > E.* (b) *Essential tones C and E, helper, D.* (c) *E > f > E.* (d) *Essential tones, E and E, helper, F.* (e) *Words a and c linked.* (f) *Essential tones of first word.* (g) *Essential tones of second word.* (h) *Words can be embedded within words. The word C > E encompasses C > d > E and E > f > E.*

Interval moods should be familiar to you from the final project in the *Interlude*. If you haven't completed the interval meditation project, do so as soon as possible.

Essential tones stand out from the rest of the tones in a melody because of repetition, rhythmic accent, harmonic support, or position as high or low note in the phrase:

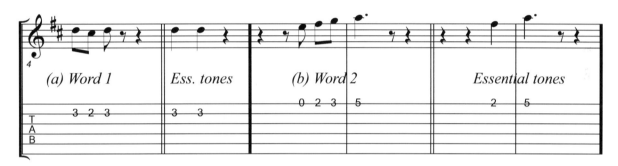

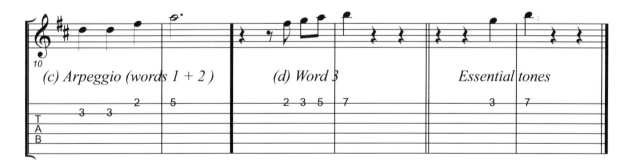

3-19. Excerpt from Bianco Fiore *(Renaissance lute piece, Cesare Negri, 1535 – 1605).*

a) **Word 1:**   **D** > **c♯** > **D**. Unison, created by note repetition and rhythmic accents.

b) **Word 2:**   **e** > **F♯** > **g** > **A**. Minor third, created by rhythmic accents, high note, harmony.

c) **Words 1+2:**   **D** > **F♯** > **A**. Together, the first two melodic words outline an arpeggio on the tonic chord.

d) **Word 3:**   **f♯** > **G** > **a** > **B**. Major third. Notice that Word 3 rhymes with Word 2. What is the effect of rhyming a major third with a minor third? Here comes the sun?

Just as accented syllables form the backbone of spoken words, accented beats form the backbone of melodic words. Notes that fall on the beat are like consonants, while the notes between beats are like vowels. While it's possible to get carried away with analogies, they do form a helpful bridge between familiar and unfamiliar worlds.

Melodic words resemble motives (also called *motifs*), such as the famous "Dit-Dit-Dit-Dah" theme of Beethoven's *Fifth Symphony* (see *Lesson 1, Ex. 1-1*). However, there's a key difference: a motive and the melodic units based on it are all similar, while melodic words based on the same essential tones may be wildly different.

The Flow of Melodic Words

Melodic words often overlap; the end of one word is the beginning of another. The first and second words in K. 545, for example, pivot around the common tone G, as did Weiss's second and third words, which pivot around the common tone F.

There is nothing mysterious or complicated about overlapping words. Almost all spoken languages have them in one form or another. They are quite common in spoken French, for example, where overlapping pronunciation is called *liaison* (lee-AY-zohn). Examples include "les amis" (the friends), pronounced "lay-za-MEEZ," and "vous avez" (you have), pronounced "voo-za-VAY."

Liaison often confuses the ears of non-French speakers at first, and so do overlapping melodic words, which seem to flow by with no breaks at all. But if you take the time to separate the melodic words in a phrase and savor each one for a moment, their cumulative meaning begins to jump out at you. After you've sorted out a few melodies this way, your Melodic I.Q. will grow and you will be able to hear the progress of thought in a phrase with new clarity.

Rising and Falling Words

Like rising or falling tone of voice, the direction of a melodic word, up or down, has a lot to do with its mood. Rising lines defy gravity, indicating surging energy or emotions, and sometimes—just as in speech—a question mark. Falling lines indicate declining energy or emotions, and at other times an increasing sense of resolve.

The first melodic word in K. 545 is the rising tonic triad (C > E > G), expressing rising emotion. The second (overlapping) word is the descending minor sixth (G > B), expressing a sad afterthought. The third melodic word, (B > C), is an example of rising scale steps with a change in harmony. In this case, the rising line represents a reassuring counterpoint to the descending minor sixth. The V > I harmony supports the movement from leading tone to tonic, while helper tones—(B > c-d > C)—add an urbane and playful melodic accent to the word.

Project: Compare your emotional response to each of the three musical words in K. 545: 1) C > E > G, 2) G > B, 3) B > c-d > C.

Weiss's first melodic word was a descending tonic triad (G > E > C). His second was a rising minor third (D > e > F-f-F), suggesting the getaway chord Dm (ii). When we simplify the third word (F-f-F > e-d > E-e-E) and fourth words (E-e-E > D-c-D), we find they outline a falling minor third (F > e > D). The line settles firmly on the question tone D, suggesting the suspenseful dominant chord.

In the examples shown so far, notice how a mix of words with and without helper tones keeps a melody interesting, while the alternation between restful tones (C-E-G) and restless tones (D-F) keeps it breathing and active.

A melodic phrase may be composed of rising and falling words. Together, they make up the broader contour of the phrase, which might resemble a rising or falling ramp, a rainbow, a bucket, a mountain peak, a flat plain, a sawtooth mountain range, a series of waves—any number of possibilities. This may make analysis more difficult, but it has little effect on composing or improvising, because of our innate understanding of rising and falling lines.

Project: Try improvising and composing a few melodic words based on the tonic triad changing to the dominant triad. Use the tonic chord's upper third (Mi-Sol), lower third (Do-Mi), or both (Do-Mi-Sol) as essential tones. Use similar parts of the dominant chord: (Sol-Ti), (Ti-Re), (Re-Fa), (Sol-Ti-Re). Use repetition, rhythmic accents, high and low notes to make the essential tones of your melody stand out.

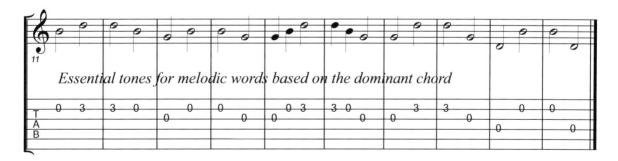

3-20. Compose with these essential tones. To create melody, link a tonic-based word to a dominant-based word with a rhyme.

The Moods of Scale Tones

The mood of individual scale tones does as much to define a melodic word as the interval between the essential tones. In K. 545, for example, the downward leap from G to B (notes three and four) has unusual poignancy partly because of the descending minor sixth, and partly because the accented tone B is scale tone 7 (Ti), which has an intense yearning to rise upward to the tonic C (Do).

All scale tones are either restful or restless, depending on their harmonic position in the key. Scale tones 1, 3, 5 and 8 are restful because they belong to the tonic chord. Scale tones 2, 4, 6, and 7 are restless. Scale tone 5 changes personality, radiating restless energy when it is part of the dominant chord.

Restful tonic chord tones 1, 3, 5, 8   Restless tones 2, 4, 6, 7, and sometimes 5

3-21. Restful and restless scale tones

In *Lesson 2*, we described the alternation between the restful tonic chord and the restless dominant as the engine of forward movement in harmony. Similarly, the alternation between essential restful and restless tones in melody is an engine that drives melody forward in time.

Restful Scale Tones

The answer tones—1, 3, 5, and 8—belong to the tonic triad. Their harmonious relationship to the tonic makes them restful, but each has a unique mood. Before reading the list of words in the right-hand column of *Table 3-1* below, try to find at least one word for each scale tone (1, 3, 5, 8) on your own. The word "restful" is all right, but seek out others, as well. Example scale tones are in the key of C major:

No.	Solfa.	Ex.	Descriptive Terms
1	Do	C	Major key: Anchored, calm, peaceful, tranquil, comfortable, strong, happy, stable, soulful, egotistical, settled, centered, sunshiny, warm, majestic, grounded, firm, conclusive, final, rooted, godly
			Minor key: Wistful, sentimental, sad, solemn, soulful (suffering), melancholy, somber, grave, mournful, tragic
3	Mi	E	Warm, emotional, sentimental, affectionate, adoring, loving, sensual, tender, human
5	Sol	G	Assertive, bold, hopeful, faithful, prideful, powerful, radiant, righteous, soaring, creative, optimistic
8	Do	C'	All of the terms that apply to the tonic an octave lower, plus lofty, heavenly, and serene, and in minor, heart-piercing

Table 3-1 – Moods of the Restful Scale Tones

Restless Scale Tones

When melodic words end with restless tones 2, 4, 6, or 7 (and sometimes 5 if the harmony is dominant), a question is left hanging in the air. According to Dr. Franklin W. Robinson,[1] all of the question tones are pulled in two directions toward neighboring tones of the tonic triad.

Tones 2, 4, and 6 tend to resolve downward (such is the gravitational pull of the tonic). Only the leading tone (7, or Ti) has a natural tendency to rise upward, since the tonic is only a half step above it, and the dominant is two whole steps below it, which results in very little pull in the opposite direction. When tone 5 (G in the key of C) is part of the dominant chord (G major in the key of C), it may leap upward or downward to the tonic, or it may remain stationary while V resolves to I.

---

1 Author of *Aural Harmony*. See *Recommended Reading*, no. 21.

$2 > 1 \qquad 4 > 3 \qquad 6 > 5 \qquad 7 > 8 \qquad 5(V) > 5(I) \qquad 5(V) > 1(I)$

3-22. Typical resolutions of restless tones. When harmonized with the dominant chord, scale tone 5 becomes charged with energy and may leap up or down to the tonic when V resolves to I.

Robinson points out the ironic nature of the leading tone, which is the *most* distant from the tonic in terms of harmonic perspective (five perfect fifths, I-V-II-VI-III-VII), *closest* to the tonic in terms of melodic attraction (one half step upward, with virtually no pull in the opposite direction, toward the dominant). It is also the only scale tone with the lighter-than-air tendency to rise. This makes 7 the most restless, yearning tone of all, a point dramatically exemplified in the Depression-era song *Over the Rainbow* (composed by Harold Arlen, 1939), in which the leading tone, appearing as the third note in the melody, tugs so poignantly at our heart strings. Incidentally, this note is the first charm note in the song, owing to its multiple reversals.

Scale tone 2 (D in the key of C) is the most airy and noncommital of all the restless tones, since it is pulled in opposite directions by the tonic on the lower side and scale tone 3, the 3rd of the tonic chord, on the upper side. The pull is roughly equal, since the root and third are each a whole step away. This causes scale tone 2 to float, perfectly suspended between two almost equally attractive goals. One of the best examples of the airy nature of scale tone 2 is heard in *Yesterday* (The Beatles, Lennon/McCartney, 1965), which begins on scale tone 2 and falls to the tonic on the second note.

When restless tones 2 and 4 defy their natural tendency to fall, resolving upward instead, they express a surge of energy, an emotional lightness of being. The progression 2 > 3 may express joy, while 4 > 5 may express faith or desire transforming into fulfillment, like a fire that smolders and then consumes in a bright flare. The helper tones will make all the difference in the character of the word, however.

Tone 6 often melts into its potent lower neighbor, the dominant, with joyful surrender (6 > 5). The pull of 5 on 6 is enhanced by the weak pull of the tonic in the opposite direction (6 is three half steps from tone 8 versus a whole step from tone 5). When 6 defies gravity, rising to 7, it adds momentum to the leading tone's natural flight toward the tonic. If 6 skips a minor third upward to the tonic (6 > 8), a popular move in country and bluegrass music, it implies frank and simple joy, since it floats upward, bypassing the step-by-step, obligated drive of the leading tone to the tonic. The flatted 6th degree found in the minor mode is particularly mournful because of the relative absence of pull in the opposite direction and the wan, tearful effect of the falling half step toward 5.

Before reading the list of words in the right-hand column of *Table 3-2* below, try to find at least one word for each scale tone (2, 4, 5, 6, 7) on your own. The word "restless" is all right, of course, but seek a few new words, as well.

No.	Solfa	Ex.	Descriptive terms
\multicolumn{4}{c}{Table 3-2 – Moods of the Restless Scale Tones}
2	Re	D	Floating, suspenseful, flying, vague, indifferent, misty, airy, wistful, wondering, wandering, questioning, inconclusive
4	Fa	F	Restrained, passive, resistant, enduring, resigned, devoted, motherly
5	Sol	G	When part of the V chord, hopeful, passionate, ecstatic
6	La	A	Happy, joyful, jolly, exuberant, colorful, tropical
7	Ti	B	Yearning, tense, unfulfilled, restless, lustful, demanding, irresistible, pulling, tugging, ecstatic

One Pair of Essential Tones, Many Meanings

We could take apart a few melodies now, translating them into plain English, word by melodic word, but this would not show the power of the melodic word concept and the various clever ways in which different composers handle the same essential tones. Only an in-depth study of one word can show how rhythm, tempo, direction, and helper tones all add focus and definition to melodic words. It will also help us develop the awakening we need to get away from randomly chosen melodic notes and begin to compose with a sense of meaning and purpose.

As mentioned earlier, most melodies begin with essential tones or an arpeggio from the tonic chord. Let's take the essential tones Mi > Sol, the 3rd and 5th of the tonic chord, for example.

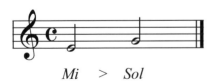

3-23. Mi > Sol, the 3rd and 5th of the tonic chord in C Major

Surely this is a flimsy foundation for any composition, let alone a masterpiece, yet Beethoven fashions the first melodic word of his immortal *Ode to Joy*, the choral from *Symphony No. 9*, out of these two tones. The word encompasses the first five notes:

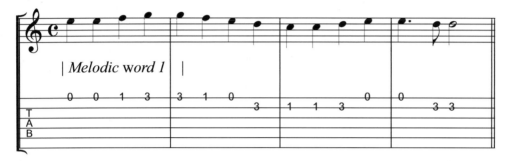

3-24. Ode to Joy, *first phrase. Original in D major.*

What is going on in this melodic word, spelled E-e > f > g-G? Beethoven anchors the essential tones E and G by repetition and rhythmic accents. The helper tone F smoothly connects them and generates forward movement, while the regularity of the tempo and rhythm indicates simplicity, honesty, directness, and reverence. The direction of the word is upward, showing rising emotion. The interval between essential tones is a minor third, expressing sadness, or—because the direction of the line is upward and gravity-defying—*longing* in the act of fulfillment. The starting tone, E (Mi), is the 3rd of the tonic chord, the tone of warm, tender feeling. The ending tone, Sol, is the 5th, the tone of faith, hope, and fulfillment. In terms of harmonic perspective, movement from Mi to Sol is movement toward the tonic (Mi is the second overtone, while Sol is the first), which generates a subtle sense of anticipation of fulfillment.

With this in mind, we can venture a definition of Beethoven's first word: "A bittersweet, reverent feeling of tenderness and longing blossoms irresistibly into a heartfelt declaration of faith, hope, and joy." The feeling inherent in the word parallels the verses of *An die Freude*, the poem by Friedrich Schiller that inspired Beethoven's composition.

This is a lot of meaning to pack into five notes, but that's precisely the point. The miracle of the musical language is that the connotations of rhythm, intervals, and tempo all occur to us automatically and instantly, thanks to the trillions of connections in our fabulous neural processing system (brains, gray matter, noggin).

Will every word based on Mi > Sol express "joy," or more specifically, "tender feeling rising to ecstatic faith and joy"? Consider a choral by Johann Schop, a seventeenth-century German violinist and composer. Notice that the first melodic word is also based on Mi > fa > Sol:

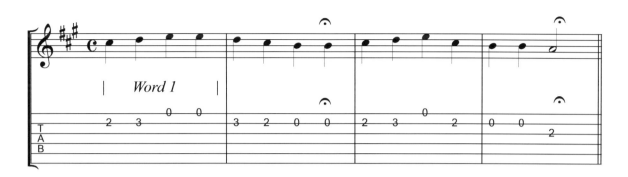

3-25. Werde Munter, mein Gemüte, *Johann Schop (1642).*

Significantly (in terms of melodic words), the title translates "Be Glad, My Soul." Schop's choral was set five times by J.S. Bach, including the famous *Cantata 147, Jesu, Joy of Man's Desiring*, in which the word "joy" crops up once again. Bach, one of the greatest masters of musical rhyme, embeds the word Mi > fa > Sol in the melody that leads into the choral:

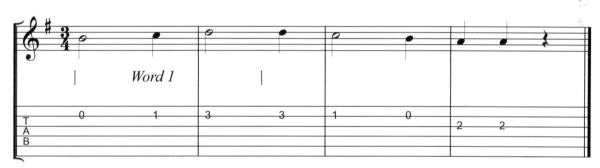

3-26. Jesu, Joy of Man's Desiring, *by J.S. Bach, (1685-1750), the choral.*

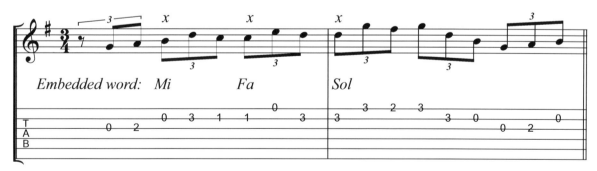

3-27. Jesu, Joy of Man's Desiring, *the introductory melody. As shown by the xs, the melody contains the word Mi > fa > Sol cleverly embedded within other melodic words parceled out in triplets. The rhythm, which should be counted, "an-a-two, an-a-three, an-a-One, an-a-two, an-a-three," etc.) underlines the embedded melodic word by accent and repetition.*

The next example comes from *Embryonic Journey*, an acoustic guitar solo by Jorma Kaukonen of the Jefferson Airplane, which debuted on the *Surrealistic Pillow* album in 1967, the Summer of Love. (Listen to the original version on YouTube or other Internet music sources.) The opening theme is based on an insistent repetition of Mi > fa > Mi, which might be interpreted as "submission or devotion to love," because of the similarity to a plagal ("amen") cadence. This is followed by a syncopated Mi > fa > Sol, which expresses joyful faith and hope of a psychedelic kind, as suggested by the droning bass and syncopated rhythms. Note the similarity to Bach.

Incidentally, as a high school student on the San Francisco Peninsula, I paid many a visit to the Haight Ashbury during the Summer of Love, lining up with my friends at the Fillmore Auditorium and Winterland to hear the Jefferson Airplane, the Grateful Dead (with Pigpen on organ), Quicksilver Messenger Service, Country Joe and the Fish, Jimi Hendrix, Cream, Janis Joplin, The Doors, Donovan, and other artists who defined the era. Listening to *Embryonic Journey* today seems to do more than any photographic essay ever could to conjure up a nostalgia-free flight into the atmosphere of the Haight in 1967. Kaukonen's poetic handling of the melodic word Mi > fa > Sol deftly captures the spiritual essence of the time and place. Flower Power lasted only one brief summer and was gone forever, but it left a few hauntingly beautiful footprints in the musical sand, and this is one of them.

Green Day's *Good Riddance (Time of Your Life)*, (Billie Joe Armstrong, Frank Wright, Michael Pritchard, 1997), puts another twist on Mi > fa > Sol. As in earlier examples, it is the first word of the melody, but the tune repeatedly backs away from the hopeful point of Sol to settle on the equivocal, floating tone, Re. This is the sound of hope unfulfilled—perhaps not denied, but left hanging. Because of the inconclusive cadencing, Mi > fa > Sol here suggests a feeling floating in memory, rather than fulfillment in a joyful present. The Mi > Sol tones appear in a similar context in *Who'll Stop the Rain* by Creedence Clearwater (John Fogerty, 1970), accompanying the lyrics, "Long as I remember…."

The purpose of these examples is to suggest the power of music to touch the emotional centers of the soul. To harness this power ourselves, we must dive deeply into the meaning of specific words from specific compositions, as we've done here in the analysis of Mi > Sol. To put it another way, we must practice writing our own dictionary of melodic words in order to become fluent in the language of music.

The Order of Tones in Words Matters

When we flip the order of essential tones in a melodic word, everything changes. Ascending intervals become descending intervals, first tones become last, and vice versa. This means that melodic words based on Sol > Mi will not mean the same thing as words based on Mi > Sol.

Such a reversal occurs in *Ode to Joy* and *Embryonic Journey*. After the assertive, syncopated statement of Mi > fa > Sol in *Embryonic Journey*, the melody continues with a reversal, the descending word Sol > fa > Mi, which incidentally includes a partial rhyme with the earlier Mi > fa > Mi. With or without musical training, one can easily hear the sweet melancholy of this reversal. While Mi > fa > Sol expresses rising hope and joy, Sol > fa > Mi expresses loss of energy, submission, and melancholy. First, Mi is not a root of Sol. Second, the movement from Sol to Mi is movement higher up the ladder of overtones, *away* from the tonic, or away from the fundamental, in terms of harmonic perspective.[2] Sol-Mi also contains the crying Fa-Mi.

Renaissance composer John Dowland (1563 – 1626) was one of England's greatest song-writers, and one of the greatest of all time. The melancholy character of his tunes is apparent in the following well-known *Fantasie*, which begins with the wistfully sad word Sol > Mi and falls through a series of rhyming figures to a happy conclusion on the tonic in the major mode. As with other great melodies, the Dowland's charm is hidden in the richness of his rhymes.

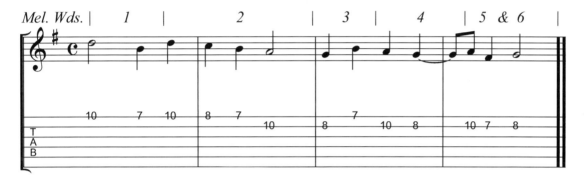

3-28. Dowland, Fantasie. *Melodic words 1 through 6 are discussed below.*

Word 1   **D > B** (Sol > Mi). Mood: Restful. A melancholy, falling minor third. The promise of Sol (D) lapses from strength into the sentimental Mi (B).

Word 2   **d > C > b > A** (sol > Fa > mi > Re). Mood: Restless, melancholy. Another falling minor third, but this time built on restless tones. The helper tone d, which is shared by both words, precedes the essential tone C. The implication of D > B, C > A is a descending scale (D > C > B > A > G; or Sol > Fa > Mi > Re > Do). The accented falling half step between C and B (Fa to Mi) is a "crying tone."

Word 3   **G > B** (Do > Mi). Mood: Restful, warm. This is a Q&A rhyme with the first two words, reversing direction and expanding the interval from a minor third to a major third. The note "B" is the first note with charm because it glows with meaning and beauty far beyond the power of a single note. As with earlier examples, this is because it is the nexus of multiple reversals.

Wds 4 - 6   (4) **A > G**, (5) **a > F♯**, (6) **F♯ > G**. Mood: Restless > restful. Words 4-6 embroider G > F♯ > G with changing tones. The embellishments rhyme with earlier words. Note the rhyme between (A > G) and (a > F♯), and the rhyme between a > F♯ and Word 1, D > B (both are descending minor thirds). The V > I return to the accented tonic G completes the harmonic journey and makes the point of the phrase.

---

2 See the *Interlude* and *Lesson 2* for background discussion on harmonic perspective.

Notice that the essential tones that form the backbone of Dowland's tune make up a cleverly disguised scale of descending thirds. Helper tones appear in alternating melodic words, constituting a rhyme.

3-29. Essential tones from Dowland's Fantasie *make a scale of descending thirds.*

The Effect of Harmony

The position of a melody note in the chord of the moment adds another layer of meaning to scale tones and melodic intervals. Restless tones may become restful and restful tones may become restless. In general, chord roots and 5ths stabilize and lose their restlessness, if any. Chord 3rds become emotionally sensitive. Chord 7ths become restless.

Chord position may lead to interesting contradictions for scale tones. For example, the ultimate pillar of strength, the tonic, becomes subdued and introspective when it is the 3rd of the VI chord (A♭-C-E♭ in the key of C or C minor), while in the ii7 chord (D-F-A-C in the key of C), as the 7th of the chord, it becomes restless.

On the other hand, the restless leading tone freezes up when it becomes a stable 5th in the iii triad (E-G-B in the key of C):

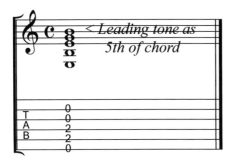

3-30. The leading tone is the 5th of the iii chord (E minor).

Contradictions such as these make for interesting tensions between layers of meaning. In the Imaj7 chord, the leading tone is a major 7th above the root, which gives it an airy, dreamy quality, somewhere between restful and restless. This may be because it continues to long to rise upward to the tonic, but the tonic is already present as the root of the chord (C-E-G-B).

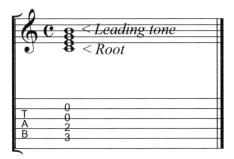

3-31. The leading tone is the 7th of the tonic C major 7 chord.

This placement of the leading tone in Cmaj7 leads to a contradiction. Like many dream symbols—flying elephants, rivers that run uphill, Cheshire cats—it is two contradictory things at once. The languid wistfulness of the leading tone in the context of Imaj7 may also result from its role as the stable 5th of a iii triad embedded in the Imaj7 chord (the minor iii chord, Em in the key of C major, which is spelled E-G-B, is the 3rd-5th-7th of the Cmaj7 tetrad).

Non-chord Tones (NCTs)

We come now to the most expressive tones of all: *non-chord tones*, also known as *nonharmonic*, *inharmonic*, and *non-harmony* tones. These are tones that do not belong to the chord of the moment. Their conflict with harmonic tones generates sparks, like steel striking flint.

Non-chord tones usually occur in three steps: chord tone (harmony) > non-chord tone (inharmonic tension) > chord tone (resolution). The tone of resolution may or may not occur with a change in the underlying harmony.

Rhythmic accent plays a large role in the expressive effect of non-chord tones. Melodic words are made from essential tones that outline an interval or chord. These supply the basic mood of the melodic word. Essential tones are often rhythmically accented and accompanied by helper tones, which add specific meaning to the basic mood of the interval. Helper tones are often unaccented NCTs, which occur between beats or on weak beats in a measure. Their discord with the underlying harmony is not conspicuous. Accented NCTs, which occur on the beat or on syncopated beats (accented offbeats), are among the most expressive tones available.

Ex. 3-32 on the following page shows the most common types of NCTs. One other type of NCT—the pedal point—has been discussed earlier (see *Exs. 2-60, 2-61*).

Play the examples and read the descriptions, then try transposing the examples to other keys and applying them to other chord progressions. If you're a guitarist, try transposing them to other chord forms and progressions.[3]

---

3 For example, apply each non-chord tone idea to the basic vocabulary of open-string chords: C, A, G, E, D, F, C7, A7, G7, E7, D7, B7, Em, Am, Dm. Or, apply each non-chord tone example to brief fragments of melody, such as Do-Re, or Mi-Re. This is valuable practice.

Ex. 3-32 – Non-Chord Tones

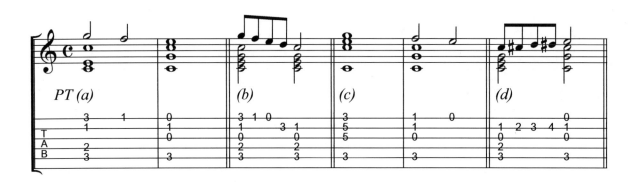

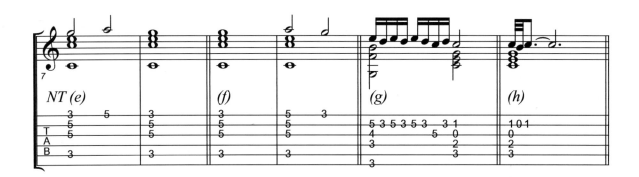

(cont. next page)

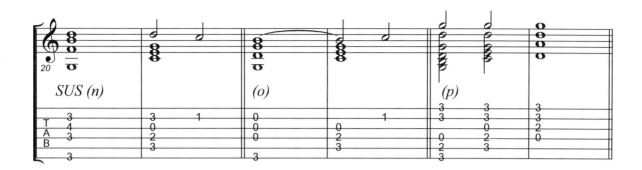

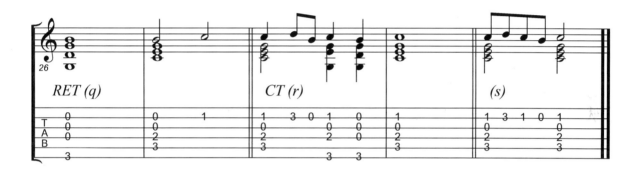

Now we'll take a closer look at each type of non-chord tone.

PT (a-d): Passing tones connect one chord tone to a different chord tone (sometimes in a different chord) by scale steps. PTs are the least dramatic of non-chord tones, particularly unaccented passing tones (a) and (b), but an accented PT (c) has considerably more impact. Chromatic passing tones (d) glide by half steps between chord tones.

NT (e-i): Neighbor tones take one step away from a chord tone and return. An unaccented NT (e) creates a slight emotional surge that melts back into a stable harmony. Accented NTs (f) lean harder on the chord tone, intensifying its emotional impact. A *trill* (g) is a rapid alternation between the chord tone (*principal tone*) and its upper neighbor (*auxiliary tone*). A mordent (h) is a rapid alternation between a chord tone and its lower neighbor. Trills and mordents are the salt and pepper of melody. They accentuate the flavor of essential tones. They also show how the speed of notes affects their meaning. The higher the speed, the less significant the individual notes become in terms of melody. *Chromatic* NTs (i) are a half step above or below the chord tone. Lower chromatic neighbors create an artificial leading tone to a chord tone. Like all leading tones, the lower chromatic NT expresses a powerful yearning for the object of its desire (the tone a half step above it). All scale tones except the leading tone may be embellished with a lower chromatic NT.

IN (j-k): Incomplete neighbor tones have only one stepwise connection with a chord tone, instead of the normal two. The other connection is a skip. The resolution (whether by skip or step) is usually in the opposite direction to the approach. (j) The IN may begin with a rest and resolve by step into a harmony tone. (k) It may begin with a skip away from a harmony tone to a non-chord tone and resolve with a step back to a harmony tone.

ET (l): The IN may begin with a step away from a harmony tone to a non-chord tone, and resolve with a skip in the opposite direction to a harmony tone. If the incomplete neighbor tone is unaccented and the resolution is in the opposite direction, as shown in example (l), the NCT is called an *escape tone*, or *echappée* (ET).

ANT (m): An *anticipation* is a non-chord tone that belongs to the next chord in the progression. The anticipation tone is approached by step and repeated after the harmony changes and the tone becomes consonant. Anticipations normally appear in soprano position (the highest voice).

SUS (n-p): A suspension (n) is a tone repeated or held over from a previous chord which then resolves by downward step to a chord tone after the harmony changes. While an anticipation (see "ANT" above) seems to hurry the arrival of a harmonic change, a suspension delays it. In modern practice, suspensions may remain unresolved (o), creating an airy, noncommittal feeling. *Yesterday*, by The Beatles (Lennon/McCartney), begins with an unprepared suspension that resolves downward from scale tone 9 to scale tone 8.

RET (q): Retardation is the reverse of suspension. A tone from the first chord is repeated or held and then resolves upward by step to a tone in the second chord.

CT: Changing tones (r)—also called *double neighboring tones* or a *neighbor group*—are two successive neighbor tones, one above and one below the preceding chord tone, which then resolve to a chord tone (usually the same one) by step. They may be accented or unaccented. Changing tones are sometimes thought of as a scale passage outlining the interval of a third, with a missing chord tone in the center (s).

APP: An *appoggiatura*[4] is an expressive incomplete neighbor tone that was popular among Romantic composers and remains popular today. *Ex. 3-33* below show that it is an accented non-chord tone approached by leap that resolves stepwise in the opposite direction to a chord tone in the new chord. The wider the leap, the more intense the emotional impact (SUS above is a kind of non-leaping appoggiatura). In the final example, notice the heightened intensity of a half-step resolution in comparison to the whole step resolutions that precede it.

---

4 Italian for "leaning tone," from *appoggiato*, the past participle of *appoggiare*, meaning "to lean on."

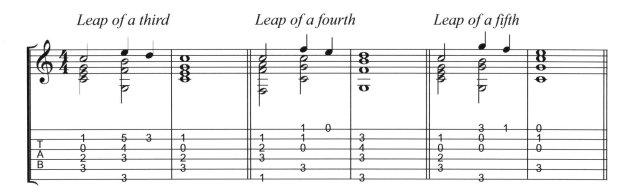

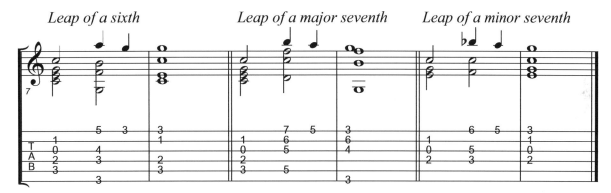

3-33. Appoggiaturas in ever wider leaps.

Non-Chord Tones and Melodic Words

Conflict is drama, and non-chord tones, particularly accented non-chord tones, are a rich source of dramatic tension. But how do they fit into the melodic words concept? For example, in the following appoggiatura, is the accented non-chord tone G a *helper* tone to the chord tone F, or is it an *essential* tone? And if G is essential, how do we classify the tone of resolution, F?

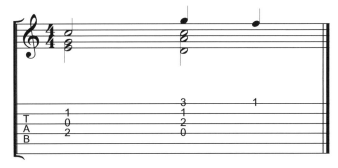

3-34. Which tone is essential, G or F?

Both sides of the argument have merit, but the best answer is "none of the above." Non-chord tones are not merely helpers: they are inextricably linked to the tone of resolution. Conductor and author Markand Thakar describes them as *agent* and *client*,[5] an especially apt metaphor that conveys how one tone implies the other so strongly that we can't deal with them separately.

Since the purpose of the melodic word concept is to get under the hood and expose the sources of meaning in melody, we must show this kinship in our notation. Wherever we have a non-chord tone that strongly implies the next chord tone, both tones will be written in capital letters (like essential tones) with a forward slash linking them. For example, the melodic word shown in *Ex. 3-34* above would be notated C > G/F (G is the appoggiatura tone, F is the tone of resolution. Put another way, G is the agent of F, which is the client.

Scale Passages

Most instrumental compositions and improvisations include scale passages that are relatively easy to perform on an instrument, but difficult or impossible to sing. These runs can be so rapid and ornate that it's difficult to find melodic words in them, but if we view them as arpeggios embroidered with scale tones, the puzzle is often easy to solve:

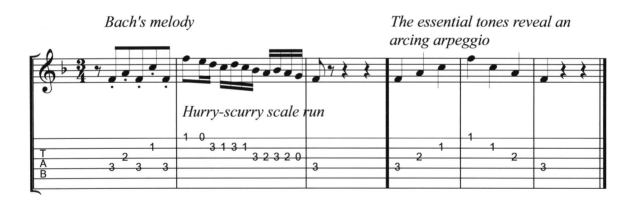

Ex 3-35. Bach, Two-Part Invention in F. *Measures 1 and 2 are in Q&A form. Measure 1 is a rising arpeggio, measure 2 is a descending arpeggio embellished with scale tones.*

Composition Versus Improvisation

Flashy scale passages and arpeggios, which are frequently found in improvisations, don't often appear in melodies. A catchy melody relies on clear, memorable motives and clever melodic rhymes. Because of this, an evocative melody is made to survive for centuries. It may even enter the cultural vocabulary.

---

5 Thakar, Markand; *Counterpoint: Fundamentals of Music Making,* Yale University Press, 1990, p. 67

Composition is executed at leisure, with careful craftsmanship and the objective of creating something that audiences will want to hear over and over again. Improvisation emphasizes spontaneity and instrumental fireworks, and while flashy instrumental passages dazzle listeners, the dazzle tends to wear off with repetition, which is why improvisers generally avoid playing anything the same way twice (and are proud of it).

These are the key differences between composition and improvisation, differences that also explain why not all composers are improvisers and not all improvisers are composers. The mindset and the training are different. Having said that, it is still desirable to cultivate both skills. Compositional ideas often arise from improvisations, and vice versa.

Composing a Melody

If we can compose an eight-measure melody in period form, we're well on our way to creating a complete musical composition. But how can we compose eight measures, when even a four-measure phrase can be a challenge?

First, you don't need to conceive of an eight-measure melody all at once. It is better to grow the melody organically, starting with as little as a two-measure section, which can be formed around just a few notes. If you can compose a two-measure section, you can grow it into a four-measure phrase by playing the Parrot Game or the Q & A Game with it, while rhyming here and there. If you have a four-measure phrase, you can grow it into an eight-measure period or a longer form by the same method. One eight-measure period is enough to grow an entire composition by Parroting or Q&A.

Finding a lively idea seems like the key to everything. An interesting idea inspires further ideas, which helps the song or instrumental grow itself. But where to get a good idea? You could wait for inspiration, but the wait might be a long one. *Lesson 4 – Secrets of Songwriting* offers a solution that provides an unlimited fund of imaginative ideas and requires no inspiration whatsoever.

The following exercises will energize your imagination for the upcoming lesson on songwriting, which will combine everything you've learned so far.

Composition and Improvisation Exercises

Save the results of your experiments. They may be useful in *Lesson 4.*

1) Compose ten melodic words based on the essential tones Mi > Sol (E > G in the key of C, but any key is fair game, including minor keys).

2) Compose ten melodic words based on the essential tones Sol > Mi (G > E in the key of C, but use any key).

3) Compose ten melodic words based on the essential tones Re > Fa (D > F in the key of C, but use any key).

4) Mix words from (1) and (2) above with words from (3) and (4) above to create two-measure sections or four-measure phrases.

5) Play a favorite song. Hit *Pause* at the end of a phrase (listen for the cadence or for the beginning of new or repeated melodic material). Compose two answering phrases in your imagination—one Parrot phrase and one Q&A phrase—and play them on your instrument. It's important to try to complete as much of the answer phrase as possible before you attempt to play it.

Focused Listening

Listen to melodies while focusing on one feature at a time chosen from the list below. Go beyond simply identifying the element—consider its emotional effect.

- Charm and reversals. For example, how soon do you hear a reversal in *I Can See Clearly Now* (no. 1 hit by Johnny Nash, 1972; Jimmy Cliff's version also charted at no. 18 in 1993)? Do you feel the charm at that moment?
- Rhythmic patterns
- Tempo
- Highest note
- Lowest note
- Scale steps
- Skips
- Phrase endings
- Melodic patterns (repetition)
- Melodic patterns (variation)
- Rhymes
- Melodic words. With the help of a score, sort out the essential tones, helper tones, and intervals. It is suggested you photocopy the score and mark it up with colored pens.

Outro

Lesson 3 contains many new ideas, but there was much more that could have been said. For example, the discussion of *Bianco Fiore* (*Ex. 3-19*), *Jesu, Joy of Man's Desiring* (*3-27*), and Dowland's *Fantasie* (*3-28, 3-29*) hinted that melodic words can be embedded within melodic words, and melodic rhymes can be embedded within melodic rhymes. Layered rhymes seem to be characteristic of all great melodies. Also, the emotional effects of rhyming was hardly touched upon here. I hope to treat these subjects and others in a future book dedicated to melody, but that doesn't mean you can't start investigating them right now. Melodic words may take a lot of explaining, but at heart they are a simple concept. All you have to do is slow down and listen carefully for them.

The discovery of charm and melodic words resulted from applying Jef Raskin's analytical method to melodic meaning. Jef asked what was the least musical event that was still musical. "Rhythm" was the answer. The roots of charm were found by listening for the least melodic event that was charming. Similarly, melodic words were found by listening for the least melodic event that was meaningful.

While it might be possible to construct elaborate theories around charm and melodic words, that was never the purpose. They have been offered simply as keys to open the doors of perception, allowing you to hear what is going on in a good melody and imitate it. Play with them and then discard them once they've served their purpose. Some readers may find them too detailed. Just remember, while the devil is in the details, so is the magic.

There will always be a difference of opinion about the meaning of melodic words, because everyone's experience of melodic words is subjective. Sorting them out, however, is worthwhile because it forces you to pay attention to what you or the composer is really saying in the language of music. Normally music goes by much too quickly to do this. We process all of the information at a subconscious level without any effort, and *that* results in the musical experience. Melodic words are a way to make your subconscious responses conscious, which enhances your ability to speak the language of melody.

Lesson 3 – The Heart of Melody lifted up the hood on the engine of music and revealed something about the way melody works. It also gave you some practical experience in forming melodic words. *Lesson 4 – Secrets of Songwriting*, will call upon you to juggle all three elements—rhythm, harmony, and melody—and *compose yourself.*

Lesson 4 – Secrets of Songwriting

I was confusing the ability to play a musical instrument with the ability to compose catchy, memorable melodies in my head. I've since learned that they are two distinct and very different skills.

– Jason Blume, songwriter, author[1]

Intro

All artists live with an unholy dread of the blank page, so let's cut right to the chase: "Where do we find a few good ideas?"

If you've been trying to write songs or compose instrumental pieces for any length of time, you've probably heard dozens of solutions to this riddle, but none that satisfied, unless phrases such as "Be creative," "Ideas are all around you," "Take long walks on the beach," or "Be sensitive, deeply" make your socks roll up and down.

Well, relax. You won't hear anything like that here. Instead, we have a nuts-and-bolts approach to finding ideas that is effortless and almost guaranteed to yield results—good, if not excellent results—all the time, whether or not you're inspired. And if the first method doesn't work, we have a few others that are not especially demanding.

Your Ideas for Nothing and Your Songs for Free

Before Jef Raskin would sign on at Apple, he insisted that they install a pipe organ that he could play anytime he wanted. Jef also used to play bocce ball in the hallways of Information Appliance, and when one of the employees objected that the atmosphere wasn't serious enough, he said, "I will never work any place that I can't play."

It was a rule I heard Jef repeat many times over the years, and I think it applies here as well. Most methods for stimulating creativity take *work*, and working at creativity is a contradiction

---

1 From *Six Steps to Songwriting Success*, *Revised Edition: The Comprehensive Guide to Writing and Marketing Hit Songs*, by Jason Blume, Billboard Books, New York, 2008. Used by permission.

in terms. We should *play* at creativity, not work at it. *Finishing* a song or instrumental may take work, but that's where craftsmanship alone is almost enough to see you through. Craftsmanship enables you to work out the implications of an inspiring idea. *Getting* an idea, or discovering one, is altogether different. Keith Richards of the Rolling Stones, one of the best pop songwriters of our time, seemed to have had the same thing in mind when he said that he never sits down with the intention of writing a song, adding "That would be fatal."[2]

So we need a method that works wonders without exertion. Fortunately, there is such a method. It's called *MC²*, or *Musical Creativity Squared*, because it exponentially increases your musical creativity without effort.[3]

MC² is easy because it relies on our ability to get things *wrong*, rather than right. Most of us get things wrong all the time, drunk or sober, without even trying. For example, have you ever misheard the lyrics to a song? Maybe you heard Creedence Clearwater singing "Who'll stop Lorraine?" when they were really singing "Who'll stop the rain?" Almost everyone has misheard song lyrics. Books and websites are dedicated to the humor that results. But here's the twist: Misheard lyrics lead to a good laugh, but misheard melodic words lead to new musical ideas. And that's the key to MC².

While an English word can only be misheard a few ways and still make sense, a melodic word can be misheard thousands of ways, and many of them are just as good as the original, if not better. And by the way, no one can tell the difference between the ideas you get from misheard melodic words and ideas that come to you via a lightning bolt of inspiration.

So how do you do it? Easy:

- Turn on some music, preferably unfamiliar music.
- Go in the bathroom, close the door, and take a hot shower.

That's all there is to it. The shower relaxes and distracts, and the water splashing in your ears muddles the sound of the music coming through the door just enough for you to mishear a few melodic words. Your ears will fill in the missing notes effortlessly and automatically, and that's where you will find your new ideas—endless new ideas.

Pattern *completion*, which is the key to MC², is the flip side of pattern *recognition*, which was discussed in *Lesson 3 – The Heart of Melody*. The same genetically programmed mechanism that allows us to see the tiger lurking in the jungle shadows or camel caravans in the clouds will allow us to hear new and intriguing melodic words by filling in the missing parts of a muffled song or instrumental.

The ideas that come to you via MC² are often so good that you'll have trouble believing that they came from you and not someone else. Naturally, you should be on guard against plagiarism, but don't rush to conclusions; your idea might be more original than you think. *Yesterday*

---

2 From an interview with former *Guitar Player Magazine* Senior Editor Jas Obrecht, editor of *Rollin' and Tumblin': The Postwar Blues Guitarists* (Miller Freeman, San Francisco, 2000).

3 With apologies to Albert Einstein, who had the first theory about MC² ($E = mc^2$).

came to Paul McCartney in a dream (talk about effortless), and for weeks afterward he was sure that he must have heard it somewhere else. After asking everyone he knew if they had heard the song before, he became convinced that it was an original, and the rest is history.

When you try to write a song, it can be difficult to find an authentic style and an original groove, but that is not often a problem with MC², because your innate talent for pattern completion summons up all of your experience with the language of music, which is probably considerably greater than your book learning, and stylistic ingredients automatically mix and mingle at a subconscious level.

Don't be surprised if the style of your ideas and the style of the music coming through the bathroom door are completely different. New styles are often a hybrid of two or more existing styles, and this seems to be a fairly common side effect of MC².

Troubleshooting MC²

You *want* a degraded, muddled sound to reach your ears in the shower, so for best results, use a rotten sound source. The best ideas seem to come from unfamiliar music. *Bad* music, badly recorded, can be a great source at times. If you have cable or satellite TV, then you probably have a dozen or more channels that play a random selection of music in diverse genres. Stations such as these are ideal sources for new ideas. If you're using your own library of tunes, then a junky MP3 or CD alarm clock with a two-inch speaker is preferable to a state-of-the-art sound system. A distorted bass speaker seems to help, too.

If the ideas don't come, you may need to take further steps to confuse your ears. For example, you can make a sound salad by playing two songs at the same time. Be sure to get water in your ears, too. You can also try singing in the shower. Singing over a misheard melody is likely to generate new ideas.

Don't expect a whole song to come to you as the result of MC². If it does, that's great, but it is more likely that you will hear a promising fragment of a melody, and that's all that you need to get started. If MC² doesn't work, try the alternative methods described below in *Three Methods for Composing From Scratch.*

Capture Your Ideas

New ideas are as ephemeral as ghosts or dreams, so it is vital to snag them before they evaporate. Keep a handheld, battery-operated tape recorder near the shower and sing your ideas into it as soon as they come to you.

It is better to sing your ideas than to play them on guitar or piano. Picking up a guitar invokes all the muscle memory and lick-based learning you've done. This reflex knowledge is a bully that will elbow out your imagination at the earliest opportunity.

If you don't like the idea of recording your voice, then go over and over the idea while you're in the shower. Lock it into your memory before you shut off the water. This will give you the best chance of transcribing it later.

Capturing ideas will be much easier if you know how to transcribe your melodic ideas quickly and accurately. Ear training is most helpful in this regard. See the section on *Perfect Pitch and Relative Pitch* in the *Interlude* for more (pp. 24-26).

The Rolling Wave Pattern

All you need to get started is two measures, a melodic fragment that spans two downbeats (with or without pickup beats) and contains as little as two melodic words. Focusing on a two-measure time span will put you in good company. Sections have been popular with composers of all kinds for hundreds of years—we've cited a few by Mozart and others already—but in the last forty years or so they have become the de facto building block of pop melody. A glance at the lead sheets (chords and melody) for a random selection of songs from the '60s through today will confirm this.

When you find sections in the scores to pop tunes, you will find that the melody often peaks around the second downbeat of the section. In measure 1, for example, the melody might begin with a couple of rests. Then the singer enters and drives toward the downbeat of measure 2. Then the energy trails off. The second half of measure 2 is often a long note. Sometimes it is just a few notes in the first half of the second measure, with rests in the latter half.

This rhythmic pattern is obvious once you see it or hear it, but to the best of my knowledge it hasn't been described elsewhere. We'll call it the *rolling wave pattern* because the energy peak in measure 2 makes it resemble a wave, a melodic and rhythmic wave that audiences can surf with pleasure.

4-1. A typical rolling wave rhythm.

The following rolling wave rhythms were extracted from hit songs. You could easily collect a dozen more in less than an hour. While you might use them as models for your own compositions, the purpose is to allow you to get a feeling for the rolling wave pattern and then apply it at will to your own melodies:

4-2. Four real-world rolling wave rhythmic patterns

One reason for the popularity of the rolling wave is that it sounds great coming from car radios and out on the dance floor. A rolling wave melodic section is surrounded on both sides by instrumentals and supported by with a strong beat. Ever since the '60s, the beat has become more and more prominent in pop. Segmenting the melody into a series of waves causes the singer to deliver the lyrics chunk by chunk, which keeps the audience in a state of suspense, waiting for the next telegrammatic, cryptic, or poetic text message.

Three Methods for Composing From Scratch

If MC² doesn't work for you, try any of the following three methods. The only disadvantage of these methods is that they take more intellectual work, so keep trying MC² every day, and keep your tape recorder handy, because it may begin to work for you in the future.

Method I — Inspiration From an Existing Melody

Many songwriters use this technique. Keith Richards, for example, says he likes to get out a Buddy Holly songbook and start to play, just to see where it will lead.

- Choose three to five notes from a melody you like. We'll choose the first five notes from Boccherini's famous *Minuet* (less the ornament). We're using music in the public domain, but obviously there are no restrictions on what music you use. Howard Roberts used to say that he liked to listen to Bartók for inspiration:

4-3. Minuet *from the* String Quintet in E Major, Opus 11, No. 5*, Luigi Boccherini (1743-1805)*

- Using your imagination and your voice, play the selected notes over and over, and as you do, play the Parrot Game and the Q&A Game with them.

The only rule is that you must go in a different direction after the selected notes. Alter the rhythm, turn a line that goes up into a line that goes down, change an answer into a question by changing the cadence, double the length of the response, cut it in half, or string it out into a sequence. Improvise against different rhythmic backgrounds. Convert country to reggae, classical to blues. Anything goes. Pretty soon, you'll have at least two measures' worth of material, which you can arrange as a rolling wave or whatever you like. Here are some variations that occurred to me—not to be taken as great composition, but as the beginnings of some new ideas:

4-4. Variations on the first five notes of Boccherini's Minuet.

Method II — Build on the Back of a Chord Progression

This is a classic way to approach composition, especially songwriting. I have attempted to enhance it somewhat by using a few ideas from *Lesson 3*.

- Choose a chord progression for the first section (*Lesson 2* offers many possible starting progressions). Suppose we choose I > ii in the key of E major, one chord per measure.

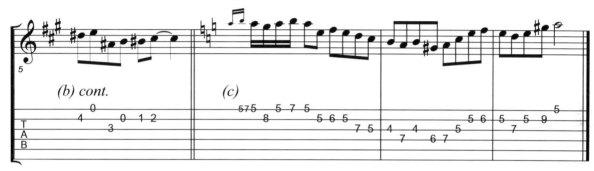

4-5. E major > F♯ minor

- Next, add a groove. Finding a groove is not difficult. If you're a guitarist, begin by turning on a favorite song and tapping your left foot to the beat. Synchronize your right hand with your foot and strum the guitar (mute the strings with the left hand) in time with the beat. After you're sure you're feeling the beat, start strumming the strings on the upbeats as well (use upstrokes) and get in tune with the rhythm. Carry on until the song is over. Then turn off the music and imitate the rhythm as best you can while using the I and ii chords in a two-measure section. Embellish the chords with hammer-ons and pull offs. Record the result, repeating it at least ten times. You now have an original jam track on which to base new melodies.

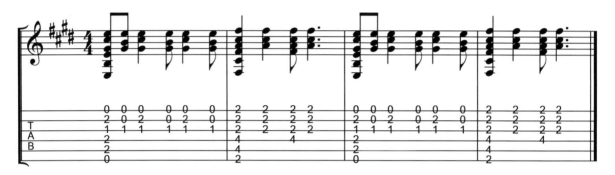

4-6. The E chord has been slightly embellished with an added 6th. Many ideas of this kind are possible on any chord.

- Choose the essential tones of a melodic word for each measure. In the example, we select tones from the I chord and the ii chord. You're not stuck with your first choice, but it does provide a starting point. In the example, we'll choose Mi > Sol from the first chord and Fa > Re from the second. The rhythm is random, but we're trying to suggest a rolling wave.

4-7. Essential tones for improvising melodic words are shown in the top line (stems up).

- Play the chords with the chosen rhythm and sing the essential tones. While you sing, try to imagine a melody weaving its way around them. Avoid using an instrument. Imitate the rolling wave pattern. Focus on the build-up to the downbeat of measure 2. Make sure that your second melodic word contains one or more reversals. For example, switch from a simple word to an ornate one, change from a rising line to a descending line, or from skips to steps.

- Keep this up for awhile, and you will find a melody that has spirit. If you do not succeed, rest and try again later. You will probably find that the idea goes on changing and developing while you're doing other things. You may also need to repeat some or all of the first three lessons of the book to reinforce your knowledge of the musical language. Eventually, you will succeed.

Sometimes it helps to work into the melody from the bass upward. When a student of Johannes Brahms brought him a new melody, the first thing he did was to play the bass line. A well-composed bass supports and inspires a well-written melody. To put it in *Compose Yourself* terms, a melody based upon a well-constructed harmonic journey will tell a story. So begin by improvising a chord progression, such as the following:

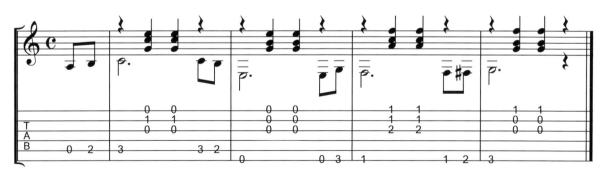

4-8. A chord progression that might occur to you.

Then develop your bass line. Put root notes on the beats, put 3rds, 5ths, and passing tones off the beat, as in the following example. Once the bass line is solid, play the progression and imagine melodies over it:

4-9. A bass line based on the chord progression, certainly not the only one possible.

Method III — Begin With Three Well-Chosen Notes

This is a backup plan for those who've had difficulty with everything else. Be sure to read *Method II* above, because this method is similar, and some of the steps described below are described in greater detail in *Method II*.

• Choose a chord progression for the first section. Let's use the blues, since it's a familiar form, and it will set up your whole song. We'll use the "fast-four" form of the blues, where the IV7 chord appears in measure 2. Measures 1-4: I7 > IV7 > I7 > I7, measures 5-8: IV7 > IV7 > I7 > I7, measures 9-12: V7 > IV7 > I7 > V7 (each chord represents a measure with four beats).

• Add a rhythm to the I > IV7 progression and record a few minutes' worth of it, as in *Method II* above.

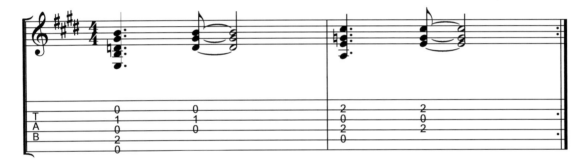

4-10. Measures 1 and 2 of a slow blues in E, chords only.

• Put one essential tone on one side of the barline, and two on the other (see *Ex. 4-11* below). Either measure can get the two tones. In *Ex. 4-11*, we put one essential tone in measure 1 and two in measure 2, but you could do the reverse. The essential tones have been chosen from the E minor pentatonic scale, which is appropriate for a blues in the key of E. Remember that scale tones 3, 6, and 7 are usually flatted in the blues, but they are mobile, meaning they can sometimes appear in non-flat form, as they would in a major scale. Scale tone 5 is sometimes flatted as well.

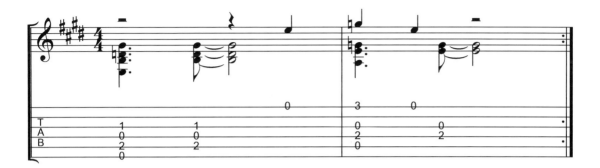

4-11. The three-note method uses three essential tones at each barline, two on one side, one on the other. Either side can get two notes.

- Proceed as you would in Method II. Sing the essential tones, or perhaps play them on harmonica, and think of helper tones. However, unlike in Method II, you can consider your job complete when you've done nothing more than changed the rhythm of the three tones.

- You can complete the entire blues in the same manner, adding one or two essential tones on either side of every barline, thinking of helper tones (or not), and changing the rhythm. It is possible to add all three essential tones to the first measure if you sustain the third tone over the barline.

Lyrics

Music or lyrics—which comes first? This chicken-or-egg riddle resembles asking which leg comes first when you walk. The same applies to "Chords or melody—which comes first?" The answer is that the composition emerges from an inner dialog, a back-and-forth discussion between the harmonic journey and the storytelling melody line, its melodic words, cadences, and rhymes. The lyrics are part of it, too. Composition can't be reduced to an assembly line.

Many songs begin as pure melody. Some begin as lyrics. Sometimes words and music are written at the same time. Since this book concentrates on *music*, and because lyrics are a major subject unto themselves, we will leave them out of the discussion for now. Suffice it to say that lyric writing should be like melody writing: playful, not planned. This is more likely to yield original, honest, and interesting results.

Song lyrics do not have to be major poems. They can be extremely simple. Many songs could be cited, but consider *It's Bad You Know* by Mississippi Delta bluesman R.L. Burnside (1926 – 2005), which was used in the soundtrack for the HBO series, *The Sopranos*. The only verse is a single sentence, about seven words. The chorus is made up of the title words and nothing else (choruses usually contain the title). Give it a listen and hear how less can be more.

Rather than work at lyrics, make up nonsense syllables or verses for your melody, and let the subject find you, rather than the other way around. That's the way Paul McCartney composed *Yesterday* (original title, *Scrambled Eggs*) and *Eleanor Rigby* (original title, *Miss Daisy*

Hawkins), among other songs. The mood of the melodic words will touch off associations that you can't dream of until you immerse yourself in the mood they create.

Candidate Ideas

Below you will find a batch of two-measure ideas generated by MC² from source material randomly selected from several different cable television music channels. None of the misheard music was familiar. Some of the keys are "difficult," but that's the way they occurred to me, and they don't sound right in any other key.

Idea 1

4-12a. An exultant, upbeat, major motif. Section-length, since it covers two downbeats.

Idea 2

4-12b. A section-length minor pentatonic idea with some possibilities—a blues, maybe?

Idea 3

4-12c. A phrase-length idea composed of two sections, ending with a closed cadence.

Idea 4 (shuffle feel)

4-12d. A blues riff, included mainly to show that not all your ideas need be highly original. On another day, something like this may spin your imagination in a new direction.

Idea 5

4-12e. Like this (130 bpm). No shuffle here, and a bit on the creepy side, but it has possibilities.

Idea 6

4-12f. Reminiscent of a sea shanty, but the source was a rock tune, which shows that misheard melodic words can lead almost anywhere.

Idea 7

4-12g. More blues. Perhaps a channel change is in order. Just remember: You may have to generate a hundred ideas before you find that one that has "it." Or, you could apply the Science of Charm. After all, look what Mozart did with "Do-Mi-Sol" (K. 545, example 3-13). One magic note is all it takes.

Idea 8

This one grew on me for several days. It began as a misheard melodic word in a frozen yogurt shop. While I was sitting and slurping, the machines were grinding away, and not much was coming over the sound system other than a heavy beat. I started thinking about flying away, getting away from there, and the melodic word Mi-Fa-Sol came to mind in the form of a melody that sounded like chorus material, so I worked backward and thought up a tune for the verse that expressed the oppressive monotony of working life. The result was something like a bubblegum rock number. Playing *As If!* can be dangerous. You never know where your imagination might lead. A sketch of my initial idea follows.

4-12h. Frozen Yogurt to Go.

Writing this was fun, but in the end it wasn't me, so I dropped it. Perhaps it would come in handy if a jingle-writing job came along. Don't laugh! Successful jingle-writers live in dream houses with edge-of-the-sky swimming pools up on Mulholland Drive in L.A. or on out-of-sight ranches in Montana with fly-fishing streams in the backyard. Nice work if you can get it.

The point has been made: With the help of MC², anyone, talented or not, can easily fill a notebook with promising song beginnings inside of a week. But *what then*? How do you finish what you've started? That's where craft and experience joins hands with inspiration.

Grow Your Songs Organically

The ability to extend an idea into a composition is not particularly mysterious. Simply apply the Parrot game, the Q&A game, and the As If game on ever larger levels. If you've got a motive, then apply these three games to expanding the motive into a section. If you've got a section, then apply them to grow a phrase. If you've got a phrase, apply them to finishing the period.

If you've got a period, then you've got a verse or a chorus, so apply the games to creating the other parts of the song. We'll discuss these parts more thoroughly below, but as you expand your melody, follow three rules:

- Everything you compose must respond to that which precedes it. The current motive, section, or phrase must rhyme with the previous motive, section, or phrase—in full or in part. Rhymes may be similar (Parrot) or contrary (Q&A). New motives rhyme by contrast.

- The essential tones of your melodic motives should be based on the harmonic journey. This ensures a long-range plan to your melody. However, avoid an obvious "one chord, one motive" pairing. It is better to stretch the motive (or melody) across the chord changes and across the barline in rolling wave patterns.

- Every addition to the song (or instrumental) must be proportional to the last. This includes major parts and transitions.

Ironically, proportionality may lead to asymmetrical phrasing. For example, a one-measure motive may be answered proportionally with a two-measure response (a three-measure phrase, all in all). Paul McCartney used this idea in *Yesterday*. The first verse is seven measures long, which is a mystery if we cling to the typical eight-measure form of pop songs as a yardstick. This has led some theorists to say that this verse is an eight-measure period with one measure "elided" (left out). But is that satisfactory? What was the motivation? In light of the principle of organic growth, McCartney's idea is simple at heart: 1 + 2 + 4—a one-measure motive, a two-measure response, and a four-measure complement to the two-measure response. Listen while reading the score and you will hear the logical unfolding.

Cadences form structural joints. Some will be weak; some will be strong. Some will be open (Questions), some will be closed (Answers). Your first cadence will probably be closed, ending on a tone of the tonic chord, such as the 3rd or the 5th, in order to establish the key. Ending on the tonic this early can be tricky, because it might sound too conclusive, but Mozart got away with it in K. 545 (*Ex. 3-13*) by placing the tonic on a weak beat. You can do the same.

Try to achieve charm within the first eight notes through reversals and rhymes. You can also take a *fragment* of your initial idea and develop it into something interesting with rhyme and reversal. This maneuver can precede or follow a presentation of your full idea. For example, if you prefer to delay the charm note, you might want to parrot the original motive or section a few times, so as to build suspense. This may take some thought, but you know how charm works, so experiment.

Continue building sections and phrases based on your original motive, but in general, it's a good idea to introduce a new melodic motive within the first phrase. The new motive should be an answer to the first motive, which may be part of creating the charm effect.

In the end, your spirit must be your guide. But the spirit has no sophisticated means of self-expression without craftsmanship and a musical vocabulary, so never quit studying.

Verses, Choruses, and Other Structural Units

The primary units of song form are *verse* and *chorus* (examples are easy to find because they are often labeled in the score). Eight measures is typical for either of these units.

Verses are the storytelling or mood-describing part of the song. The *chorus* sums up the moral or the message and often contains the title of the song. If you remember your fifth-grade English composition class, the chorus is like the topic sentence of a paragraph, while the verses contain the supporting evidence. Alternatively, verses may tell a story or describe a set of circumstances that proves the point described in the chorus. Just as when composing a paragraph or telling a story, the chorus can precede the verse or follow it. Rather than following a preconceived formula, let your song tell you the most effective way to present your ideas.

Verses have the same melody and harmony, but the words differ from verse to verse, since they tell a story or develop a theme. The harmony and melody of the chorus contrast with the verse. The words are the same in each repetition of the chorus. The chorus often steps up the emotional energy by rising to a higher range of notes. The highest note of the melody often occurs in the chorus, as well as a catchy motive called the *hook* that anchors the song in memory.

Popular songs must be singable, which means they are usually confined to the range of an octave, with most rhythmic values in the whole-note, half-note, quarter-note, and eighth-note range. Sixteenth notes sound agitated. Instrumental pieces are usually loaded with them.

A song may also include one or more of the following structural units:

- **Intro**: A musical introduction that establishes the mood of the song and leads into the first verse. For an outstanding example, listen to the intro of *Like a Rolling Stone* (Bob Dylan, 1965), selected as the No. 1 song of all time in *Rolling Stone*'s "500 Greatest Songs of All Time" in 2010.[4] Intros may differ from the song itself, as in *Stairway to Heaven*.

- **Outro**: The ramping-down, fading-out music that concludes the song. The outro often contains a line or a key word from the chorus. Think of Bobby Darin riffing on "sailin'" at the end of *Beyond the Sea* (1959). An outro may also be purely instrumental, as in the chaotic jam that concludes *Strawberry Fields Forever* (Lennon/McCartney, 1967). The classical counterpart of the outro is the coda, a dramatic prolongation of the conclusion of a piece.

- **Pre-chorus**: A transitional section or phrase that intensifies anticipation of the chorus. Also called the "build" or the "climb."

- **Bridge**: An extended digression, often in another key, in the middle of a song that provides relief from the repetition of verses and choruses. Bridge melodies contrast with other parts.

- **Instrumental break**: A solo instrumental—flashy, or soulful, or both—usually played over the same chord progression as the verse.

---

4 According to the founders of *Rolling Stone*, which debuted in 1967, the magazine was named for a Muddy Waters song by the same name, not for Dylan's masterpiece.

Song Form

The ordering of the structural units of a song determines its overall form. One of the most common song forms in use these days is *verse-chorus*, whose parts line up as follows:

- First verse
- Chorus
- Second verse
- Chorus
- Instrumental break
- Chorus
- Chorus

As the composer, you aren't obligated to write the instrumental break. Unless you've composed a classic riff or solo, just write "8-bar instrumental break," and let the sax or lead guitar player do their thing. Your primary concerns are a well-constructed verse and chorus.

Listeners expect some kind of a peak moment in a song, a surging release of emotion, and the chorus is usually where that occurs, with the help of ironic or emotion-drenched lyrics, high notes, intensified rhythm, harmonic thrills, and the hook. Hold your highest note in reserve, and avoid repeating it (look at a few song scores to confirm this rule).

The principle of organic growth—consistent application of the Parrot Game and the Q&A game to your original section—ensures unity and variety. Melodic rhyme can lend profundity even to the simplest of melodies. After all, what is so complicated about *Twinkle, Twinkle Little Star*? Nothing. Yet *Twinkle, Twinkle* is a delightful, immortal song. Mozart liked it enough to write a series of twelve variations on it (*Variations on Ah! Vous dirai-je, Maman*, K. 265/300e, 1781 or 1782). He was about twenty-five years old at the time.

The Gulf

The disastrous oil spill in the Gulf of Mexico formed a constant backdrop of doom and dread for ninety days in 2010. The following melody came to me some forty days into the crisis while I was idly fooling around with the chord progression Am > F > E, interpreting it with a reggae rhythm. As it began to develop, I recognized the source of its ominous edginess and titled it *The Gulf*.

The *Intro* (four measures) sets the rhythm and the style, but harmonies have been omitted for the rest of the song, because it would distract from the melody, which should be capable of standing on its own. The middle section—the chorus—is in the relative major (C major). The tune is self-explanatory, even without lyrics.

The Gulf

A Tribute to the Readers

The composition on the cover came to me around dawn at the conclusion of an all-night writing marathon. It appears more or less in full below as a graduation tribute to all who made it through the four easy lessons. Tempo: brisk march (half notes at 84 bpm).

Fanfare for Recorders, Crumhorn, Lute, and Tabor
(arranged for one guitar)

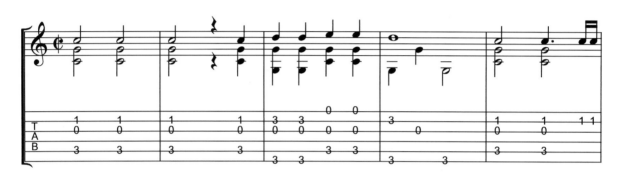

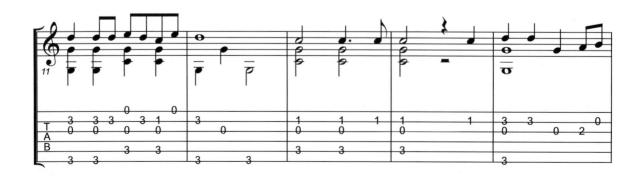

Music from past centuries can be a rich source of inspiration. Some English Renaissance tunes, for example, sound almost like modern pop. You may be familiar with *Scarborough Fair* (Simon & Garfunkel, 1968), which is more Medieval, but go to YouTube and check out *The Fairy Round* by Anthony Holborne, performed by Luteplayer80, and *Philip's Dump* by Philip Van Wilder; performed by Swedish lutenist Magnus Andersson (a *"dump"* is a circle dance). Both pieces swing nicely, particularly the latter, which even sports a few tangy blue notes.

Focused Listening

Obtain a fake book and listen to as many songs as possible, focusing on the structural units: intros, outros, verses, choruses, and others. A *fake book* is a collection of simplified song scores that provides enough information for a professional musician to "fake" an accompaniment. The score includes chords and melody. Verses, choruses, and other parts of the song are often labeled. Also listen to the songs listed in the *Interlude* (interval examples) and *Lesson 2* (chord progression examples).

As you become more familiar with the parts of a song or instrumental piece, you can adapt them to your unique needs. You always have the freedom to modify a standard song form, and if the change is well-motivated, audiences will love it.

Many songwriting books offer formulas. While it is good to write a few songs according to recipe, it is best to forget all about formula when you compose and deploy the structural elements *as needed* in order to achieve your purpose, which is to communicate feeling.

Outro

Renaissance lutenist John Dowland—acknowledged as one of the greatest songwriters of all time—was one of Jef Raskin's favorite composers. One day at work, Jef threw a few switches on the DX7 synthesizer, transforming it into a credible replica of a lute, and began to improvise a beautiful song in the style of Dowland, replete with the lush ornaments and scale runs that characterize Dowland's lute compositions.

"Did Dowland do that, or did you?" I asked.

"I never memorize music," he answered. "I don't know a single piece. But I remember styles. Just pick any three notes, and I'll make it sound like Dowland."

Thinking back, it would have been better to choose three related notes, but for some reason I tried to throw Jef a curve ball by picking the toughest group of notes I could imagine. Two of them didn't belong to the same key, and the third was an awkward interval away from the other two. I figured Jef would have trouble living up to his boast, but in short order he had turned them into a melodic motive and developed them into a Dowland lute piece, as promised. Then came the fun part. In the middle of playing the Dowland improvisation, Jef flipped a switch and the DX7 mutated into an organ. The three notes became the subject of a Bach fugue. A minute of that and flip, the organ became a piano and the three notes became the theme of a Mozart piano sonata. *Flip*, Beethoven. *Flip*, Chopin. *Flip*, Brahms. *Flip*, Tin Pan Alley. Through it all, the same three notes could be heard as the heart of the theme. He ended in a humorous take off on the Las Vegas piano lounge style, complete with dazzling arpeggios and flourishes.

Three notes and five hundred years of music—flip, flip, flip—and Jef had never missed a note or broken his stride. That was musical fluency at its finest.

We are surrounded by popular music all of our lives, which makes composing a song an easier, more attractive goal than, say, composing a sonata or a fugue. But now that you are familiar with harmonic perspective and melodic words, the Parrot Game and the Q&A Game, melodic rhyme, organic growth, and artistic values such as unity and variety, perhaps you'd like to try your hand at something else. Jazz is a next-door neighbor to pop, and instrumental compositions often derive from dance music, so the leap might not be as far as you think.

But before you gain musical fluency like Jef's, you'll need to know more about music theory and style. The game you're playing is at least seven hundred years old, and there's a lot to learn about it. Check the *Recommended Reading* list at the back of the book. It might give you some ideas for the next stop on your journey.

Coda

Music is enough for a lifetime, but a lifetime is not enough for music.

– Sergei Rachmaninoff

Congratulations! You have come a long way on the path to creative musicianship. Your rhythmic consciousness? Alert. Your sense of harmonic perspective? Awakened. Your perception of melodic words? Sharp and getting sharper. The proof? You composed a song.

Before *Compose Yourself*, one note or chord might have sounded as good as another. Now you have reasons to choose *this* chord instead of *that* chord, or *this* note instead of *that* note. The choice isn't as arbitrary as it once was because you are developing the sensitivities and discriminative powers of an artist, a composer.

"How long will it take to master the art of composition?" A natural question to ask. On the day of my first lesson with Jef, it was the first thing on my mind. I thought he'd say a couple of months. Half a year, maybe. His answer knocked the wind out of my sails.

"About as long as it took you to learn your instrument in the first place," he said.

Thinking perhaps he'd misunderstood, I reminded him how many years of study I had behind me, all the pieces I'd learned and analyzed, all the improvisation, all the composing I'd done for my first book—a lifetime of work. I thought Jef would just throw a switch, converting music *in* to music *out*.

"This is something else," he said. "It's going to be like building a new instrument from scratch, an instrument made entirely of imagination."

Jef had a gift for saying simple things that would keep you thinking for years. This was one of them, and it became the theme of *Compose Yourself*. Musical imagination. It has little to do theory. It has little to do with playing fast. It has little to do with licks or tricks. But without it, you're nothing. With it, you have everything.

Jef had it. Howard did, too. The episode in North Hollywood[1] proved that beyond a shadow of a doubt, as if there ever was one. Where did HR get such a high Musical I.Q.? I think he found it where any of us might find it—on a walk in the desert.

When HR was trying to explain the Sonic Shapes concept to me, he told me a story about his teenage years, how he used to listen to Top 40 radio, then go for a walk in the desert around Phoenix, trying to figure out how he would play the music he'd heard. Then he would go home, pick up the guitar, and try out the fingerings he had imagined. He said that this was how he taught himself to associate musical sounds with geometric shapes on the fretboard. He also said it was how he eliminated "clams" (wrong notes) from his soloing. I think it taught him much more than that. On those long walks in the desert, Howard also taught himself the musical language. He did that by imagining musical sounds—rhythm, harmony, and melody—and arranging and rearranging them in the theatre of his mind.

If you've ever taken a walk in the desert, you know it is enveloped in a vast, mysterious, delicately perfumed silence. If you can imagine that silence, then you know where to find your music. Yours and no one else's. It's out there, waiting for you. And now you're well-equipped to walk in this unknown country.

---

1 See the *Outro* to *Lesson 2*.

Recommended Reading

The list below represents a "best of" selection compiled from decades of reading, studying, and collecting music publications. The selections have been divided according to the four lessons of *Compose Yourself*. The list includes a few out-of-print books that are worth pursuing (many such books were left out, as they are simply too rare). Apologies are tendered in advance if any important works have been omitted. This is only a selection from a long and distinguished honor roll, and by no means an exhaustive list.

Difficulty levels defined:

> 1 – Easy: no knowledge of sight reading or theory required
> 2 – Average: about the same as *Compose Yourself*
> 3 – Above average: must know sight-reading, theory, and have keyboard facility
> 4 – Difficult: intense abstract content; requires solid background in theory and keyboard

Lesson 1 – Juggling Rhythm

1) **Top recommendation**: Dworsky, Alan and Sansby, Betsy. *A Rhythmic Vocabulary – A Musician's Guide to Understanding and Improvising with Rhythm* (includes CD). Dancing Hands Music, Mel Bay, 1997. A book for all instruments, establishes absolute certainty about the division of time within the measure. Starts simple, but gets complex by the end. Difficulty level: 1.

2) Arnold, Bruce E. *The Big Metronome.* Muse Eek Publishing Company, New York, NY, 1999. (See muse-eek.com, click "Books" in the left-hand column of the home page and

scroll down to "Books for time studies.") Dedicated to developing the inner time sense over multi-measure time spans. Difficulty level: 3.

3) Artzt, Alice. *Rhythmic Mastery – An Imaginative Guide for Guitarists*. Chanterelle, Mel Bay, 1996. Addresses common problems guitarists have in reading and performing rhythm. Difficulty level: 2.

4) Dworsky, Alan and Sansby, Betsy. *World-Beat & Funk Grooves – Playing a Drumset the Easy Way* (includes two CDs). Dancing Hands Music, Mel Bay, 1999. Fascinating rhythms, and who needs a drumset when you can use a couple of upside-down coffee cups, and a pair of spoons? Difficulty level: 1

5) Marshall, John. *World Beat Encyclopedia* (for guitar, includes CD). Alfred Publishing Co., 2003. Will greatly enhance your rhythmic vocabulary. Difficulty level: 3.

6) Phillips, Mark. *Sight-Read Any Rhythm Instantly*. Cherry Lane Music Company, 2002. An easy introduction to rhythm reading. Difficulty level: 2.

Interlude – Elements of Harmony

7) **Top recommendation**: The relative pitch ear training course at PerfectPitch.com. Quite simply has no peer. When you get to the site, click the "Relative Pitch Ear Training" link underneath the "#1" in the home page banner (there are no tabs; the text itself is a live link). Difficulty level: 1, but it requires perseverance, like all good things.

8) Eskelin, Gerald R., DME. *The Sounds of Music: Perception and Notation* (CD included). Stage 3 Publishing, Woodland Hills, CA, 1998. Generally available at Borders and Barnes & Noble. The author has a unique outlook, well-founded on teaching experience. Visual charts help to organize aural perception. Difficulty level: 1.

Lesson 2 – Harmony

Standard textbooks for college harmony classes include Piston, Kostka, and Benward. All are excellent, but expensive and daunting for those who are self-teaching. The following titles are less well-known, but every bit as helpful for students who want to take their Harmonic I.Q. to the next level.

9) **Top recommendation**: Sessions, Peter Lynn. *The Functions of Chords for Pop, Jazz, and Modern Styles*. P&R Press, www.pandrpress.com, 350 pages, 2002. Sessions' enlightening, scientifically-based theory of chord functions is a major leap forward, comparable to Rameau's *Treatise on Harmony* (1722). As a professional technical writer, musician, and music instructor with decades of experience, he has done a masterful job in making his unique and revolutionary ideas accessible. Coincidentally, Peter was my first guitar

teacher, and I well remember his creative teaching methods and expertise in music theory, which was already impressive way back then. Difficulty level: 2.

10) Aldwell, Edward and Schachter, Carl. *Harmony and Voice Leading*, Fourth Edition. Harcourt, Brace, Jovanovich, College Publishers, 2010. A Schenker-influenced introduction to four-part harmony makes this a logical follow-up to Williams's *Harmony and Voice Leading* (see below). Considered by many to be the best textbook of its kind. While the current edition is extremely expensive, used copies can be found for a reasonable price, especially of earlier editions. CDs are available. Difficulty level: 4.

11) Bernstein, Leonard. *The Unanswered Question – Six Talks at Harvard*. Harvard University Press, Cambridge, Massachusetts, 1976. Interesting insights into tonality and music as a language. A DVD of Bernstein's lectures is available. Difficulty level: 3.

12) Cadwallader, Allen and Gagné, David. *Analysis of Tonal Music – a Schenkerian Approach*, Second Edition. Oxford University Press. One of the best introductions to the ideas of the influential German theorist (also see 17 below). Requires knowledge of four-part harmony and voice leading. Difficulty level: 4.

13) Kachulis, Jimmy. *The Songwriter's Workshop – Harmony* (includes CD). Berklee Press, Boston, MA, 2005. Covers modern harmony in the context of songwriting. Exercises include "Rewrite the Hits"—an excellent idea. Difficulty level: 2

14) Lieberman, Maurice. *Creative Counterpoint*. Allyn and Bacon, Inc., Boston, 1966. A practical workbook that enhances your knowledge of harmony with principles of counterpoint. For advanced students only. Must know piano. Difficulty level: 4.

15) Ligon, Bert. *Jazz Theory Resources, Vols. I and II*. Advanced harmonic and melodic concepts with numerous examples from jazz and classical sources. Somewhat deficient in how-to exercises, but unique in its depth and very worthwhile. Difficulty level: 3.

16) Mathieu, W.A. *Harmonic Experience – Tonal Harmony From Its Natural Origins to Its Modern Expression*. Inner Traditions International, Rochester, Vermont, 1997. A richly detailed, 563-page unified field theory of harmony, replete with mystifying terms such as the "didymic comma in dronality," and diamond-lattice diagrams of extended chord families. Difficult, but fascinating! Stresses exercises designed to help you experience the theoretical concepts. One caveat: You must know the keyboard well enough to play through accidental-laden examples quickly and efficiently or you will become bogged down. Difficulty level: 4.

17) Porter, Steven. *Schenker Made Simple*. Phantom Publications, in association with Player Press, Inc. (P.O. Box 1132, Studio City, CA 91614-0132), 2002. Dr. Porter was a student of Carl Schachter and Felix Salzer (see 22 below), who in turn were students of Heinrich Schenker. Porter is eminently qualified to teach Schenker's theories, but he is well aware

of how daunting the terminology and diagrams can be to beginners. With the help of vivid analogies and simple examples, he brings these erudite subjects within reach, without sacrificing depth. Dr. Porter suggests studying his companion volume, *Harmonization of the Chorale* (1987), as preparation for *Schenker Made Simple*. Finest, most accessible introduction to Schenker I have seen. Fully lives up to its title. Difficulty level: 3.

18) Pratt, George. The Dynamics of *Harmony – Principles and Practice*. Oxford University Press, New York, NY, 1996. A thin book with great depth, *The Dynamics of Harmony* stresses the role of dominant relationships in tonal harmony, using scores by Mozart, Bach, and Schubert. (Caution, you will need to procure supporting scores.) Difficulty level: 4.

19) Ratner, Leonard G. *Harmony – Structure and Style*. McGraw-Hill Book Company, Inc., New York, NY, 1962. Begins with a simple analysis of melodic cadences based on scale tones 4, 7, and 1, and continues with three-part and four-part writing, along with all the standard tools of tonal harmony, but continually develops the theme of melody and musical form. Difficulty level: begins at 2, progresses rapidly to 3.

20) Ricigliano, Daniel A. *Popular & Jazz Harmony – Revised Edition*; Donato Music Publishing Co., New York, NY 10011, 1967, 1969. Unfortunately a rare book now, this remains a classic, nuts-and-bolts introduction to popular harmony. Cites numerous song titles to illustrate progressions. Difficulty level: 2.

21) Robinson, Dr. Franklin W. *Aural Harmony, Part I*. Now a rare book, *Aural Harmony* was published by G. Schirmer in 1918. It is available in a modern edition from Brouwer Press and BiblioBazaar. A revised edition exists, which includes *Part II* on chromatic harmony, but it is difficult to find. Robinson is concerned with classical four-part harmony and voice leading, so his book is not for pop-oriented readers. While his writing style is dated, his novel ideas and passion for music are timeless. Difficulty level: 3.

22) Salzer, Felix and Schachter, Carl. *Counterpoint in Composition – The Study of Voice Leading*. Columbia University Press (paperback), Morningside Edition, 1989. If you want to understand the connection between counterpoint and the classical masterpieces, this is your book. Schenker-influenced (see no. 17 above). Difficulty level: 4.

23) Williams, Jr., Edgar W. *Harmony and Voice Leading*. Harper-Collins College Outline, Harper Perennial, New York, NY 10022. One of the best, most readable, yet comprehensive introductions to classical harmony and voice-leading principles, informed by a Schenkerian perspective, but not at all difficult to understand. This survey provides the *why* as well as the *what*. Used copies available on Amazon.com. Difficulty level: 2.

Lesson 3 – The Heart of Melody

24) **Top recommendation**: Cooke, Deryck. *The Language of Music*. Clarendon Paperbacks, Oxford University Press, New York, NY, 1959. Examines music as a medium for the communication of emotion, an idea that provoked critics at the time, but continues to have legs. Includes a discussion of the emotional effects of intervals (pp. 51-90), and "Some Basic Terms of Musical Vocabulary" (pp. 113-167), which dovetails with the melodic words concept. Written for a cultured audience, but if you can handle the scholarly prose, the difficulty level is only a mild 2.

25) Kachulis, Jimmy. *The Songwriter's Workshop – Melody* (CDs included). Berklee Press, Boston, MA, 2003. Melody in the context of songwriting. Includes the relationship between melody and verses, chord progressions, and motivic development. Difficulty level: 2.

26) Ligon, Bert. *Connecting Chords With Linear Harmony*. Houston Publishing, Inc., Lebanon, IN, 1996. This was a close runner-up to the top recommendation. According to the author, almost all melodies and improvisations boil down to three outline frameworks. Ligon provides ample evidence of this with quotes from the masters of jazz composition and improvisation. Working with these tools will greatly enhance the organization, interest, and storytelling power of your melodies. Difficulty level: 3.

27) Meyer, Leonard B. *Emotion and Meaning in Music*. The University of Chicago Press, Chicago, 1956. Meyer can be trusted for original insights into the musical language. The prose style alternates between average (level 2) and difficult (level 4).

28) Narmour, Eugene. *The Analysis and Cognition of Melodic Complexity – The Implication-Realization Model*. University of Chicago Press, 1992. The author's *Analysis and Cognition of Basic Melodic Structures* should be read first. Narmour's theory is based on the work of Leonard B. Meyer (see no. 27 above) and cognitive science. While it comes as close as music theory gets to astrophysics, if you patiently absorb the underlying axioms and definitions, you will come away with some powerful insights into the inner workings of melody. Narmour provides a refreshing alternative to Schenker (he is also the author of *Beyond Schenkerism – The Need for Alternatives in Music Analysis*; University of Chicago Press, 1977). Difficulty level: 4+.

29) Perricone, Jack. *Melody in Songwriting – Tools and Techniques for Writing Hit Songs*. Berklee Press, Boston, 2000. In spite of the airy feel of the page layout, this is a detailed technical discussion of melody that is intriguing, but confusing at times. If you keep reading and keep working through the assignments, you will come away with valuable insights that will sharpen your craftsmanship. Difficulty level: 3.

30) Siegmeister, Elie. *Harmony and Melody, Vols. I* and *II*. Wadsworth Publishing Company, Inc., Belmont, CA, 1966. Unlike most other authors in this genre, Siegmeister was a com-

poser. In these two very readable volumes, he covers the usual subject matter of four-part harmony, but constantly shows the reciprocal relationship between harmony and melody. Apparently out of print. Inexpensive used copies were found on Amazon and eBay. Difficulty level: 4.

31) Szabolcsi, Bence. *A History of Melody*. St. Martin's Press, New York, NY, 1965. Traces melodic style from earliest European history through the early twentieth century, but more important, provides a wealth of melodic ideas to recycle in your own music.

Lesson 4 – Secrets of Songwriting

32) **Top recommendation**: Chase, Wayne. *How Music Really Works! The Essential Handbook for Songwriters, Performers, and Music Students*. Roady Black Publishing Inc., Vancouver, British Columbia, Canada, 2006 (sample chapters available at website: howmusicreallyworks.com). One of the miracles of Chase's insightful 889-page book is that he successfully takes on the whole panorama of music theory and practice without once resorting to musical notation. Written in a clear, conversational, entertaining style. Compatible with *Compose Yourself*, and includes much more detail on many subjects. A third edition is planned for 2010. Difficulty level: 1.

33) Appleby, Amy. *You Can Write a Song* (includes CD). Amsco Publications, New York, NY, 1991, 1995. Simple but effective. Sections are brief and easily understood. All new information is followed up with a call-to-action that any amateur musician can handle. The CD invites improvisation and creativity. Difficulty level: 2.

34) Blume, Jason. *Six Steps to Songwriting Success, Revised Edition: The Comprehensive Guide to Writing and Marketing Hit Songs*. Billboard Books, New York, NY 2008. Difficulty level: 1.

35) Brandt, Matthieu. *Songwriting on Guitar – The Complete Creative, Technical, and Reference Compendium for Composing Songs on Guitar*, Truefire.com, 2010. In fifty-seven video lessons lasting roughly eight hours, singer/songwriter Brandt covers all aspects of songwriting on guitar in great detail. Example videos are posted at Truefire.com. Difficulty level: 2 to 3.

36) Citron, Stephen. *Songwriting – A Complete Guide to the Craft*. Limelight Editions, NY, New York, 1985, Fourth Limelight Edition, 1995. Complete, detailed. Currently stocked by Borders and Barnes & Noble. Difficulty level: 2.

37) Josefs, Jai. *Writing Music for Hit Songs – Including New Songs From the '90s*. Schirmer Books, New York, NY, 1989, 1996. Straightforward, easily read introduction to theory in the context of songwriting. Considerable thought given to melody. Difficulty level: 2.

38) Webb, Jimmy. *Tunesmith – Inside the Art of Songwriting*. Hyperion, New York, NY, 1998. Thoughtful, detailed, and filled with practical wisdom, considered a bible by many songwriters. Webb, who penned such hits as *By the Time I Get to Phoenix, Galveston, Up, Up and Away*, and *MacArthur Park*, mingles insightful discussion of theory with anecdotes and history of songwriting. Engaging and readable.

Improvisation

Improvisation is dependent on genre and instrument, so it is difficult to make up even a partial list of what is available. However, the resources listed below are stand-outs:

39) Guitarists should check out Truefire.com, which has consistently produced high-quality lessons in every major genre and offers courses with top players through Truefire TV.

40) Cosmo, Emile de. *The Woodshedding Sourcebook – The Ultimate Practice Method for All Concert Instruments* (includes CD). Hal Leonard, 1997. Arpeggio and melody studies are matched with multiple rhythms to produce tons of variations. Great technique and Musical I.Q. builder. Difficulty level: 3.

41) Frank, Dave and Amaral, John. *Joy of Improv, Vols. I* and *II* (includes CDs; suitable for all instruments), Hal Leonard, 1997. If I had to pick one book on jazz improvisation to take to a desert island, it would be *Joy of Improv*. Everything in the course is based on the literature, not on theory. Sequencing and solo exercises build great technique. An idiomatic jazz vocabulary is built through scat singing with the classics. The work is challenging, but fun and musical. Anyone who wants to excel should heed their advice on practicing. Difficulty level: 3 to 4, based on the commitment required.

42) Schlieder, Frederick. *Lyric Composition Through Improvisation*, C.C. Birchard & Company, Boston, New York, 1927 (out of print). An intensely disciplined piano improvisation method by an author with a profound and passionate love of classical music. Like Raskin (who had never heard of Schlieder until I brought the book to his attention), Schlieder put rhythm first and foremost, although for different reasons. Schlieder had a great talent for describing musical values in metaphorical terms and emphasized emotional values, as well as formal structure. The title cited here covers the first year of Schlieder's improvisation course, which apparently had a nationwide following. Difficulty level: 3.

For Guitarists Only

In addition to the books listed below, see nos. 35 and 39 above.

43) Agresta, Ralph. *Chords and Progressions for Rock Guitar*. Amsco Publications, New York, NY, 1997. Builds a vocabulary of licks, rhythms, and progressions linked to real-world rock. A fun and practical way to enhance your harmonic I.Q. Difficulty level: 2 to 3.

44) Bogdanovic, Dusan. *Counterpoint for Guitar – With Improvisation in the Renaissance Style and Study in Motivic Metamorphosis.* Bèrben, Ancona, Italy, 1996 (website: dusan-bogdanovic.com). Bogdanovic is a brilliant composer with great depth of learning that shines through every page of this remarkable book on a complex, demanding form of composition and improvisation. Solves innumerable problems of translating contrapuntal practice to the fretboard. Replete with examples from the Renaissance, and compositions by the author. English/Italian text side-by-side. Patience, persistence, and knowledge of classical guitar technique required. Difficulty level: 3 to 4, based on the commitment.

45) Bosman, Lance. *Harmony for Guitar – Revised Edition.* Musical New Services, 1991. Survey of four-part harmony through the modern period, for classical guitarists. Uses classical guitar compositions for illustrations. Well-written, easy to read. Difficulty level: 2.

46) Kolb, Tom. *Chord Progressions for Guitar* (includes CD). Musicians Institute, Hal Leonard, 2003. Genre-linked chord progressions. Further widens your rhythmic and harmonic vocabulary.

47) Roberts, Howard. *Jazz Guitar Styling of Howard Roberts*, Mitch Holder & Patty Roberts, Mel Bay Publications. Includes solos and remembrances of HR. Demands chops. Difficulty level: 3.

48) Roberts, Howard, and Hagberg, Garry. *Technique/Improvisation/Musicianship/Theory, Vol. 1*, Guitar Solo Publications, catalog number AM10014. Deep, thorough, meticulous, and remarkable. Difficulty level: 3.

49) Rooksby, Rikky. *How to Write Songs on Guitar – A Guitar-Playing and Songwriting Course – Revised.* Backbeat Books, San Francisco, CA, 2000, 2009. Rooksby has authored a virtual library of books on songwriting, for keyboard as well as guitar. The title listed here has sold over 100,000 copies. Well-written and well-researched, all of them are worth checking out. The information is quite complementary to *Compose Yourself.* Quality of illustrations, pages, print, and color are outstanding. Style: conversational. Includes numerous song titles illustrating key concepts. Difficulty level: 2.

50) Sprague, Peter. *The Sprague Technique.* Satyam Music, 1989. A thorough method for mastering harmony and scales for jazz guitar, by a great player. Includes a valuable listening list in back. Order through PeterSprague.com, where you can also check out his transcribed solos and original compositions on CD. Difficulty level: 2 to 3.

Acknowledgments

Howard Roberts was fond of saying that writing a book was like giving birth to a Sherman tank, and he was right. It's my pleasure, then, to acknowledge the assistance and encouragement of numerous midwives, doctors, attendants, and friends.

Compose Yourself would never would have been written without the support of my sweetheart, Susan O'Neill. Susan came up with the *Compose Yourself* title, listened patiently for years to repeated readings of countless drafts and music theory lectures, and always picked up my spirits during the inevitable spells of doubt and discouragement.

Dr. Han Kim—also a friend and associate of Jef Raskin—understood my commitment to the project early on, even when he was my boss and our company was under excruciating deadline pressure. Even years later, he took an active interest, which says a lot about Han, who has always been an understanding and optimistic friend. Without him, it's doubtful the book would have seen the light of day.

Jef's brother, Michael—like Jef, an excellent musician—read an early draft of the book and made me rethink everything that had gone into it from the ground up. An "*Arrrgh*" is in order, but without his helpful criticism, *Compose Yourself* would have been much less than it is.

Thanks to all those who provided feedback on early drafts, including Aza Raskin, Bob Cañete, Dick Karpinski, Jim Rafferty, Peter Sprague, and my father, who won a scholarship to a music conservatory as a kid, but decided to go into science instead. Even now, at age ninety-one, he talks about getting a keyboard and learning to compose.

Perry Hoffman suggested the four-lesson format. Thanks for a most excellent idea, Perry.

In the *Prelude*, I singled out Jef Raskin and Howard Roberts as inspirations, but I am profoundly indebted to all of my teachers. It would be hard to find a better classical guitar instructor and friend than Michael McChesney, West Valley College, who introduced me to the South Bay

Guitar Society and master classes with world-class artists such as Manuel Barrueco, Roland Dyens, Oscar Ghiglia, Berta Rojas, David Russell, Marc Teicholz, Ben Verdery, and many others. In addition, Michael allowed me to recruit volunteers for experimental classes in the *Compose Yourself* method from the ranks of students in his classes through the 1990s and early 2000s. Many of these students were most helpful, especially David Lundgren and Scott Swink.

Similarly, I would like to acknowledge and thank my other teachers, including Dr. Michael Andrews (Stanford, Pleshakov-Kaneko Piano School, Palo Alto), Dr. David Barton (UC Santa Barbara), Phil Ienni, Peter Madlem, Peter Lynn Sessions, and Marc Teicholz.

I am especially grateful to John and Bill Gilbert for making the best classical guitars in the world, and for understanding why, with considerable sorrow and regret, I had to sacrifice mine in to back the publication of a book.

The South Bay Guitar Society (sbgs.org) is one of the best organizations of its kind. I want to thank the entire group, especially Jerry Snyder, for allowing me to address a couple of meetings on *Compose Yourself* concepts and recruit volunteers for an experimental class.

Many thanks to Tad Yosten, who helped me acquire Finale, which was indispensible to finishing the project.

Thanks to Kevin Owens and Jas Obrecht of *Guitar Player* for their advice on copyright questions.

Most of the book was written on a laptop at a local Starbucks. Many thanks to baristas Abbey, Alisha, Alty, Danica, Jim, Justin, Michelle, and Susie for making me feel comfortably at home, even though I monopolized one of the best tables in the house for three years.

A special thanks to Mike Robbins for playing Franz Liszt and saying it was easy to write a pop song. Wherever you are, Mike, I hope you're still surfing and writing songs.

Finally, I'd like to express my gratitude to English composer Thomas Morley (1557 – 1602). I was fifteen when I discovered the Dover paperback edition of Morley's classic, *A Plain and Easy Introduction to Practical Music* (1597) high up on a shelf at Kepler's Books, Menlo Park, California. "Eureka!" I thought as I grabbed it. "*This is it!* The secrets of composition!"

What I found inside has been an inspiration to me ever since, because it was neither plain, nor easy, nor practical. Morley convinced me that teaching musical creativity must have been a problem for a long, long time, maybe even an insoluble problem, which made the pursuit of a new way of thinking about it seem all the more worthwhile.

About the Author

Born and raised in the San Francisco Bay Area, David Alzofon became entranced with music at age five upon hearing his father play a couple of notes on the violin. He began playing trumpet in fifth grade, but fell in love with the guitar in high school. His first guitar teacher was Peter Lynn Sessions, who introduced him to Elizabeth Cotten's *Freight Train* and Luis Milan's *Pavans*, initiating a lifelong devotion to! folk baroque and classical guitar.

After graduating from the University of California, Santa Barbara, College of Creative Studies, in 1972, he returned to the Bay Area, where he began a career in writing while continuing to study music in college, and jazz guitar, owing largely to the influence of his talented cousin Chris Grampp and jazz virtuoso Bill Courtial, owner of Guitars Unlimited, Menlo Park.

In the mid-1970s and early 1980s, he lent editorial assistance to jazz guitarist Howard Roberts on Howard's popular jazz improvisation column in *Guitar Player* magazine, where he later became a full-time assistant editor. In 1981, Simon & Schuster published his first book, *Mastering Guitar*, an instruction book in the form of a novel.

In the mid-1980s, he left *Guitar Player* to become Publications Manager at Information Appliance Inc. (IAI), a start-up company founded by Jef Raskin, creator of the Macintosh. Jef, who had been a music professor at UC San Diego before emigrating to Silicon Valley, was later to provide the lessons that formed the basis of *Compose Yourself.*

A twenty-year career with a variety of Silicon Valley start-ups followed, including NeXT, DIRECTV Broadband, and BZWeb, a small start-up that designed an award-winning user interface for a Samsung cell phone. He also wrote electronic novels for Synapse and Broderbund.

Little did his employers know, but it was all to support the author's incurable addiction to music.

Mr. Alzofon currently resides in San Diego, where he teaches guitar, drinks four shots of espresso a day, and plans further volumes in the *Compose Yourself* series.

NOTES

Made in the USA
Lexington, KY
19 December 2015